Redefining
Development

The Policy and Practice of Governance

Maria Ivanova, series editor

Redefining Development

The Extraordinary Genesis of the Sustainable Development Goals

Paula Caballero with
Patti Londoño

LYNNE
RIENNER
PUBLISHERS

BOULDER
LONDON

Published in the United States of America in 2022 by
Lynne Rienner Publishers, Inc.
1800 30th Street, Suite 314, Boulder, Colorado 80301
www.rienner.com

and in the United Kingdom by
Lynne Rienner Publishers, Inc.
Gray's Inn House, 127 Clerkenwell Road, London EC1 5DB
www.eurospanbookstore.com/rienner

Library of Congress Cataloging-in-Publication Data
Names: López Caballero, Paula, author. | Londoño Jaramillo, Patti,
    author.
Title: Redefining development : the extraordinary genesis of the
    sustainable development goals / Paula Caballero, with Patti Londoño.
Description: Boulder, Colorado : Lynne Rienner Publishers, Inc., [2022] |
    Series: The Policy and Practice of Governance | Includes bibliographical
    references and index. | Summary: "A first-person story tracing the
    improbably successful struggle to achieve acceptance of the Sustainable
    Development Goals—and thus transform the global development
    agenda—against all odds"— Provided by publisher.
Identifiers: LCCN 2021055193 (print) | LCCN 2021055194 (ebook) | ISBN
    9781955055253 (Hardcover : alk. paper) | ISBN 9781955055260 (Paperback :
    alk. paper) | ISBN 9781955055475 (eBook)
Subjects: LCSH: Sustainable Development Goals. | Sustainable development.
Classification: LCC HC79.E5 L667 2022 (print) | LCC HC79.E5 (ebook) | DDC
    338.9/27—dc23/eng/20220223
LC record available at https://lccn.loc.gov/2021055193
LC ebook record available at https://lccn.loc.gov/2021055194

British Cataloguing in Publication Data
A Cataloguing in Publication record for this book
is available from the British Library.

Printed and bound in the United States of America

The paper used in this publication meets the requirements
∞ of the American National Standard for Permanence of
Paper for Printed Library Materials Z39.48-1992.

5 4 3 2 1

We offer this book to the source of it all:
our teachers and mentors

Contents

Foreword

In my opinion, the adoption of the Sustainable Development Goals (SDGs) is the most important achievement of the United Nations in this century and a great example of what can be accomplished when one knows what one is pursuing. Colombia knew what it was pursuing and was able to play a decisive role in the conception of the SDGs, which were adopted as a global agenda at the UN General Assembly in 2015. This book is the story of how—through meticulous and effective multilateral diplomacy—what very few (almost no one) thought possible was achieved: getting the world to agree on a new development paradigm.

The story starts in February 2011, when my minister of Foreign Affairs, joined by her deputy minister, Patti Londoño, and by Paula Caballero, the director for environmental, economic, and social affairs at the ministry, presented their idea: replace the Millennium Development Goals with more ambitious ones that would involve the developed countries and an important environmental component. I remember Paula appealing to my ego when she said, "President Santos, this is your great opportunity to lead something truly momentous worldwide." I thought the idea was great, and I did not hesitate to give it my support. Paula and Patti worked tirelessly, always with the unconditional support of the Ministry of Foreign Affairs.

Every head of state is concerned about his or her legacy. During my government, we achieved unprecedented improvements in economic and social indicators. As has happened in so many countries, many of the social and economic gains of the first two decades of this century were erased by the dire combination of the pandemic and poor governance. What no one will ever be able to erase, and what will forever remain in the history books as part of our legacy, is the initiative described in this book—and promoted by Colombia—to create the SDGs and all that this new concept of development means for the world.

Multilateral diplomacy is not a simple affair. Life has given me the opportunity to take part in many international negotiations, and I have witnessed firsthand how difficult it is to reach an agreement in such a diverse world and how complex international diplomacy truly is. This further highlights the extraordinary achievement of the United Nations unanimously adopting the SDGs.

My first experience of multilateral diplomacy was in London in the 1970s, when I was the Colombian delegate to the International Coffee Organization. More than 100 countries had to reach an agreement every year. Those were truly pitched battles. My boss at the time, Arturo Gómez Jaramillo, CEO of the National Federation of Coffee Growers, was a great teacher. He was called the "coffee czar" for his knowledge and authority on this matter and for his exceptional negotiating skills. Some of his lessons were to always put yourself in the shoes of the other, have infinite patience, never lose sight of your objective, avoid (price) wars at all cost, win over and protect the small countries, not allow yourself to be provoked, and remember that if everyone feels a bit frustrated after an agreement is reached, it means that the agreement is a good one. I also learned from the exceptional Brazilian diplomats, elegant and smooth in form, but majestic and tough in substance. This book highlights how, when hosting the Rio+20 Summit in June 2012, the Brazilian chair quite brilliantly managed to consolidate the summit's final agreed text, giving rise to the concept of the SDGs.

These and many other meaningful experiences over the years have made me a passionate supporter of multilateralism. To mention just a few, I learned much from being a student assistant to well-known Harvard negotiation professor, Roger Fisher; from participating in the establishment of the World Trade Organization in Marrakesh, Morocco, in 1994; and from chairing the Eighth United Nations Conference for Trade and Development (UNCTAD) in 1992. This last event gave rise to one of the most enriching conversations of my life when I handed over the UNCTAD presidency to Nelson Mandela in 1996 when he was elected president of the Ninth Conference. Also a formative experience, years later, as Colombia's minister of Finance, I was at the launch of the Millennium Development Goals in Mexico in 2002.

It is unfortunate that so many have tried to weaken or minimize the importance of multilateralism. This is a serious mistake. The pandemic has reminded us that no one is alone in this world—"no one is safe until everybody is safe"—and if we want to survive and make progress, for example, in the face of the existential threat of climate change, we had better recognize our interdependence and the need to work together. Rather than weaken it, it is crucial to strengthen multilateralism.

Generally presidents and ministers take the credit for important achievements. But the actual work is usually done behind the scenes, by the valuable people who don't appear in the picture—people like Paula Caballero and Patti Londoño, along with many others, as shown in this book.

Paula was the first one to raise the idea of replacing the Millennium Development Goals with the SDGs. She presented it to our minister of Foreign Affairs, who embraced it and appointed Patti, her deputy, to work with Paula. My role was to give them political support. For that purpose, I dedicated myself to selling the idea to all of the heads of state with whom I met, and the minister did the same with her peers. During my tenure as president, I had more than 600 meetings with heads of state and high-level officials, including Pope Francis, who first heard about the SDGs during a visit from Colombia's ambassador to the United Nations, Néstor Osorio Londoño, when he presided over the UN Economic and Social Council. I always mentioned the SDGs, like a mantra.

In this book, Paula and Patti describe their journey, step by step: the partners and allies they found (Guatemala and Peru were the first); the opponents they had to persuade or neutralize; the decisive role of the presidents of such groups as the G77 and China and of UN officials, whom they had to encourage; the difficult decisions of when to compromise or give in and when to stand firm; the subtle and delicate work to reconcile the traditional demands of rich countries, regarding transparency and the correct use of resources, with the aversion of developing countries to conditionality; and the seemingly endless meetings to craft the wording of the texts. In a nutshell, this book is the chronicle of the extraordinary diplomatic and negotiation work carried out by these women. They deserve the recognition of their country and the entire world. For any student of multilateral diplomacy, their book serves as a handbook on how to do things right.

The SDGs were formally approved as a global agenda at an historic session of the UN General Assembly on September 25, 2015, chaired by Mogens Lykketoft, who was also the speaker of the Danish legislature. The General Assembly Hall burst into jubilant applause when the resolution was adopted without a single objection or abstention. I felt immense joy because the nations of the world had been able to agree to work for a better, more peaceful, fairer, more sustainable future, with concrete and measurable goals.

Upon my return from New York, I told my cabinet that I wanted our country to be not only the first to turn the SDGs into law but also the first to take them beyond the national level, that is, to take them to each state and municipality so that those governments could incorporate the goals into their respective development plans and assume them as their own. Thanks to the work of several ministers, coordinated by the National Planning Department, we succeeded. UN Secretary-General Ban Ki-moon congratulated us with great enthusiasm. When we signed the Peace Agreement with the Revolutionary Armed Forces (FARC) in Cartagena in 2016, he said that these two achievements set Colombia as a true example worldwide. In the General Assembly, he mentioned that Colombia was the best news in the complex world that he had to deal with.

With the pandemic and the dreadful economic and social setback suffered by the world, the SDGs have become much more relevant. Covid-19 has shown us ever more clearly the extreme fragility of our planet, the only home we have. It has also unveiled the shortcomings and obstacles that we must overcome to achieve a new development model that "leaves no one behind" and allows us to preserve what remains of our biodiversity, which is essential if we are to stop global warming, undoubtedly the greatest existential challenge that humanity faces.

A new postpandemic social contract is needed because we cannot go back to business as usual, neither in the global arena nor between countries. It can easily be achieved if our work revolves around the SDGs. Everything is there: the social, economic, environmental, and institutional aspects. The work must be done by all: governments, civil society, the private sector, Indigenous peoples, traditionally marginalized minorities. This great tool, this visionary and holistic concept of development, is the result of an impressive effort and a demonstration of effective diplomatic tactics, which Caballero and Londoño describe so well in this book.

The role that Colombia played in the creation of the SDGs will forever remain part of the legacy of our government. To these two great women, along with my minister of Foreign Affairs, goes my infinite gratitude, extended to so many other people who contributed to making the impossible real. The world will be better because of your great work.

—*Juan Manuel Santos*
former president of Colombia and 2016 Nobel Peace laureate

Acknowledgments

The journey to the Sustainable Development Goals (SDGs) was complex and intense. So many participated in making the SDGs and the Open Working Group two key outcomes at the Rio+20 Summit that an exhaustive list that does justice to the myriad efforts and contributions is impossible to collate. Thus, this effort to acknowledge all those who played an important part in the process will, of necessity, fall short. To those who are not explicitly mentioned here, know that your work and efforts live on in the SDGs.

From the very beginning, in Colombia the SDGs idea had the full support of President Juan Manuel Santos and Minister of Foreign Affairs María Ángela Holguín. We remain forever grateful for their trust in us and for facilitating and lobbying for the SDGs, sharing our conviction and determination. In addition, Frank Pearl, minister of environment and sustainable development, and Néstor Osorio Londoño, ambassador to the United Nations in New York, were resolute advocates.

The SDGs idea matured over time, as did our relentless informal diplomatic process, with the consummate dedication and creativity of our team at the Ministry of Foreign Affairs: Carolina Aguirre, Heidi Botero, Faryde Carlier, Isabel Cavelier, Alicia Lozano, Ángela Rivera, David Rodríguez, and Claudia Vásquez; and likewise Andrea Guerrero, Jimena Nieto, María Alejandra Riaño, and Gianina Santiago at the Ministry of Environment and Sustainable Development.

Only the perseverance and visionary commitment to the SDGs idea of a remarkable group of negotiators allowed it to ultimately prevail. A key group of friends worked tirelessly behind the scenes and behind the microphones: Yeshey Dorji, Bhutan; Jimena Leiva and Rita Mishaan, Guatemala; Damaso Luna, Mexico; Kitty van der Heijden, the Netherlands; Marianne Loe, Norway; Farrukh Khan, Pakistan; Victor Muñoz, Peru; Anders Wallberg and Annika Markovic, Sweden; Franz Perrez, Switzerland; Majid Hassan Al Suwaidi, United Arab Emirates; Chris Whaley, United Kingdom; and John Matuszak, United States. Farrukh Khan of Pakistan played a leading and decisive role in getting final agreement on both the SDGs concept and the Open Working Group.

Throughout the process, key staff at the UN played a decisive role. Within the Executive Coordination Team of the UN Conference on Sustainable Development (UNCSD), Brice Lalonde, Liz Thompson, and Henry de Cazotte were allies from the early days, encouraging us to persevere and providing guidance. The Secretariat staff at the UN Department of Economic and Social Affairs (DESA) deserves special recognition; throughout the process, they tracked the tortuous evolution of the negotiation text, tirelessly working to craft consensus text that was regularly issued by the co-chairs and, in the final days, the draft outcome document that Brazil proposed. The team, led by Nikhil Seth, director of the Division for Sustainable Development at DESA, with the support of David O'Connor, chief of the Policy and Analysis Branch, helped deliver success at Rio+20, combining sharp and incisive political understanding with deep technical expertise to help steer the process.

Starting in late 2011, many in the UN system began to gravitate to our bold, shiny SDGs proposal. Many leaders helped pave the way: Achim Steiner, then UN Environment Programme (UNEP) executive director, now UN Development Programme (UNDP) administrator; Olav Kjørven, then director of the Bureau for Development Policy at UNDP; Janos Pasztor, then assistant secretary-general in the Executive Office of the Secretary-General; and Alicia Bárcena, executive director of the Economic Commission for Latin America and the Caribbean (ECLAC). Bruno Moro, resident representative, and Silvia Rucks, country director, in the UNDP Colombia country office believed in our idea from the early days and provided critical support. Surendra Shrestha, then with UNEP, produced the first-ever SDGs buttons that we distributed at Rio+20. Several renowned authorities in the sustainable development field were early champions of the idea and helped further and position it, including Ida Auken, Manish Bapna, Don Chen, Felix Dodds, Georg Kell, Ashok Khosla, Jonathan Pershing, Jeffrey Sachs, and Darren Walker. In the final days of the Rio+20 process, the

Brazilian hosts played their hand in support of the post-Rio option that we had striven for to develop the SDGs.

In addition to those who played key roles in supporting Colombia's efforts to position and gain acceptance of the SDGs, we want to express our gratitude to the many colleagues who gave us interviews for this book. We thank Carolina Aguirre, Carlos Berrozpe, Dominique Bichara, Henry de Cazotte, Elizabeth Cousens, Felix Dodds, Kimo Goree, Mohamed Khalil, Olav Kjørven, Farrukh Khan, Marianne Loe, Alicia Lozano, Annika Markovic, John Matuszak, David O'Connor, Néstor Osorio Londoño, Janos Pasztor, Franz Perrez, John Podesta, Janez Potočnik, Ángela Rivera, Hugo Schally, Nikhil Seth, Todd Stern, Kitty van der Heijden, Anders Wallberg, and Chris Whaley.

We do not presume to capture in our book all of the recollections and experiences of the SDGs journey. We aim to spur greater research and scholarship around the Rio+20 process, and we hope that this book is just the first of many.

Several friends and colleagues read the manuscript and provided invaluable insights and guidance. For this we express special thanks to Farrukh Khan, Maria H. Ivanova, John Matuszak, Victor Muñoz, Franz Perrez, Nikhil Seth, and Chris Whaley. We thank our editor, Pia Kohler, for her dedication and generosity in supporting our work and for her rigorous and perceptive reviews.

Note on
Appendixes

Other than the first two appendixes, the appendix documents that follow the main text are direct transcriptions of negotiation
texts and concept notes. In an effort to maintain authenticity, all gram-
matical and typographical errors have been left unchanged.

1

The Sustainable Development Goals: The Roadmap for Our Time

The remarkable and largely unknown story of the struggle—against many odds—to achieve global acceptance of the Sustainable Development Goals (SDGs) speaks to the extent to which they shattered the existing paradigm and ushered in a new understanding of development. The transformation that they represent proves that the boundaries of what is possible are fluid and that determination, perseverance, and vision can deliver unexpected shifts. The SDGs fundamentally changed the development agenda, moving from a narrow, siloed suite of goals to be delivered almost exclusively by developing countries to a vibrant, inclusive, and universal framework. The SDGs spawned a more integrated understanding of the world, demanding that all dimensions of development be comprehensively and synergistically tackled. Today, they form the backbone of the international development agenda and guide the actions of governments, companies, and coalitions.

Intended as a primary source, this book is a firsthand account of the process, led by two women from the Global South who unexpectedly crafted and launched a new global initiative. It recounts the improbable journey to frame and get acceptance of the SDGs concept throughout 2011 and then provides an insider's perspective of the negotiation process during the first half of 2012, culminating at the UN Conference on Sustainable Development (UNCSD) known as Rio+20, as told by practitioners deeply familiar with the halls, rooms, and procedures of the United Nations. It includes a rich trove of negotiation documents, rarely available to the public, and uncovers a deeper understanding of how agreements unfold through multilateral negotiations. It shows how a country like Colombia, which has not traditionally been a major player in shaping the global agenda, can radically alter established processes and expectations with a combination of experience and boldness, geopolitical savviness and technical knowledge, to create a new understanding of global relations. We share the story of how we challenged the status quo because now we all need to do so again to implement the SDGs as they were envisioned: far-reaching, resolute, and uncompromising. We must surmount incumbency, entitlement, and inertia across all systems to deliver the radical solutions needed to address the convergence of crises the world faces today. This book aims to inspire and incite.

It Took a Village

This book is the chronicle of what it took to conceptualize and frame an implausible idea and then position it internationally and get agreement at a historic summit at the level of heads of state. It is the story of a notably diverse group of diplomats and practitioners that we brought together to create an upwelling of support and build a movement. First and foremost, the SDGs were only possible thanks to the unflagging support of Patti Londoño—then vice minister for multilateral affairs in the Colombian Ministry of Foreign Affairs. Between the two of us, we had decades of experience in government and in multilateral affairs, and we were well versed in navigating the international system. Together, Patti and I led a rogue operation that ultimately sidelined the formal agenda for Rio+20 and succeeded in creating the pathway for redefining how we understand and think about development.

This book is a first-person narrative because I led many of the processes, events, and negotiations in New York and other cities detailed in the book. This was a journey undertaken jointly with Patti, who was a fellow "conspirator" and master strategist from the very beginning. Hence the plural "we" is used throughout the book to convey this close partnership. "We" also conveys the fact that we were both government officials and thus represented the vision and position of the Colombian government. Finally, "we" reflects the fact that there was an exceptional team supporting our efforts.

The book also tells the story of how an enlightened government saw the extraordinary potential in the SDGs concept and supported it to make it a reality. The SDGs became possible because we benefited from the unconditional support of President and Nobel Laureate Juan Manuel Santos and Minister of Foreign Affairs María Ángela Holguín. President Santos is a savvy political leader with a long-standing track record in the international arena and a keen appreciation of the value of technocratic approaches. Likewise, Minister Holguín, who has years of bilateral and multilateral diplomatic experience and discerning political judgment, immediately grasped the full scope of this idea. Without the full backing of a president who was willing to support disruption in the international system and a minister who understood the need for it, the SDGs would have never seen the light of day.

This is also the story of a team. At the ministry, I led the Directorate for Economic, Social and Environmental Affairs, where I benefited from the commitment of a group of talented and dedicated experts who played a vital role in shaping and framing this new concept and navigating the uncharted pathways of informal diplomacy. During the long, lonely months of 2011 during the struggle to position the idea, they believed in it. As negotiations got underway in 2012, we strategized constantly and worked together to navigate the complex international political waters. In parallel, they orchestrated and led extensive consultations at the national level to build ownership and flesh out this concept.

The story of the genesis of the SDGs is also the story of a movement. As government representatives of Colombia, Patti and I may have led the process, but without the resolute and vibrant support of a cohort of fellow negotiators and friends, the SDGs would not have been successful. Hailing from countries from both the Global North and the Global South, individual delegates worked tirelessly to position and advance the SDGs' cause in their own governments and in their respective political groups. All brought innovation, insights, and information as we worked together to build the SDGs concept and achieve progressive agreement. Several countries provided funding for key international consultations that unlocked the process. Civil society played a decisive role, and from the outset we consulted with and gave representatives a leading place at the table. Many constituencies embraced the SDGs proposal early on and created momentum around it. Getting the SDGs to become a reality literally took a village.

The SDGs Genesis

In bringing to light the tough journey to get agreement on even the concept of the SDGs, this book invites reflection on what it takes to drive and advance the urgent and imperative reset needed across our societies and economies to stem and reverse the systemic devastation that characterizes the epoch of the Anthropocene. That our fractured and ultimately short-sighted approach to growth has given rise to a new geologic epoch should be enough to give us pause and force a reflection not just of the scale of what we have done but more so of what we need to do now. The word "Anthropocene" in itself should be a call to action, with the SDGs a vital tool. They are no silver bullet, but they do provide a lens through which everyone from all walks of life can better understand the complexity of development and the immensity and depth of the interlinkages and trends. Something that drove us to persevere with our proposal was the sense that without a framework like that of the SDGs, the world would be a darker, more obtuse place.

SDGs implementation is inherently linked to tackling the climate crisis; the science is clear. We have just a few years to radically alter our productive systems and consumption choices, to change how we recognize and value natural and social capital. We often hear about 2050 as the target year we need to focus on. But 2050 is now: the world of 2050 is defined by what we decide to do right now. We must align our economies and societies with pathways that can effectively deliver net zero by 2050 while tackling the massive impacts that the climate change phenomenon is already wreaking around the world. Climate action demands alignment and unwavering sustained commitment to the Paris Agreement targets across all sectors, all cities, all landscapes, and all countries. For that the SDGs provide a blueprint, laying bare key arenas of development and priority actions.

SDGs implementation is also about decisively stemming the biodiversity crisis. Protecting biodiversity is also fundamentally about changing our value systems and mindsets. The actions needed to safeguard the vast and still largely unknown web of life of this small planet need to happen across all productive sectors. Action on effective biodiversity protection and sustainable management cut across vast swathes of the SDGs, not just the two goals that explicitly speak to "life on land" and "life below water." A fundamental aim of the SDGs is to disabuse humans of the notion that environmental issues are somehow distinct from economic and social realms, even as the latter two are often prioritized at the expense of the former.

The SDGs are also inherently about equity. Equity within countries, equity between countries, equity across generations. The interlinked crises of the Anthropocene will limit our capacities to respond to global human needs and undermine hard-won development gains. The Covid-19 pandemic has merely laid bare yet again the structural inequities of our societies and economies and, in many cases, the absence of a value system to drive resolute action. Millions continue to be left behind, and many millions more across an entire generation risk slipping into poverty. Growing inequality is thus also a reminder that 2050 is now, that our actions today determine—as never before—the world of tomorrow.

Yet rather than unleashing the deep changes that these interlinked crises demand, and despite the potential for the SDGs to launch radical shifts, in many ways their implementation has so far followed well-trodden trails. We are hopeful that we can spur more dramatic action by opening a window onto the remarkably difficult process we undertook with many friends and colleagues to convince nations to accept the SDGs idea.

Indeed, the story of the SDGs' genesis is profoundly relevant today. The commonly held assumption that the SDGs were a logical and inevitable sequence to the Millennium Development Goals (MDGs) belies the stark struggles that took place across governments and within governments and across constituencies.[1] In obscuring the origin struggle, the SDGs' disruptive potential has yet to be fully recognized and embraced. In fact, the SDGs are a roadmap to a viable planetary future if we deploy and implement them as intended.

There are four key attributes that make the SDGs revolutionary. First, the goals broke down the concept of separate and distinct "pillars" around which human activity has been structured and conceived, with primacy afforded to the economic and social pillars. Instead, the SDGs spoke to "dimensions"; they emphasized integration, the need to assess and understand the effects, trade-offs, and win-wins of actions, policies, and investments across sectors. The SDGs are the first comprehensive, integrated metric to guide and drive sustainable development pathways.

Second, the goals ushered in a conceptualization of development as a universal agenda, relevant to and actionable by all countries of the world and by all constituencies, from government to private sector to civil society. Thus, they changed the prevailing idea of "development" as a "lack of" that only a subset of countries had to tackle and on which their precursor, the MDGs, had been predicated. The SDGs set the stage for an unprecedented depth and scale of collective action to finally address the unconscionable destruction of the planet's global commons and effectively include those who have been historically marginalized. The Covid-19 pandemic, which evidenced with stark precision our societies' and economies' interconnections, has also cast a spotlight on pervasive inequalities that are now exacerbated.

Third, the SDGs brought together two separate agendas in the multilateral system and created a process that enabled the remarkable and complex negotiation process of the SDGs framework to come to fruition. This combining of two arenas is proof that it is possible to change the formats and architecture of tracks across the UN. This success still has high resonance today, notably as a clarion call to unify the SDGs, biodiversity, and climate agendas at global and national levels. They are one and the same.

Fourth, the SDGs process broke with established UN formats and created an innovative, science-based forum for developing an actionable, sensible metric—what came to be known as the Open Working Group. This was the most bitter front of the negotiations, a reflection of the degree to which it deviated from well-known, comfortable political processes.

We discuss these four disruptions in more detail below.

Driving Disruption

At first glance, there may appear to be a logical sequence from the MDGs to the SDGs: a narrow set of social goals (see Appendix 1) inevitably progresses to a more ambitious framework that encompasses the complexity of development. Nothing could be further from the truth.

In the decade since Rio+20, there has been broad and growing awareness that we are at a planetary, economic, and social inflection point. Study after study documents the relentless pace of biodiversity loss and deforestation, the grim trajectory of climate change, and the exhaustion of fish stocks, soil, and groundwater.[2] Acidified oceans increasingly become cesspools of plastic and waste. Air pollution silently kills millions. Even before the Covid-19 global pandemic, gains in poverty eradication faced enormous hurdles. Almost half of humanity—3.4 billion people—lived on less than $5.50 a day in 2018 and faced high risks of sliding back into poverty.[3] Extreme poverty is increasing in sub-Saharan Africa and by 2030, "under all but the most optimistic scenarios, poverty will remain in double digits."[4] In parallel, income inequality has increased in most developed countries and in some middle-income countries, including China and India, since 1990.[5]

Yet as a global community, we are still largely pretending that we will bring about the necessary shifts across all systems—food, energy, transport, health—while eradicating poverty, merely through small tweaks to our business-as-usual models and pathways. The painful inadequacy of our collective climate commitments attests to this: under a carbon-intensive pathway, increases in global average temperatures could exceed 3°C over preindustrial levels by the end of the century. The Covid-19 pandemic has shown just what disruption can mean, but despite calls for a "green recovery," rather than capitalizing on the crisis, humanity is simply slipping back into old habits.

First SDGs Disruption: The Need for Integration
Relentless innovation over the past centuries has transformed our world and societies. Until just a generation ago, humanity was mesmerized by a sense of inevitable progress toward ever greater prosperity. It was tacitly assumed to be our entitlement as a species that was held to be above all other species and beyond the laws of nature by dint of intelligence, consciousness, language, and opposable thumbs. In the developed world, prosperity was a birthright, and children expected to be better off than their parents. In the developing world, the lifestyles of the richer quintiles of the global population beaconed while great (albeit uneven) strides were made in poverty eradication. Development was the rallying cry: socioeconomic progress at any cost. Environmental impacts, when considered at all, were seen as inconvenient hurdles. Environmental issues were outliers, optional and discretionary, to be considered only insofar as they did not deter development and prosperity. This idea was consolidated in the concept of three distinct and separate pillars of development: economic, social, and environmental.

The first global conference on the "human environment" in Stockholm in 1972 captured and translated the nascent understanding of planetary boundaries implicit in the first photographs of Earth from space, which made the stark reality of our cosmic isolation tangible. The ensuing years gave rise to ever more distinct environmental movements and the concept of sustainable development. Twenty years later, at the 1992 Earth Summit in Rio de Janeiro,[6] the gradual realization of the need to protect the planet's natural assets and comprehensively tackle the many fronts of development generated Agenda 21,[7] a first attempt at a far-reaching development framework. The Earth Summit also generated the three so-called Rio conventions: the Convention on Biological Diversity (CBD), the UN Framework Convention on Climate Change (UNFCCC), and the UN Convention to Combat Desertification (UNCCD). For its part, Agenda 21 spawned an impressive institutional outburst that sought to consolidate and capitalize on a fully integrated agenda, with commissions for its implementation established across countries and at many scales of governance. But these efforts gradually fizzled out, and the notion of the three distinct pillars of sustainable development became more entrenched.

Growth remained the imperative. Humans first, and no-holds-barred development to enable developing countries to catch up with the others. For its part, the environmental movement evolved and came to emphasize the need to "mainstream" environmental considerations into other sectors, to work with communities and deliver local benefits. But this mainstreaming remained an outlier in key conversations and movements, marginalized from the imperative to deliver continuous growth across governments and the private sector. The rallying calls for sustainability and equity hinted at the systemic transformations needed, but there was never a real commitment to changing the comforts of the status quo, the lifestyles of the entitled, or the drive for growth. It is said that we measure what matters; tellingly, the value of natural and human capital did not figure into the calculations of decision-makers across public and private sectors. Gross domestic product remained the guiding North Star; only the total economic output achieved by a country was measured, thus ignoring the natural and human capital that are the actual foundation of all well-being and ignoring the effects or externalities of unbridled growth.

This divide inherent in a vision of development that privileges economic growth at the expense of the environment was manifest in the distinct communities that evolved. In the wake of the Earth Summit, many countries, including Colombia, established or consolidated a Ministry of the Environment. These novel institutions, almost without exception, became cabinet laggards, ministries with inadequate funding and little political clout, with an agenda widely considered at odds with the imperative of growth, development, and prosperity nominally advanced by other sectoral ministries and by the development community. The development cooperation agendas privileged social and economic issues, consolidating the divide with environmental issues. Across governments, aid agencies, multilateral financial institutions, and philanthropies, the view was largely cemented that environmental issues were optional or a brake on development. The interaction between the socioeconomic pillars and the environmental pillar was perceived by many as a zero-sum game.

Our SDGs proposal sought to shatter the status quo around these pillars. By creating a referent framework that reflected and translated the complexity of development, we aimed to hold up a mirror to guide decisionmaking at all levels. The three pillars had ensconced the majority into a comfortable worldview with blinders that made it possible to advance on single tracks with willful disregard for spillover impacts and trade-offs across sectors or geographies. We were convinced that the

SDGs framework would force stakeholders at all levels, across all walks of life, to consider where their actions fit in in the full scheme of development; to consider whether their actions were in fact, sustainable. SDGs would provide a common language and grammar for countenancing and taking ownership for the comprehensive scope of what development entailed. We feared that in the absence of such a holistic systemic referent, the narrow, marginal understanding of development would continue to prevail, bolstering an untenable status quo.

The SDGs idea brought to the fore a sharp, actionable, systemic vision. We called for deep structural shifts to truly deliver on goals first envisioned in a minimalist fashion in the MDGs: not just eliminate hunger but transform food systems; not just tackle a few infectious diseases but create functional health systems that all could access. As Colombia argued from the outset, the SDGs aimed to create the systems and mindsets to effectively deliver on the MDGs and beyond.

Second SDGs Disruption: The Need for Universality

According to the widely prevailing narrative at the start of the millennium and crystalized in the MDGs, developed countries had achieved prosperity and were called on to support less developed countries in advancing toward equivalent prosperity. For their part, developing countries were called on to emulate the pathways of already industrialized nations and advance "development." Within this broad understanding, there was agreement that the overarching priority and imperative was to eradicate poverty, so poorer countries and marginalized people had to be prioritized. Building on earlier work, the Development Assistance Committee of the Organisation for Economic Co-operation and Development (OECD), largely an organization of the world's industrialized nations, compiled a list of goals and targets in 1996 to guide official development assistance (ODA). This list gained currency across the bilateral development community and leading multilateral organizations and in 2001 dovetailed into the MDGs, which were actually referred to in official documents as "the internationally agreed development goals, including those contained in the Millennium Declaration."[8] At the UN International Conference on Financing for Development, in Monterrey, Mexico, in 2002, member states agreed to mobilize financial resources and build new partnerships between developing and developed countries to meet the MDGs targets. In principle, the MDGs were thus a partnership. But they were an uneven one.

The MDGs in fact cemented the divide between countries—between those whose main responsibility was to provide resources and those that had an implementation responsibility. Moreover, although the MDGs were powerful in driving change across a few select and critical fronts of development—the Global Alliance for Vaccination is a potent example—in general, their approach was minimalist. The MDGs embedded a pro-poor approach that wholly sidelined, for example, the fact that to effectively eradicate poverty or hunger for the long run, systems change is imperative. There was no space to acknowledge shared issues—such as deep pockets of poverty in developed countries—or to tackle the threats to the global commons. Nominal consideration was given to environmental issues under MDG7,[9] but only two of the four targets MDG7 encompassed were actually focused on environmental issues and were so broad as to be largely ineffectual.[10]

This sharp division in how countries were characterized was reinforced in international negotiations by another concept that came to have far-reaching influence. In 1992, the United Nations Framework Convention on Climate Change (UNFCCC) enshrined the principle known as common but differentiated responsibilities (CBDR) and respective capabilities, as defined in Article 3.1: "The Parties should protect the climate system for the benefit of present and future generations of humankind, on the basis of equity and in accordance with their common but differentiated responsibilities and respective capabilities. Accordingly, the developed country Parties should take the lead in combating climate change and the adverse effects thereof."[11] Furthermore, Article 4.1 in the section of commitments states that "All Parties, taking into account their common but differentiated responsibilities and their specific national and regional development priorities, objectives and circumstances" should undertake a range of actions and policies.

This principle became such a mainstay of negotiations in the sustainable development arena that it came to be known simply as CBDR-RC or CBDR. Under UNFCCC, the CBDR principle acknowledged that all states have a shared obligation to address environmental effects. However, given disparities in industrialization timelines, nations that first industrialized have higher historic responsibility for environmental degradation and greenhouse gas emissions. Thus, those states also have a higher degree of responsibility to deliver on halting climate change and must do so sooner than developing countries. The principle also recognized that there are disparities in terms of the resources that countries have to deliver on the convention's objective. Reflecting CBDR, parties to the convention were divided into "Annex 1" and "non–Annex 1." Annex 1 generally referred to developed countries,[12] and non–Annex 1 to developing countries. Under the convention, Annex 1 countries have greater and obligatory responsibility to deliver on mitigation action. Developing countries do not have this obligation as such.

Simplistically, CBDR could be interpreted to mean that industrialized nations had a primary responsibility to act to reduce emissions and provide financing for other nations who needed to achieve the same prosperity in a world that had since woken up to the implications of climate change, for them to reduce their emissions. Over time, the CBDR principle contributed to a bifurcated view of a world of antagonistic responsibilities and acrimonious worldviews. CBDR took on a life of its own beyond the UNFCCC and came to be invoked across many negotiations by members of the G77 and China.[13] Even though CBDR was invoked as part of a broader negotiating tactic, for many in the G77 and China, it was a cardinal principle that encompassed several key tenets. First, it implicitly reaffirmed what a major emerging economy at one point called the "right to development": given the primacy of eradicating poverty and achieving robust growth, developing countries should have the same right that industrialized nations had had to develop with no regard for environmental and climate considerations. Second, it obligated developed countries to take a decisive lead with regard to action on environmental issues. Third, it conditioned more ambitious efforts by developing countries to the provision of resources by developed countries. It also had the unfortunate consequence of lumping developing countries together in the same category even if they had negligible emissions or were among the top emitters in the world.

The SDGs challenged those dichotomous worldviews. A new agenda was proposed that called on all countries to act across a comprehensive framework encompassing the main arenas of development. This universal aspect of the Colombian proposal was initially looked at askance. How could such a framework possibly apply to developed countries that had already resolved all development issues? There were different readings of the concept of universality and from our perspective, it spoke to two of them. First, given the interdependence of our globalized society, many conditions and factors that underpin societies' well-being are driven by processes or systems beyond the purview of individual countries. These range from climate change and pandemic diseases to trade flows and the global financial system, and they call for different forms of collective and national action. Second, although there are marked national differences based on where countries were situated across a spectrum of development parameters, development issues are relevant to all countries. For example, in 2017 one in five children in rich countries lived in relative income poverty, and on average, 12.7 percent of children lived with a respondent who is food insecure.[14] Research has shown that "high-income countries are still far from delivering for their children the vision held out by the SDGs. Income inequality is growing, adolescents' mental health is worsening and child obesity is increasing. Not a single country does well on all indicators or has shown positive trends on all fronts."[15] As we often said when trying to explain our idea, the SDGs were about "inequality between nations, inequality within nations, and inequality across generations." If the new global agenda was to result in structural change and a systemic transformation of development trends, then it had to be universal. For us, the SDGs posited a revolution in responsibility for all.

Third SDGs Disruption:
The Need to Align Tracks at the UN

The MDGs evolved from a track firmly embedded in ongoing processes related to traditional development assistance, which was core to the architecture and raison d'être of the UN. In 2011, when Colombia decided to propose a brand-new framework, the end date of the MDGs in 2015 was still years away. Progress was being made across the targets, but those four years of implementation were crucial to achieving them around the world.

Since the MDGs' formal launch in 2002, a comprehensive development architecture—domestic, bilateral, and multilateral—had consolidated around them. Developing countries built them into national development agendas, and a vast range of stakeholders, from multilateral financial institutions to bilateral donors and philanthropies to think tanks and nongovernmental organizations, structured their development assistance and programs around the MDGs. The agencies and ministries that managed international development assistance were keen champions of the MDGs. Philanthropic organizations took them up, and they inspired incredibly successful coalitions. The MDGs were pinned to walls in national ministries and aid agencies around the world. The MDGs were a nice, short, crisp list focusing on a few salient social goals. They were easy to understand and comfortably confirmed the prevailing status quo—that only developing countries had development issues and a need to act on them. Surprisingly, it was generally overlooked that they had not resulted from an inclusive multilateral process but from a UN Secretariat–led initiative to capitalize on a Millennium Declaration and had been developed by UN experts.

In this context, any proposal that could be interpreted as moving away from or undermining the MDGs was sure to meet with fierce resistance, although in truth we woefully underestimated just how fierce that resistance would be. The many constituencies that were married to the MDGs were adamant that the goals were tackling the "real" core development issues and must not be eroded in any way. They endlessly intoned that the MDGs were "unfinished business," and many affirmed that the MDGs would need to be carried on beyond their nominal end date of 2015. The UN and many others were focused on accelerating MDGs implementation.[16] We were told time and again that no one should have the temerity to propose anything else until 2015. In any case, why worry about post-2015 when it was still only early 2011? This resistance did not end even after the adoption of the SDGs proposal at Rio+20. These tensions spilled over into the deliberations of the Open Working Group, where the SDGs framework was defined (2013–2014).

The process that had created the MDGs was thus completely separate from the Rio track that began in 1992 that had spawned the lion's share of the international multilateral environment legal framework. Given the prevailing worldview that regarded the international development agenda as wholly distinct from the environmental one, these two tracks had unsurprisingly run parallel to each other for almost two decades. Efforts had been ongoing in the environment community to link the environment to "human development," but even so, it still constituted a fundamentally separate track in the UN. Under normal circumstances, such distinct tracks never meet in international arenas, and their separation fueled mindsets that locked in divergent visions of development.

Thus, when Colombia proposed that a major outcome of the Rio+20 Summit could be a revamped, truly global metric, a successor to the MDGs no less, those that did not dismiss it as blasphemous dismissed it as a sheer impossibility, the pipe dream of a negotiator who did not understand the system or the history. The reasons were legion: historically, these were two distinct tracks; the MDGs still had four years to run, so no one could dare to propose a successor; and what would happen to the MDGs after 2015 was something exclusively for the development community to propose after due diligence in the form of extensive assessments of MDGs implementation, gaps, and "emerging issues." To top it off, the agenda for Rio+20 had already been locked in with a formal UN resolution.[17] In short, we were repeatedly reminded that it was a conceptual and procedural impossibility.

Yet this is exactly what we achieved in Rio de Janeiro in June 2012.

Fourth SDGs Disruption:
Inclusive, Science-Based Decisionmaking

What made this alignment of agendas so powerful and transformative was the fact that at Rio+20, countries not only committed to negotiating the SDGs, they also agreed to establish a radically different format for negotiating the goals, the Open Working Group (OWG). If the SDGs had been negotiated under a more traditional UN format, the world would most likely have ended up with political declarations couched as a metric or a cookbook of recommendations doomed to be shelved. The drive to create this format spawned some of the most bitter negotiations in the entire process, which gives a measure of how radical the OWG proposal was seen to be.

Colombia advocated for the unique negotiation format of the OWG and it proved central to crafting a globally relevant and actionable SDGs framework. Rather than being driven largely by political consider- ations, the OWG allowed for a major intergovernmental negotiation based on science and the multisectoral expertise that each country could bring from their capitals. Moreover, the format aspired to be transparent and participatory, one that all constituencies and stakeholders could fol- low. We were convinced that the SDGs negotiation process had to be not just intergovernmental but also open and inclusive of all stakehold- ers to achieve universal consensus and, above all, ownership around an ambitious and forward-looking agenda.

After months of fruitless negotiations on the format, the final agree- ment that Colombia and Pakistan brokered at Rio+20, which the Brazilian presidency ultimately supported, proved to be transformative. As we advocated, rather than having the new body be "open-ended" and operate under the aegis of the UN General Assembly rules—and thus be led by the traditional political negotiation blocs—the body would be open so that all nations and constituencies could follow the proceedings even if they were not a formal member of the new body. Moreover, proceedings would be livestreamed so that it would be radically transparent. This format finally routed the other standard option that had been favored: a small, closed high-level panel appointed by the Secretary-General. This time around, nothing would be negotiated or agreed to behind closed doors.

Multilateralism in Crisis

If the SDGs faced an uphill battle to gain acceptance because of how disruptive they would be, the context in which they were proposed and developed was itself a significant hurdle. The negotiations for Rio+20 took place at a point when the import and value of multilateralism was being deeply questioned.

During 2011 when we proposed the SDGs concept, the fallout from the 2008 financial crisis and the food crisis was still unfolding. Confidence in global governance had been severely damaged. In the context of multilateral environmental negotiations, the implosion of the Fifteenth Conference of the Parties (COP) of the UNFCCC in Copenhagen in 2009 due to perceptions of a lack of transparency and inclusivity further fractured trust in the international system. Ultimately the Copenhagen Accord was not adopted by the parties and was left in limbo, and "Copenhagen" was ominously invoked in meetings around the world for the next few years as a dire warning of where exclusive processes would lead. Distrust in multilateralism peaked.[18]

One bright spot in the international arena was the Tenth COP of the CBD held in Nagoya, Japan, in October 2010, weeks before the Cancún UNFCCC COP. There, countries adopted a 2011–2020 Strategic Plan for Biodiversity, which included the Aichi Biodiversity Targets (five goals, twenty targets, each with a respective suite of indicators).[19] We took this as proof that the international community was able to jointly define and commit to measurable priority actions.

Book Overview

This book covers the period from early January 2011 through to the Rio+20 Conference, which culminated on June 22, 2012, and focuses exclusively on the journey from the first conceptualization of an idea we called the SDGs through to their final acceptance in Rio+20. (See the Timeline.) In the context of the Rio+20 negotiations, it maintains a tight focus on the negotiations around the section on the SDGs in the Zero Draft and does not cover the complex discussions around the many other tracks within the negotiations.

The book ends with the conclusion of the Rio+20 Conference and does not describe the process that followed on the composition of the OWG or its deliberations. Many books have already been written about that remarkable exercise.[20] Co-chairs Csaba Kőrösi of Hungary and Macharia Kamau of Kenya did a brilliant job in structuring and leading a process of progressive understanding and enlightenment around the many thematic arenas that were tackled. The intensely participatory process they established was exactly what we had envisioned when we fought for an open process rather than an open-ended one. Seldom has a

UN process generated so much ownership and a sense of shared account-ability and responsibility by legions of constituencies.

We do not purport to provide a comprehensive analysis of the many and diverse consultations, initiatives, and research that were percolating in the run-up to Rio+20. In the preceding years, there were various processes and discussions as many organizations and individuals were thinking about how to understand and broach the multiple challenges humanity was facing and how to craft solutions and pathways. In 2010, UN Secretary-General Ban Ki-moon had established a High-Level Panel on Global Sustainability, which issued a report in early 2012.[21] He also established a UN System Task Team on the Post-2015 Develop-ment Agenda in September 2011, which led to a wide range of consul-tations and reports.[22] For the latter, Ban turned to the Department for Economic and Social Affairs (UNDESA) and the United Nations Devel-opment Programme (UNDP) to help shape the process. There were var-ious reviews of the MDGs and proposals for undertaking gap analyses to identify and prioritize the issues that needed to be tackled, both exist-ing and emerging.[23] There were numerous documents outlining what Rio+20 could focus on and deliver, such as the United Nations Confer-ence on Trade and Development (UNCTAD)'s *Road to Rio+20* and a wide range of papers by UNDP, UNEP, and UNDESA. When one reviews all this literature and takes the pulse of the consultations and analyses that were ongoing, it is even more notable that in the end it was the SDGs that captivated the world.

Our book aims to contribute to the extensive literature on this period by providing a firsthand account of a decisive contribution to the international development agenda whose genesis is largely unknown. The SDGs were a minuscule part of the massive Rio+20 negotiation, which covered all the main thematic arenas of sustainable development. Yet in the end they endured and became the cornerstone of international development, resonating with governments, the private sector, civil society, and academia around the world. We trust that by casting light on the richness of the historic Rio+20 process negotiations, others will want to further explore and analyze them.

In telling our story, this book is a primary source. Beyond the scenes from the UN General Assembly broadcast every fall with cere-monial takes of heads of states and governments, we provide insights from the backrooms of negotiations, formal and informal, that take place across meeting rooms, in corridors, and even in cafés.[24] It also provides the reader with access to negotiation materials, which are sel-dom available to the public. When negotiations are unfolding at a rapid pace, there are often versions of proposed language that are informally circulated in the negotiation rooms or more formal versions put forward by those leading or facilitating the negotiations to try to craft consensus language. Most of these documents were only available to those directly involved in the negotiations, and many are designed to be ephemeral—once an issue is resolved, interim negotiation drafts are discarded. These materials, set out in the appendixes, will enable readers to better understand how the UN works and the intricacies of a negotiation track.[25] Only by being able to read these documents can one understand the pace and scope of a negotiation: the appendixes provide a unique insider's perspective of how negotiations evolve. In addition to this, we include the many concept papers that Colombia presented with other countries and other relevant documents. These shed light on the evolution of the process as these were political documents that we issued based on deep listening across constituencies and that aimed to guide the discussions and negotiations. For ease of reference, we include the relevant SDGs sections of the final, formally agreed Rio+20 outcome document, *The Future We Want*.

Finally, but most important, Appendix 2 provides a succinct introduction to negotiations at the UN for readers who are not so familiar with multilateral processes. For some, it may even be helpful to read this appendix before delving into the story.

We have included a timeline of the events we describe in the book and a schematic of the time period covered by each chapter.

In Chapter 2, we show how informal diplomacy outperformed politically imposed limitations and expectations. A narrow framing for Rio+20 was eclipsed by our innovative and creative proposal to transform the way we understand development and agree to a global evidence-based agenda with universal commitments. The transition from the MDGs to the SDGs, now seen as evident and intuitive, was a challenging minefield that proved just how difficult it is to set a paradigm shift in motion. From the outset, innovation and tenacity helped make the SDGs a reality.

In Chapter 3, we deal with the challenges inherent in motivating countries from all over the world to consider a proposal that was an outlier. In so doing, we defied the formal blueprint for Rio+20. It describes how we used a blend of backroom outreach, hallway lobbying, and formal settings to position our proposal. Furthermore, we explain why getting the SDGs into the Zero Draft of the Rio+20 summit was a major breakthrough in advancing the adoption of a new framework by the international community.

In Chapter 4, we present an analysis of the international consultations and tools that we deployed to enable the full range of stakeholders to unpack and understand what the SDGs proposal was about. We examine the main areas of contention that would come to define the negotiations. This chapter is aimed at enabling the reader to understand the framing of the proposal and its importance. Describing the genesis of support for our proposal, we explain how we established a core group of countries to help drive the process.

In Chapter 5, we provide an overview of the political economy of the negotiations, introducing the key players and analyzing the dynamics among them. It recounts the initial round of preparatory negotiations and how we continued to capitalize on informal diplomatic channels even as we shifted to formal proceedings.

In Chapter 6, we bring to life the complex negotiations in New York, delving into the architecture and perils of the format. We describe the difficulty of advancing on the various negotiation tracks, providing insight into constituencies' positions. Well-intentioned efforts backfired, evidencing the widely divergent expectations around our brave agenda. We delineate the challenges of the three negotiation rounds held in New York from March to June 2012 (see Timeline). We track how the relevant passages of the negotiation text ballooned, seemingly out of control.

In Chapter 7, we cover the same timeframe as in Chapter 6 but focus on a close analysis of the main negotiation tracks in the SDGs process. We describe the evolution of the text through several rounds of negotiations. This chapter is extensively documented with the actual negotiation texts. This allows us to offer a unique insight into what might be considered the equivalent of "how the sausage gets made" behind the scenes in international diplomacy. This more technical analysis of the negotiation draft may be of greater interest to more specialized or academic audiences.

In Chapter 8, we take the reader to Rio de Janeiro in June 2012, providing an insight into the backroom negotiations there. We document how the final text was gradually crafted through a combination of informal diplomacy, trust, and sheer negotiation clout. We narrate the final stressful hours in which agreement seemed evasive in the midst of highly politically charged positions, and we share a development that almost derailed the whole SDGs process. We would like the reader to understand the remarkable story of what it took to get a final consensus outcome.

In Chapter 9, we focus specifically on the fraught process that ultimately delivered what came to be known as the OWG. We discuss why establishing a technical, evidence-based body to develop the SDGs framework after Rio+20 became an essential component of our transformative proposal. To the end, there was opposition to the establishment of the OWG, an institution that has since been credited as instrumental in bringing about the SDGs adopted in 2015.

In Chapter 10, we conclude by sharing a few lessons that are relevant for implementing the SDGs as they were envisioned to drive deep changes across systems and mindsets. We point to the audaciousness of the SDGs story as evidence that transformation is possible and necessary for humanity to finally find the balance of sustainability and equity.

Notes

1. The MDGs were proposed to UN member states by the Secretary-General in his report *Road Map Towards the Implementation of the United Nations Development Declaration* (A/56/326, September 6, 2001), a year after the Millennium Declaration was adopted in 2000. More information on their elaboration and impact is included in Appendix 1.

2. Brondizio et al. (2019); Pirlea et al. (2020); World Economic Forum (2021).

3. Lawson et al. (2019).

4. World Bank (2018), 3.

5. UNDESA (2020).

6. The full name of the Earth Summit was the UN Conference on Environment and Development.

7. Agenda 21 resulted from the Earth Summit. Rio+20 Summit of 2012 was a continuum of the efforts to build more sustainable development pathways at a global level to address the environmental, social, and economic challenges the international community needs to tackle together.

8. See additional information on the MDGs in Appendix 1.

9. MDG7: Ensure Environmental Sustainability, was added at the last minute when the UNDP administrator was asked whether the new framework being developed at the UN included anything on the environment and the notable gap was redressed.

10. MDG7: Target 7.A: Integrate the principles of sustainable development into country policies and programs and reverse the loss of environmental resources; Target 7.B: Reduce biodiversity loss, achieving, by 2010, a significant reduction in the rate of loss; Target 7.C: Halve, by 2015, the proportion of the population without sustainable access to safe drinking water and basic sanitation; and Target 7.D: Achieve, by 2020, a significant improvement in the lives of at least 100 million slum dwellers.

11. The 1987 Montreal Protocol on Substances That Deplete the Ozone Layer is widely recognized as an earlier formulation of the CBDR principle; see Stalley (2018).

12. Annex 1 included industrialized countries that were members of the OECD in 1992 and countries with economies in transition, which encompassed states of the former Soviet Union and those of Central and Eastern Europe.

13. The G77 and China is the main negotiating group of the developing world with 134 countries from Asia, Africa, and Latin America and the Caribbean, and during the negotiations for Rio+20 it played a major role in channeling the views

and voices of the Global South. It is commonly a counterpart to the European Union and Others, that represent the views of the Global North in negotiations. In this book, when we mention "the Group" or "the G77 and China" we are referring to the Group of 77 and China.

14. UNICEF (2017), 13 and 17.

15. UNICEF (2017), 52.

16. UNDESA (2011).

17. UN General Assembly Resolution A/RES/64/236, December 24, 2009.

18. For more on the Copenhagen COP, see Meilstrup (2010).

19. The goals addressed issues including biodiversity loss, promotion of its sustainable use, and safeguarding ecosystems, species, and genetic diversity. Each goal has targets, such as making people aware of the value of biodiversity, eliminating incentives harmful for biodiversity, developing incentives for conservation, implementing plans for sustainable production and consumption, sustainable management of fisheries and agricultural activities, and others that can be found in the CBD. See http://www.cbd.int/sp/targets.

20. Dodds et al. (2014, 2017).

21. UNSG (2012).

22. United Nations (2012).

23. UNDESA (2011, 2012b); UN System Task Team (2012).

24. Many books and articles have been written about UN negotiation and decision-making. See Hawden and Kaufman (1962).

25. As the negotiations advanced, the Zero Draft grew exponentially. Thus the appendixes of this book only include negotiation texts for the section on the SDGs.

2

The Merits of
Informal Diplomacy

*Setting a paradigm shift in motion is no easy feat, especially when few
are initially convinced of the merits of an idea. In this chapter, we detail
how varied avenues of informal diplomacy were used to overcome fierce
resistance and build support for a proposal, now seen as evident and
intuitive, to move away from the Millennium Development Goals toward
a universal, comprehensive development agenda.*

The Unexpected Beginning
In the final months of 2010, the agenda of international multilateral
environmental agreements (MEAs) was in full swing with both the
Tenth Conference of the Parties (COP) to the Convention on Biological
Diversity in Nagoya, Japan, and the Sixteenth COP of the UN Frame-
work Convention on Climate Change (UNFCCC) in Cancún, Mexico.

Having led the delegation to both COPs as the recently appointed
director of Economic, Social and Environmental Affairs in the Ministry
of Foreign Affairs of Colombia, I took away key lessons. Nagoya, where
the world agreed to the Aichi targets, offered proof that it was possible
to get agreement on an ambitious global framework. The lessons from
Cancún in December were more complex. There the Mexican team masterfully managed the COP presidency, restoring trust in the process and
bringing it back from the abyss of distrust that was the legacy of COP 15
in Copenhagen. They proved that through extensive and transparent consultations, it was possible to craft pathways for consensus, overcoming

ideological divides across parties, notably the entrenched and intractable positions that underpinned a bifurcated vision of the world. The 1997 Kyoto Protocol under the UNFCCC had cemented states into two camps by separating them into Annex 1 and non–Annex 1 countries. In Cancún, after two weeks of exhaustive consultations and negotiations, the Mexican presidency presented a comprehensive outcome text, a finely balanced package that navigated the parties' diverse and often antagonistic ambitions. After Copenhagen, the climate regime needed an agreement to move forward. The consensus text was presented as a take-it-or-leave-it solution. In the early hours of the morning, after lengthy and exhaustive deliberations in the final plenary session, and despite the objection by Bolivia, the Mexican presidency finally declared that one country could not effectively veto the process and gaveled it through. At that moment, there was cheering in the conference room. Yet just six weeks later, at the next round of climate negotiations, there was deep bitterness across the G77 and China Group over how consensus had been reached. Mexico was rightly celebrated for steering the climate negotiations back on track, but a few probing questions about the validity and legitimacy of multilateral processes lingered. A significant number of delegates from both the Copenhagen and Cancún COPs would participate in the Rio+20 process discussed in this book, and these two COPs highlighted both the dividends of aiming high around a clear and common vision as well as the minefields of multilateral negotiations.

The upcoming twentieth anniversary of the famed 1992 Earth Summit, at the highest political level with the participation of heads of state, thus seemed the perfect opportunity to garner global political will around a renewed commitment to a compelling and truly actionable agenda for sustainability and equity, one that was fit to help deliver on the urgent agendas we were collectively designing and endorsing. Thus, when I joined the government in late 2010, I was surprised to learn that the focus of the upcoming Rio+20 conference was on two issues that meant little to the broader global public.

The first was the concept of a "green economy." This was current in Europe but poorly understood and mired in controversy in many other constituencies, especially those from the Global South. There were acrimonious discussions around its very definition. The UN Environment Programme (UNEP) defined a green economy as one that was "low carbon, resource efficient and socially inclusive," one that would make trade and environment mutually supportive and encourage sustainable domestic investments.[1] Most developing countries eyed it with apprehension, fearing it was shorthand for all manner of conditionalities that would affect their competitiveness and limit access to markets. There was little hope of meaningful consensus that would drive real change on the ground.

The second pillar focused on the International Framework for Sustainable Development (IFSD) and had at its core the aim to revitalize the Commission on Sustainable Development (CSD) and "upgrade" UNEP into an autonomous agency in the UN.[2] This pillar was underpinned by a conviction that improving the architecture of governance was necessary to advance sustainable development in all its complexity. The debacle in the CSD in May 2011 (see Chapter 3), which stridently failed to get agreement on a consensus package, bolstered this view. A few European countries in particular were keen on the UNEP upgrade, with support from a few African countries. Conversely, other developed countries were of the strong persuasion that no new institutional entities were needed; all that was required, they argued, was to improve the functionality of the UN Economic and Social Council (ECOSOC) and CSD.[3] The United States was firmly opposed to the creation of a new entity. In the end, upgrading UNEP proved to be one of the most intractable issues in the Rio+20 negotiations.

The agenda for Rio+20, with these two issues at its core, had been locked in with a UN resolution, which meant all 193 member states had formally signed off on it. In short, it was written in stone. Yet neither of these two prioritized issues had real potential for incentivizing action across societies and the global economy, to inspire the deep transformations at a scale so urgently needed on a planet facing historic and relentless degradation, which remained so stubbornly inequitable at many levels.

So in early January 2011, I convened a small group of government colleagues for a brainstorming session at the Ministry of Foreign Affairs on what Colombia could propose for Rio+20 to generate the kind of historic traction that had been the hallmark of the Rio conference in 1992. The group met in a small, cold room just off the historic Patio of the Palms, an interior courtyard with a palm tree and a walnut tree, both centuries old and (according to legend) planted by Simon Bolívar. At that meeting, I proposed that Colombia could advance a new set of global goals, like the MDGs, which had set targets for 2015, but this time covering all critical areas of development.

Despite shortcomings, the MDGs had been singularly effective in bringing about significant progress on a range of fronts and mobilized broad coalitions behind specific targets. However, the MDGs were short-sighted and narrow, and they sidelined economic and environmental issues without which even the already prioritized goals could never be fully realized. The idea was that Colombia would propose a new set of goals that would encompass the many dimensions of sustainable development. As the attendees explored the idea, possible names were discussed. An initial rubric of "Global Environmental Objectives" was considered—a play on the Global Environment Outlook reports periodically issued by UNEP. This first idea was eventually discarded given that the whole point of the proposal was to go beyond "environmental" considerations to embrace all the dimensions of development. Thus, "Sustainable Development Goals" was a much better fit. We were envisioning a more comprehensive framework that would be equally relevant and applicable to all countries.[4]

To make this idea a reality required sign-off from the ministry. This was, after all, a proposal to shape a new global agenda. I shared it with Patti Londoño, then deputy minister of Foreign Affairs, who immediately embraced it and also got the minister's support. Thus the adventure began.

Walking the Hallways

Rather than position the idea through a formal UN process, we decided to advance our cause through a bottom-up, informal approach. This proved to be a crucial decision, central to our eventual success. Patti and I knew the UN and its negotiation processes well, and we recognized that an attempt to disrupt the system by spearheading a formal process from within would have been an exhausting and ultimately fruitless task.

Even though we embarked on what ultimately proved to be a radically disruptive pathway, we were nevertheless determined to build a framework resulting from the active engagement of member states in negotiations. Our aim was to get the Sustainable Development Goals (SDGs) to become a core element of the final Rio+20 outcome. The MDGs had been crafted by the UN Secretariat through a top-down process in which member states were not even consulted, one that consolidated the view that developed countries' only responsibility was to provide resources while that of developing countries was to act on a narrow set of largely social priorities. We wanted to ensure that the idea we were advancing could come to fruition in a radically different way.

Two preparatory meetings for Rio+20 were already scheduled for March 2011 to confirm the timeline for the eighteen months of the preparatory process that would culminate in the Rio+20 Summit.[5] This timeline centered on preparing a synthesis report on sustainable development that assessed progress on various fronts, gaps, and emerging issues. Colombia did not participate in these March meetings; from our perspective, this process could only yield incremental changes and would not give rise to a bold, bright new framework for transformation.

At the end of January 2011, just a few weeks after that first meeting in Bogotá that gave life to the SDGs concept, I went to New York to take part in the Ninth Session of the UN Forum on Forests. It was my first trip to New York since joining the government, and it was to be the first of many meetings on the margins of which I canvassed the SDGs idea. I started to wander the hallways of the "New Lawn Building"—the temporary conference and meeting venue set up in the UN compound on the banks of the East River in New York while the UN Headquarters building was refurbished—with copies of the initial SDGs proposal. Unfortunately, we did not retain a copy of our very first document proposing the SDGs, and thus we could not include it among the appendixes.

The initial reactions should have been deeply discouraging. The idea was dismissed as ludicrous and utterly impractical, or at best met with skepticism. At that juncture, having just come back to government, my network was quite small, and I was only familiar with delegates I had recently met at the Nagoya and Cancún negotiations. I was widely seen as a newcomer with an absurd idea, an outsider who did not know the ropes or the system or what was possible (or impossible). Time and again I was reminded that the agenda for Rio+20 had already been locked in through a formal resolution. I was also reminded that the MDGs were not part of the Rio+20 process and had their genesis in a completely different track in the UN—thus any type of interaction, let alone convergence, between the two was impossible. Moreover, it was underscored that the MDGs still had several years to go until their 2015 endpoint and were "unfinished business," so no one could propose anything to replace them until 2015. In addition to these insurmountable formal and procedural reasons, I was often told that the MDGs worked because they focused on a few core and salient issues and that it was ridiculous to suggest such a broad agenda. Early on, reactions were more bemused than aggressive as it was clear that this idea had absolutely no possibility of advancing.

Among the few delegates who were willing to even discuss the proposal, only three colleagues (Jimena Leiva of Guatemala, Ye-Min Wu of Singapore, and Damaso Luna of Mexico) reviewed the proposal and provided guidance: to stand a chance of advancing, it had to be embedded in the legacy of the Rio Conference in 1992, so it was essential to link it explicitly to one of its key outcomes, Agenda 21. So one night during the Forum on Forests negotiations, back at my hotel, I rewrote the proposal, structuring it around the chapters of Agenda 21 in hopes of making it more palatable to other governments.

The resulting document, just three pages long (see Appendix 3), was the first of many versions of SDGs-related documents that were drafted at The Pod hotel on 51st Street, off Second Avenue. I joked that we should put a plaque outside the hotel that would read "The SDGs were born and bred here." After getting clearance from my ministry to proceed with this version, I went back to haunting the hallways the following day.

The revised proposal reiterated that

> The Government of Colombia considers that Rio+20 constitutes a critical opportunity for the international community to agree on a concrete approach that transcends intellectual debates and delivers means for measuring—in accordance with the contexts and priorities of each country—both advances as well as bottlenecks in efforts to balance sustained socio-economic growth with the sustainable use of natural resources and the conservation of ecosystem services. There are experiences, such as the MDGs, that indicate that when there are objectives to guide the international community's efforts towards a collective goal, it becomes easier for governments and institutions to work together to reach them.

It went on to affirm that "Colombia is proposing that a key outcome of the Rio+20 process be the definition and agreement of a suite of Sustainable Development Goals (SDGs), equivalent to the MDGs."

These SDGs would translate the green economy/sustainable development debate into tangible goals, thus shifting away from broad political debates. We included a reference to the concept of green economy to demonstrate that as proponents we were aware of the established process. The text went on to clearly establish a pathway forward from Agenda 21, affirming that the SDGs would provide a "logical sequence and structure" to the process and guiding principles agreed to in 1992. The chapters around which Agenda 21 was structured were outdated, so the concept note proposed an "initial refocusing, clustering and additions," such as changing the chapter on atmosphere to focus on climate change mitigation and adding a new chapter on adaptation.

To jump-start the discussion—and drive home the fact that the international community had already once agreed to a broad, far-reaching agenda—the paper outlined issue areas taken from Agenda 21 around which objectives could be structured, including "combating poverty" (chapter 3), "changing consumption patterns" (chapter 4), "demographic dynamics and sustainability" (chapter 5), "protecting and promoting human health" (chapter 6), and so on. I made a point of focusing equally on social and economic issues. Crafted as a political document, the paper pointed to Agenda 21 as proof that the international community had already agreed to a framework and that it was feasible and straightforward to do so again. Notably, the paper did not explicitly state that this was a universal agenda. We knew the process was going to be long and battles had to be sequentially and carefully picked.

Throughout the first half of 2011, I traveled often to New York, given that my portfolio included a range of development issues. As I started to get to know more delegates, I changed the modus operandi. The time-worn Vienna Café, a mainstay of the UN complex for delegates, had been resurrected on the second floor of the temporary UN building. Rather than wandering the hallways, I made it a habit to set up shop in the Vienna Café in between negotiations and meetings. It was the only place for food and beverages in the building (besides a few vending machines on the first floor) and was an obligatory pass-through for the negotiation rooms on the second floor. All manner of ruses were used to bring colleagues to my table to explain the idea. Slowly, a small cohort of supporters started to bring others to my table, enthused about the idea. Although the number of adepts remained negligible considering the UN's 193 member states, a respectable number of people started to at least understand the concept. There were a few hard-won early victories of renowned pioneers and advocates of the sustainability agenda who were dragged to the table but walked away convinced that it was a new, real opportunity. However, this did not lead to widespread acceptance. The idea was still deemed too far-fetched, unattainable, and irrational. Besides, who was Colombia to propose what would be, in effect, a new global agenda?

Why Colombia?

From the start, our proposal met with unmitigated incredulity and as time passed, open animosity. The idea of a new set of goals was met with derision as the MDGs were "the gold standard" and still had several years to go, until 2015—until *at least* 2015 as many emphasized. Many questioned with exasperation why Colombia was even bothering to prepare for Rio+20 when "it was still so far away." Indeed, many increasingly asked "Why Colombia?": as in, "Why is Colombia, a nondescript developing country, aiming to propose and lead on a global agenda?" Looking back, it is still surprising that so many people asked this, as though we had usurped some unwritten right. The answer was and still is, why not?

In this multilateral setting, being Colombian conferred strengths for building bridges across constituencies. Colombia has a long and rich history in the G77 and China and was well respected among its members, even though over the previous decade we held positions that were increasingly at odds with those of the majority in that coalition. At the same time, in 2011 we started the process to join the Organisation for Economic Co-operation and Development (OECD), one of President Juan Manuel Santos's priorities since his first day in office.[6] In international negotiations, we were known for our progressive, well-documented positions. We were thus a country working across the geopolitical spectrum that could not be readily shoehorned into a specific niche. This gave us much wider political play. If a developed country had proposed the idea, concerns that surfaced around potential conditionalities would have been exacerbated, and it is possible that the proposal would not have flown, in UN parlance. Coming from a developing country, it was more feasible to avoid the perception that it was an agenda for limiting the growth opportunities of the Global South.

Colombia is a country of unexpected contrasts and a wide spectrum of regional realities that have evolved over the decades, laying bare the need to tackle development in a more integrated, multisectoral way. It also offers stark lessons about the impacts of failing to do so, as its fifty-year internal conflict evidenced. At the same time, even though our conflict has been indelibly linked with the illicit drug market and the human rights issues that it has spawned, Colombia is a country with strong institutions and a vibrant democracy. By 2010 we had walked back from the edge of the abyss of a failed state and were garnering support and recognition for our dogged and stalwart efforts to get the country back on track. Our history imbued us with a sense of how imperative it was to put forward a more ambitious, meaningful, and transformative global agenda. We believed then, as we do now, that our one shared destiny meant that we have the responsibility to act together.

As seasoned negotiators, Patti and I were convinced that our deep understanding of Colombia's complex history and present-day realities equipped us to understand and sort through conflicting ideas and build bridges to reach global consensus. In this context, the understanding and learning derived from our complex domestic reality helped us identify positions, difficulties, obstacles, and opportunities. Being Colombian has at times been difficult and painful: one saw the immense opportunities of a land of seemingly endless riches and hard-working people so often derailed by the impacts of harsh revolts against entrenched inequalities.

One overriding lesson is that solutions cannot be piecemeal. Nothing is purely economic or social or environmental. Sustainability and equity are two sides of the same coin. As Colombians, we had a perspective on development and conflict that gave us a dogged conviction that the world needed the SDGs. And we were determined that the process had to be radically different from that which had spawned the MDGs. Being Colombian actually prepared us for a journey of hurdles and difficulties and ultimately made it possible for the SDGs to become a fundamental linchpin for our time.

From MDGs to SDGs: A Transition
As I canvassed our idea, many retorted that only developing countries had issues related to development and that any development agenda should therefore focus exclusively on them. There were deep and valid concerns that a more far-ranging framework would detract attention from what were viewed as core development needs and that the SDGs were thus a formula for the irredeemable dilution of development priorities and commitments. Others—the few who actually listened to what we were proposing during those early days and thought it through—queried what development targets could possibly mean for developed countries. No one knew how to even think about "development" in terms of developed countries. The MDGs had cemented the divide between "developed" and "developing" based on their minimalist, propoor vision.

Colombia was deeply committed to the MDGs and methodically tracked progress in achieving them. Colombia was recognized by the United Nations Development Programme (UNDP) as one of the countries that had been widely successful in delivering on the MDGs. We agreed that the MDGs had delivered significant progress on the prioritized targets around the world and played a decisive role in galvanizing action around fundamental development issues. The MDGs stood out in the landscape of development assistance. But we also strongly felt that they were woefully inadequate for the challenges ahead as they reflected a narrow agenda that was unable to deliver the system-wide changes and broad structural transformations that were needed. Many of the global gains in poverty eradication attributed to the MDGs were largely achieved in China. Continued poverty eradication in the future, on a planet facing degradation and scarcity of natural resources, climate change and climatic variability impacts, food insecurity, rapid and often unplanned urbanization, and landscapes of increasing fragility, insecurity, and polarization would be much more challenging. For that, an agenda that embraced the complexity of development was needed.

Box 2.1   Moving Beyond Internationally Agreed Development Goals

In the context of the United Nations development agenda, there are a range of internationally agreed development goals that stem from the many multilateral instruments that have been adopted by countries over the past decades and include goals and commitments defined in the context of major UN conferences and summits starting in the 1970s through the 2000s. The MDGs were part of these goals because they were understood as part of a wider development agenda. These cut across the outcomes of conferences and summits, ranging from social development, population, education, employment, racism, women and gender equality, aging, children, health, food, HIV/AIDS, human settlements, landlocked developing countries, least developed countries, small island developing states, sustainable development to human rights, financing for development, information and communication technology, and governance.

In the years before Rio+20, there were many discussions and papers on "internationally agreed development goals" that covered different agendas that had their own timeframes and strategies. For example, an important UN-led project, *Back to Our Common Future,* noted that "Sustainable development scenarios produced for Rio+20 by various research groups have explored a broad range of sustainability goals."[7] These were entirely different from the SDGs but were sometimes confused with the SDGs, especially in the early years. The SDGs we envisioned were a stand-alone comprehensive framework—transformative in nature and highly ambitious in scope. In hindsight, we consider this one of the most meaningful achievements of the SDGs proposal.

There were deep misunderstandings about what the MDGs encompassed and what we were aiming for with the SDGs idea (see Box 2.1). Even the fact that we were proposing not to eviscerate the MDGs but to incorporate them into more integrated and far-reaching goals after 2015 was taken precisely as proof of the threat that the SDGs posed. Over the months of negotiations, and indeed well into the process launched in 2013 to define the details of the SDGs framework, there was opposition to the establishment of a single health goal, for example. In one exchange, I was emphatically informed that Africa would never agree to merge the three MDGs health goals under one goal. It was perceived as giving up three goals for just one. We saw this as trading in three incomplete goals for one comprehensive goal. For instance, the MDGs did not include a goal on noncommunicable diseases, which are the greatest and growing public health care burden for developing countries (before Covid-19).

As the months went by, the idea that a country from the Global South had proposed out of the blue started to gain adherents, but by the same measure, opposition grew. Interestingly, precisely because of the resistance, our proposal started to force some to consider what might happen in 2015 and how the MDGs process would be taken forward. This cohort started to rally behind a vague concept that many came to refer to as "MDG+" and that gradually became invested with diverse meanings but a single endpoint. First and foremost, the concept was rooted in the conviction that the MDGs would and should essentially be rolled over in 2015 and continue to be the linchpin of the international development agenda. This was predicated on the fact that in several developing countries, many of the MDGs targets would not be met and that the MDGs already focused on the most important development issues. Most MDG+ advocates recognized that a few changes or updates would be needed in 2015 to adjust the targets and accommodate lessons or new developments or "emerging issues," but the MDGs architecture was to remain essentially intact. What was envisioned was the preservation of the MDGs status quo for at least another fifteen years, or until the majority of developing countries achieved the targets, which were understood to be the core metric of development.

This idea was anathema to us. It locked in a mindset and a framework that excluded the systemic shifts so urgently needed to reverse the degradation of resources, rampant inequality, inexorable rise of greenhouse gas emissions, wasteful consumption and unsustainable production, and untenable growth models. It locked in a bifurcated vision of the world that would make it impossible to tackle global public goods issues. It locked in a paternalistic vision of development that effectively negated empowerment and agency. Despite the global process that aimed to implement and monitor improvements in aid quality and its effect on the ground, and despite establishing principles such as ownership, alignment, harmonization, and mutual accountability, the MDGs cemented a donor-driven framework. Certainly, the MDGs had given rise to remarkable partnerships, but these were, in the big picture of development trajectories for the coming decades, small drops in an ocean of structural needs.

Nevertheless, the MDG+ idea gained strength. From the perspective of the traditional development community, it resolved the threat posed by the SDGs idea. All that was needed was a reaffirmation of the primacy of the MDGs and an acknowledgment that they would need to be rolled over as unfinished business and updated based on judicious assessments. Thus, the perceived derailment of the MDGs and a decade of investments and efforts would be avoided, and the basic core priorities would be maintained. As this was a completely separate process from the one that started in Rio de Janeiro in 1992, and Rio+20 would take place a full three years before the MDGs' initial due date in 2015, some contended there was at most a need to reaffirm the primacy and relevance of the MDGs in Rio+20. In the months of arduous negotiation recounted in this book, what Colombia and its closest allies did was steer the process away from this short-sighted proposition.

Fortunately, in many (if not most) governments, there were widely divergent positions regarding MDGs, MDG+, and the SDGs. Although generalizations in this case are fraught with imprecision, environment ministries gradually came to adhere to the SDGs proposition. Most development ministries or agencies were largely and firmly in the MDG+ camp. Thus, within the same government, some viewed the SDGs as the stepping-stone toward an agenda of integration and structural change, whereas others considered them an imminent threat and unwelcome distraction from critical issues. I have often noted that at some level, Colombia did not negotiate the SDGs with 193 governments but with hundreds of individual delegates and constituencies. Often it was the case, especially in 2011, that a country's position would shift 180 degrees depending on which delegate, from which ministry, was participating in a meeting.

The depth of this divide ultimately played out in an interesting and unexpected way in the final hours of negotiation in Rio de Janeiro (these events are detailed in Chapter 8). In several key donor countries, the development community had been convinced early on that such an absurd proposition would ultimately never be accepted. Thus, they mostly left the negotiations in the hands of environment ministries that were largely supportive of the SDGs for two key reasons. First, it enabled them to move out of the straitjacket of MDG7, which purported to be about the environment but tackled two social issues and two environmental ones. Second, it opened up access to funding in development agencies. It created a window whereby environment ministries would potentially be able to wield greater power. This enabled the SDGs process to advance, by the time we got to Rio, to a point of no return.

As will be seen, this proved decisive in the final hours of negotiation. It also explains why there were marked changes in the composition and leadership of many delegations from the Rio+20 negotiations in 2012 to the Open Working Group in 2013.

Dogged Determination

In those early months of 2011, the harder the going, the more convinced we were that the SDGs were what the world desperately needed. The more opposition, the firmer our government's backbone.[8] It was fast becoming clear that the process was going to be more complicated and difficult than we had ever anticipated. We had not expected such forceful and deep-rooted opposition to an idea that had seemed so simple, good, and self-evident. But there was no turning back. We were determined to orchestrate a process that would ensure the SDGs were adopted—and that this be achieved through a strong multilateral process. We knew that when consensus is finally reached through a comprehensive multilateral process, there is real ownership.

From our perspective, many governments and delegates were in a sort of bind and could not see beyond the limited contours of the existing frameworks and positions and politicized language. For many, the mere thought of trying to get such a radical change as envisioned in the SDGs through the UN system and its processes was dissuasion enough. It was not just the complexity of what Colombia was proposing but also the fact that it would upend the divide between developed and developing countries, a cornerstone of most negotiations in the environmental arena.[9] The framework we lobbied for embodied a universal agenda—applicable to all countries and for which all countries were accountable. For years, the UNFCCC negotiations had run aground precisely because parties could not move beyond the divide reflected in CBDR. Even those who were rooting for the SDGs lamented that ultimately the proposal would never see the light of day given these entrenched positions.

In May 2011, a failed multilateral process shone a stark light on the depth of the divisions in international fora on sustainable development, and Colombia's proposal seemed all the more quixotic and unreachable. On May 15, 2011, the CSD imploded. It was a debacle charged with significance for the process we were trying to lead. Because this was the last CSD meeting before Rio+20, it seemed to signal that the international community was unable or unwilling to come together to deliver the agreements and commitments to advance the sustainable development agenda.

Established after the first Rio Earth Summit in 1992, the CSD was tasked with ensuring effective follow-up of Agenda 21. After the Rio+10 conference in 2002, which took place in Johannesburg, South Africa, CSD was also tasked with follow-up on the Johannesburg Plan of Implementation.[10]

In May 2011, CSD convened for the second meeting of a two-year cycle, focused on a thematic cluster that included sustainable consumption and production, mining, transport, and waste management. After two weeks of negotiations, high-level meetings, and dialogues, there was full agreement on most tracks by the time of the final plenary on May 14, notably including the Ten-Year Framework Program on Sustainable Consumption and Production. Even so, in the end, a few outstanding and very contentious issues—on the inclusion of language on "the rights of people living under colonial and foreign occupation," on text referencing "developed countries taking the lead," and on the principle of CBDR—blocked the proceedings. One of the areas around which there was clearly no consensus was the concept of "green economy," one of the two formally defined pillars of UNCSD.

After an all-night session of intense but fruitless consultations, and despite the best efforts of the bureau and the chair who put forward a consensus package, agreement ultimately proved impossible. The plenary spilled past the last day of the meeting. After efforts during successive early morning plenary sessions to find a way forward, Saudi Arabia requested a quorum count.[11] It was found that there was no longer a quorum; after two weeks of intense deliberations, the CSD session simply fizzled out, concluding with a text in brackets and no resolution.

The CSD debacle evidenced the deep divisions that underlay discussions around sustainable development issues and the attendant role and responsibilities to deliver on new pathways. Make no mistake: if it had not been for Colombia's proposal and dogged perseverance, the international community would most likely have ultimately agreed to a mildly revamped version of the status quo, an "MDG+ world" in 2015.

Given the complexities of formal negotiation processes, our informal diplomacy was essential for building the momentum to create a new way forward.

Notes

1. UNEP (2011).

2. The CSD is another key development in the context of the Rio Earth Summit of 1992, also known as the United Nations Conference on Environment and Development (UNCED). The CSD was created by UN General Assembly Resolu-

tion 47/191 of December 22, 1992, to follow up the UNCED. After Rio+20, member states agreed to create the High-Level Political Forum to track implementation of the 2030 agenda and the Sustainable Development Goals (SDGs), and with this decision the CSD was replaced.

3. The Charter of the United Nations of 1945, chapter III, article 7, established its principal organs, namely, the General Assembly, the Security Council, the Economic and Social Council (ECOSOC), the Trusteeship Council, the International Court of Justice, and the Secretariat. Chapter X, articles 61–72, deals with the composition, functions and powers, voting, and procedure of the ECOSOC.

4. It is interesting to note that this name did not sit well with many. Throughout the process, I was intermittently pressured to change the name, something that I refused to do. Over the coming years, and indeed even after 2015 when the SDGs were a reality, many attempted to rename them—mostly with the intent to eliminate the word "sustainable." Concerted efforts were made to call the SDGs the "Global Goals" or the "Global Development Goals."

5. Summary of First Intersessional Meeting of UNCSD (March 10–11, 2011) and Summary of the Second Session of the Preparatory Committee (PrepCom) for UNCSD (March 7–8, 2011).

6. In May 2018, the OECD issued the invitation to join, and Colombia became a full member in April 2020.

7. UNDESA (2012a).

8. As I became obsessed with the SDGs, Patti used to joke and call me a Rottweiler, saying that I had bitten into the idea and would simply never let go.

9. In the negotiations of the Basel, Rotterdam, and Stockholm Conventions, for example, there is no G77 and China coordination.

10. The Johannesburg Plan of Implementation of the World Summit on Sustainable Development 2002 contained eleven chapters with recommendations on issues such as poverty eradication, consumption and production patterns, and health, and it established roles for the main organs, such as the General Assembly, the ECOSOC, and the CSD. It also provided a needs assessment for the different regions in terms of sustainable development.

11. A minimum of twenty-seven members of the CSD constituted a quorum, and at that point there were only twenty-four delegations in the room.

3

Getting Governments
on Board

Informal diplomacy drove our effort to include the Sustainable Development Goals (SDGs) in the Rio+20 outcome, as the tight timeframe required us to get other governments on board in time for the SDGs to be included in the text that would form the basis of negotiations in the six months leading to the Rio+20 Summit. Ensuring the SDGs were included in the Zero Draft, the compilation of suggestions and priorities that would be the starting point of intense negotiations from January 2012 onward, was our "make-or-break" moment. For this to happen, we engaged and lobbied in multiple settings, formats, and meetings and took every opportunity to introduce and convince our peers of the merits and value of our SDGs proposal.

The Very First Meeting

After months of intermittent meetings in the Vienna Café, we decided that it was time to have a proper consultation on the SDGs. By then most of the delegates who had relevant portfolios, notably those in the Second Committee of the UN General Assembly, had heard of the proposal.[1] Our idea was still regarded as an improbable outlier. We felt it was vital to bring together a group of delegates to discuss the proposal so we could gauge more clearly where various delegates—it would have been a stretch to have referred to "governments" at this point—stood on the proposal. We had spent months trying to stitch together a sense of the main issues or concerns, and we hoped that the meeting could be a timely way to take stock. We thought that by bringing delegates together, some kind of momentum could be generated, some nascent coalition could be identified. On May 27, 2011, I convened the first informal intergovernmental consultation on the SDGs. It took place at the Colombian Mission to the United Nations in New York.

Delegates from Botswana, Brazil, Chile, China, Egypt, France, Guatemala, Mexico, Singapore, Spain, Switzerland, the United States, and Uruguay attended, thus ensuring representation of all the UN regional groups. The meeting went better than I had anticipated, although ultimately there was no clear way forward. In hindsight, it was telling that at this first meeting some of the core issues that came to define—and plague—the negotiations already surfaced (see Appendix 4).

All participants emphasized that poverty eradication had to remain the overriding goal. Egypt said that this could be a major outcome of Rio+20 and that it could integrate the Millennium Development Goals (MDGs) agenda, affirming that it was important to think beyond 2015.[2] Together with Guatemala, they noted that an SDGs framework would provide benchmarks and quantifiable targets for sustainable development issues. Mexico declared the SDGs an excellent idea and said it would be a way to measure the seriousness of political commitments. The delegate liked that it was so well grounded in Agenda 21. China said that the Colombian proposal was good, but that monitoring and Means of Implementation (MoI) would be key.[3] The US delegate said the Colombian paper had caused an impact in Washington, and there was a growing sense of the need to provide messages relevant to the next generation. I affirmed that there was a value in having goals with clear deliverables and said there was merit in at least embarking on the process.

However, others expressed concerns that the SDGs could try to "substitute the MDGs" and said that it was key to differentiate between developing and developed countries. One suggestion was that there be different types of targets, "bottom-up for developing countries and top-down for developed countries." Just what this meant was never clarified. Switzerland pointed to the MDGs review process and said it should be a starting point for thinking about a future framework. Several delegates queried how the MDGs community and the UN Department for Economic and Social Affairs (DESA) would see the proposal.[4] Guatemala affirmed that there could be a strong linkage to the MDGs, and that some SDGs would simply reaffirm the MDGs, as appropriate. All agreed that in any case, the goals would need to be voluntary.

I was especially keen to hear the views of Brazil, the future host of Rio+20. The delegate raised a series of questions. How could the issue areas be clustered? How would MoI be integrated? How to reflect common but differentiated responsibilities (CBDR)? As others had done, he affirmed that poverty reduction had to remain the cornerstone.

Spain agreed with the need to merge environment and sustainable development but considered that it was important to understand why and how this link had failed to be made: it was in Agenda 21, but had fallen to the wayside. Several colleagues thought that a thorough gap analysis was needed first to better understand what had worked and what had not in terms of sustainable development. The GEO Report was highlighted as an example of the kind of analysis that was needed.[5] However, France thought this could become a blame game, and Brazil underscored that responses to development challenges would have to be understood as contingent on "respective capabilities."

In fact, most of the G77 and China members started out their interventions by emphasizing the need to ensure that any new framework would be under "CBDR and respective capabilities," while other delegates that did not belong to the group strongly objected to this. There was, however, a degree of agreement on the need to build on the principles outlined in Agenda 21. Concerns around MoI were linked to the CBDR discussion. Most agreed that these had to be central to any new proposal, but a few delegates said it would be important to better understand what this could concretely translate into.

The need for a strong monitoring framework was highlighted several times. The United States said that going forward it would be important to look beyond government action and involve the private sector, academia, and civil society.

France said that the issue of sustainable development was encompassed in the "green economy" pillar and insisted that a proposal like the SDGs had to be embedded in this pillar. There was strong resistance—which France maintained to the end—to create a separate SDGs track in the preparatory process for Rio+20. Another concern that many delegations brought up was that "other negotiations" could get caught up in the process, a stark if indirect reference to the climate change negotiations. Some mused about the need to include climate change in the Rio+20 discussions, worrying that doing so could negatively affect the UN Framework Convention on Climate Change (UNFCCC) negotiations. There were persistent gentle reminders to Colombia that the themes for Rio+20 had already been defined in UN Resolution A/64/236, with the implicit message that new tracks or proposals could no longer be put on the table at this stage.

I was exhilarated after the meeting. Through their participation, representatives from key governments had at least signaled that our idea had some value. I felt this gave us a firmer runway for exploring and maturing the proposal. Concerns had been discussed in a collective setting where delegates from key constituencies could hear each other out, and I felt confident that we had a good sense of the emerging geopolitical map and the political economy of the SDGs. My consultations over the preceding months had already surfaced these issues, and now they were confirmed. I heard the strong subtext of concern regarding what Rio+20 could deliver and the need to ensure concrete and tangible outcomes. Many were concerned about the level of ambition: the UN resolution said nothing fundamentally meaningful in terms of how the international community could face the myriad challenges that cut across environmental, social, and economic dimensions. The road ahead was incredibly challenging, but as far as Colombia was concerned, there was a way forward.

The Proposal Gains Traction

In June 2011, during the UNFCCC negotiations in Bonn, I continued Colombia's advocacy work. In the hallways there was a marked and palpable change. Colleagues and delegates started to approach me to express informal support for the idea or to ask for more information and insights about what it entailed. Many affirmed that Rio+20 desperately needed to deliver concrete and tangible results. It finally seemed that the proposal was getting traction. It was notable that so many representatives from nongovernmental organizations and civil society groups came forward with earnest support.

I sought out André do Lago, a colleague I had come to know well across the various negotiations, who led the Brazilian delegation in the UNFCCC negotiations. We met in a small café in the lobby of the Maritime Hotel in Bonn, where the climate change negotiations were taking place. He expressed interest but also reminded me of their role as the presidency of Rio+20. I took the confirmation of interest as an endorsement but at that point did not fully calibrate what other considerations or concerns the Brazilian delegation might have as the incoming host country of the conference.

The growing encouragement we received was tempered by the hard reality of the UNFCCC negotiations. At that juncture, a deep fracture in the climate change negotiations for an eventual post-Kyoto regime centered on whether to maintain the differentiation between countries. The Kyoto regime was grounded in the division between Annex 1 and non–Annex 1 countries; this had been a linchpin of the process from its early days. Battles were being waged across the climate change negotiations that hinged on whether the post-Kyoto regime could demand obligatory action from all countries, not just industrialized countries with a responsibility for historic emissions, and how to manage the differences in financial capacity and emissions trajectories. Given these, a key concern for many was the role that the emerging economies of Brazil, China, India, and South Africa would play. In other words, the core question was whether a post-Kyoto regime would be universal, and what we were proposing was precisely a universal framework.

And yet. From our vantage point, convinced as we were that the world needed the SDGs framework, we saw the proposal as the only actionable option on the table given that the discussions around the two agreed pillars for the Rio conference had limited purchase.

In June 2011, UN Secretary-General Ban Ki-moon visited Colombia to support President Santos's Law on Land Restitution and Victims, which aimed to create conditions for providing effective redress and livelihood options to victims of the decades-long internal conflict. During the visit, President Santos told the Secretary-General about Colombia's initiative for Rio+20 and explained the level of ambition and the universal ambit of the SDGs proposal. The Secretary-General responded positively to the initiative and mentioned that he would take it up with his team in New York. To the best of our knowledge, there was no follow-up, most likely because at that point the agenda for Rio+20 was viewed entirely through the mandate of the UN resolution. At that early stage, there was no indication that the SDGs would turn out to be the most transformative outcome at Rio+20 and one of the major legacies of Ban Ki-moon's tenure. In fact, many UN staff's first recollection of hearing about the SDGs was at a meeting in Solo, Indonesia.

Around this time, the government of Indonesia decided to host a High-Level Dialogue on the International Framework for Sustainable Development (IFSD) July 19–21, 2011, in Solo. We saw it as an opportunity to formally present the SDGs to the UN. As far as we knew, this was the only global UN-related meeting in the coming months or the remainder of the year on Rio+20, so it offered a unique entry point. It seemed our best bet because it was jointly hosted with the UN and participants included UN Under-Secretary-General and Secretary-General of the Rio+20 Conference Ambassador Sha Zukang, as well as representatives of many member states, intergovernmental organizations (IGOs), and major groups, plus key UN system entities.

As stated in the event's report, its objective "was to support the preparatory process for Rio+20 by providing a forum for delegates and invited experts to share views and hold frank discussions, in a non-negotiation context, on the pros and cons of various options and proposals." Although the focus was exclusively on IFSD, we figured that any setting worked to position the SDGs.

On arrival, I went to both the Indonesian delegation and the UN Secretariat to request permission to present our proposal. Getting access to a printer and making copies for everyone proved challenging, so only a few copies were on hand. On the second day I was allowed to take the floor, and I described the proposal, underscoring that Colombia's hope was that others would support it. To my surprise, there was no opportunity to discuss it. At the time there was interest in an initiative of the Secretary-General on a suite of sustainable energy goals, and many saw this as a compelling development. But there was no vision for an overarching framework beyond energy. After I finished my presentation, the agenda moved on after a comment by the chair. According to the report summarizing the discussions, of the eight "Main Points of Progress in Discussions," the SDGs were singled out:

> *Sustainable Development Goals* (SDGs): There was a significant interest in the discussion on the Sustainable Development Goals. In the context of goals related, in particular, to the sustainable energy goals advanced by the [UN]SG's Advisory Group, there was a feeling that negotiating specific goals would bog down the negotiations. However, there may be a good chance for an agreement in principle on the development of Sustainable Development Goals.

However, the final Solo message, which highlighted seven key messages, did not include any mention of the SDGs. It mentioned the need to "ensure that the economic, social and environmental pillars work together with each pillar integrating the goals of the other two pillars," but said nothing about how this was to be done. The report missed the point of the proposal entirely and zeroed in on the three goals that had already been identified on sustainable energy, which became the cornerstone of the Sustainable Energy for All initiative. It was within the safe boundaries of the status quo.

Sha Zukang's concluding remarks made no mention of the SDGs. In his comments on "strengthening integration among 3 pillars," he referred to "one significant proposal [which] is the formation of a sustainable development council." Despite this, I viewed the proceedings as positive for two reasons. The first is that with our presentation, the SDGs proposal had been acknowledged in a UN setting on Rio+20. The second one is that on the margins of the meetings, the momentum around the SDGs was really starting to pick up.

In the hallways, I continued seeking meetings with every delegation—ranging from the willing to the downright reluctant—as well as stakeholder representatives. There was growing concern that the conference, as it had been conceived and defined in the relevant UN resolution, would deliver nothing of bearing for the world. A welcome sign that the tide was starting to turn was that a few delegations, including the European Union, asked me for meetings. There were bilateral meetings with delegations that suddenly wanted to better understand the proposal and who had started to see it as a real possibility for Rio+20. We knew that once delegates became interested in an innovative idea, there is a chance for success.

In Solo, the representative for Guatemala, Rita Mishaan, confirmed her government's interest in supporting the SDGs proposal. Felix Dodds, the executive director of the Stakeholder Forum, an important civil society organization platform, told me this proposal could be a key Rio+20 outcome and encouraged Colombia to hold the course. There was a growing sense of hope that the proposal would prosper.

The following month in August 2011, Brazil held an informal preparatory consultation for Rio+20 in Rio de Janeiro at the imposing Palácio do Itamaraty. A small group of delegates were invited. When I wrote to ask for permission to present the SDGs proposal, I was informed that it was an open, informal consultation and that countries could discuss whatever they wanted to. On the first morning of the two-day meeting, I presented it, this time armed with multiple copies of the proposal, which I duly distributed. There were other topics on the agenda, but the entire meeting started to gravitate around the concept of the SDGs. It was amazing to hear delegates from Cuba to Norway welcoming the proposal, keen to explore its dimensions and implications. Rita Mishaan from Guatemala once again expressed interest in supporting the proposal.

However, as the discussions progressed that first day, I realized that the proposal as written, with its strong linkages to Agenda 21, was confusing and that a simpler text focused only on the SDGs concept was needed. The discussions kept straying into an assessment of Agenda 21 and the relevance of some of its chapters, rather than focusing on the characteristics and strengths of the SDGs. Did Colombia want to revamp Agenda 21? By then we had realized that despite a lot of lip service to Agenda 21, no one actually cared that much about it. It was dated.

That night, I wrote a new concept note that would do double duty: help streamline the discussion and enable Guatemala to formally endorse the proposal. This was a major breakthrough and a key next step. This two-page proposal (see Appendix 5), now put forward by two governments, focused on the importance of a measurable outcome with goals, targets, and indicators. It reiterated that "a key outcome of the Rio+20 process [was] the definition and agreement of a suite of Sustainable Development Goals (SDGs)." Reference to the journey from 1992 was maintained to emphasize that the new proposal was rooted in agreements and a vision already subscribed to by the international community. The proposal was no longer tied to an evolution of Agenda 21 but rather aimed to show that it was a sensible next step on the pathway that had begun in 1992: "The SDGs could provide a logical sequence and structure to the process launched almost 20 years ago: in 1992 the guiding principles were agreed to as well as a roadmap for sustainable development; in 2002 a Plan of Implementation was defined; and now in 2012 we could consider identifying goals in order to better identify gaps and needs and provide for more structured implementation of the principles and goals defined 20 years ago."

Cognizant that a major hurdle was the relationship to the MDGs, the note stated simply that the "SDGs and the MDGs should be fully complementary" and suggested that both processes, defining the SDGs and revising the MDGs, could be convergent. We did not dare at this stage suggest a single process as we knew that one of the overriding fears of many delegations was that the SDGs would overshadow the MDGs and impede their full realization. Crucially, however, the note went on to underscore that "while the MDGs applied only to developing countries, the SDGs would have universal application." Given that these were highly political documents, this transformative affirmation was quietly understated.

Beyond sketching out the SDGs concept, the paper reflected the overriding concern we had from the outset regarding the need to establish a process to develop the framework after Rio+20. Knowing full well how protracted UN processes are, the paper called for "gaug[ing] a practical level of ambition for the development of the SDGs by June 2012" and proposed that "a reasonable deliverable . . . at Rio would be agreement on a suite of Objectives at a broad level." It clearly stated that "the expected results at the Rio Summit would be two pronged: 1) a definition of thematic objectives and, 2) an agreement on a mandate to subsequently define (post-Rio) how these Objectives would be further developed. . . . There would not be a need to prejudge the outcome in the remaining months leading up to Rio."

The SDGs proposal, now sharper and more succinct, took center stage during the second day of the consultations in Rio de Janeiro. There were intense and substantive exchanges, and even though many voiced concerns about the implications for the MDGs, there was a broad sense of emerging support from several quarters. Many underscored that Rio+20 needed to have powerful, tangible outcomes and the SDGs framework could well be what was needed. Even though no one in the Brazilian delegation expressed explicit support for the proposal, in his concluding remarks Luiz Alberto Figueiredo Machado, executive secretary of the Brazilian National Commission for Rio+20, said that Rio+20 could not be just about principles but needed tangible results. I interpreted that as Brazilian support for the proposal.

The next milestone on the journey was the Regional Preparatory Meeting for Latin America and the Caribbean on UNCSD at the headquarters of the Economic Commission for Latin America and the Caribbean (ECLAC) on September 7–9, 2011, in Santiago, Chile. Alicia Bárcena, executive secretary of ECLAC, was an early and energetic supporter of the SDGs and immediately assessed their potential. Arriving a day early to the meeting, I met with Bárcena in her office, where we strategized on options for structuring the SDGs and ways of positioning them in the months ahead. She pledged unconditional support.

For Colombia, this regional meeting was a unique opportunity to substantively discuss the proposal in a formal UN setting, even if a regional one. Colombia had submitted the Colombia-Guatemala paper well ahead of time so that it would be an official conference document. We had an overriding objective at this meeting: to get widespread support from all countries in the Latin American and Caribbean region so that it could be presented as a regional contribution to Rio+20. Colombia hoped it could be a proposal from the whole region, not just a few countries.

Unfortunately, despite strong support from many delegations, this ultimately proved impossible, and not because of substantive issues or concerns. One delegation that had enthusiastically supported the SDGs just two weeks before in Rio de Janeiro now eviscerated them. Often a change in a country's representation, especially when different delegates were sent to a meeting, meant that the country's position could do a 180-degree turn. One delegate was incensed that the proposal from Colombia-Guatemala was a formal conference document.

Firm supporters like Guatemala and Mexico spoke strongly in favor, arguing yet again for the need for a concrete and compelling outcome in Rio+20. On the sides, the ECLAC Secretariat did the rounds, discussing the proposal with various delegates, but to no avail. In the end, the final decision text made no reference at all to the SDGs proposal and "agree[d] that the Conference must apply itself to the task for finding a new world production and consumption paradigm and understand that this may be referred to as a 'green economy'" and "decide[d] that a new international covenant must be forged aimed at addressing development asymmetries." There was a reiteration of well-established demands of developed countries, including the "historical commitment to set aside 0.7% of their gross national income for [official development assistance]." There was an energetic focus on the MDGs, which were to be fulfilled at all costs. There was nothing new.

Despite the difficulties in getting full agreement in the Latin American and Caribbean Group, the SDGs had been formally presented and discussed, and we saw this as another positive step forward. A decisive development was the strong support from Caribbean countries, who argued for the need to have a tangible outcome in Rio+20 in 2012. Their support would be critical less than two months later.

Getting a Foothold

Back in March 2011, the second session of the Preparatory Committee for UNCSD had set November 1, 2011, as the deadline for all parties and constituencies to submit their inputs and recommendations for the basic negotiation text for defining the Rio+20 outcome. The document based on these inputs would be known as the Zero Draft. In July 2011, the co-chairs issued a guidance note on this invitation.[6] The structure of the Zero Draft would include the two pillars defined in the UN resolution. Beyond that, only issues that made it into the Zero Draft would be part of the Rio+20 outcome. Therefore, at this point, it was essential that enough member states and constituencies include the concept of the SDGs in their submissions to the UNCSD. The entire undertaking hung in the balance.

For the next two months, all our efforts focused on ensuring that the SDGs would make the Zero Draft. Although we had received positive signals of support from many stakeholder groups and government representatives (albeit the latter from governments who also had delegates opposed to the concept), we were trying to get an entirely new issue on the agenda of a process that many considered already locked in. At best, as delegates from France and a few other countries suggested, we might be able to slot in a mention under the Green Economy pillar. We also knew that many countries and constituencies, especially from the traditional development arena, were determined to "protect" the MDGs from the SDGs.

Throughout September and October 2011, we lobbied relentlessly for the SDGs ahead of the deadline. There were still endless questions from most governments and concerns over the MDGs' "unfinished business," over a brand-new "universal" agenda, over a framework that integrated all core areas of development. After the disappointing outcome in ECLAC with nothing close to regional endorsement, we occasionally despaired. But it also galvanized us to maximize the next big opportunity: the UN General Assembly, held every September in New York with the participation of the heads of state of all member states and around which thousands of representatives of many major stakeholder groups, constituencies, and organizations congregated.

The briefings for both the foreign minister and the president during their many bilateral meetings during the General Assembly included a strong appeal in support of the SDGs. We programmed numerous bilateral meetings with delegations that were supportive and with those skeptical and resistant to the proposal. We organized small consultations. We tried to drum up interest in the countries and with representatives we had targeted to invite to a consultation we were planning to hold in Bogotá.

My team generated a steady flow of talking points, briefings, and concept notes for members of government, so that the SDGs would be raised in as many international and bilateral meetings as possible. Papers explained the Rio process since before 1992, the relationship between the MDGs and the SDGs, the many benefits of adopting a metric for sustainable development, and the importance of a tangible, broadly galvanizing outcome from Rio+20. I spent hours each day sending emails and making calls trying to drum up support and gauge the probabilities of getting the SDGs into the Zero Draft.

I was in especially close contact with members of the UNCSD Executive Coordination team, in particular Brice Lalonde, Liz Thompson, and Henry de Cazotte. During my frequent trips to New York, I had begun to meet with them regularly. Given that a key role of this team was to support ambitious and tangible results, early on they saw that the SDGs offered the possibility of a galvanizing outcome at Rio+20. In our conversations, they helped us better understand the dynamics around the process.

Across the UN system, opinions were varied, and there were divisions over specific aspects. For example, many thought the best outcome would be a mandate for deciding on a process without defining specific thematic areas. There was a concern that only experts could provide the substance needed to define goals and targets. Others considered that there was a need to debate the themes. Still others believed that leaders attending Rio+20 would want decisions on actual goals, not just on processes. Within the UN, there was an important cohort that was strongly wedded to the MDGs and perceived the SDGs as a threat that would derail established work programs and priorities. Several colleagues in New York confirmed to us that Brazil was supportive of the concept and wanted to be heavily involved in the goals. They underscored that they were hearing that civil society wanted concrete outcomes to bring back from Rio+20. A constant referent was the platform on sustainable energy established by Secretary-General Ban Ki-moon that had identified a suite of concrete goals and would eventually lead to the establishment of the Sustainable Energy for All initiative.

The UNCSD Bureau had also warmed to the idea of the SDGs.[7] At its seventeenth meeting on September 11, 2011, reference was made to the SDGs in their minutes for the first time. One of the summary bullets recorded, "The idea of setting sustainable development goals was considered relevant in measuring the performance of sustainable development. It was noted that the Rio+20 Conference could perhaps set a process to further elaborate on these goals." However, the "Key expectations from Rio+20" prioritized "a process for transitioning towards a green economy; better coordination and cooperation among UN system entities; and scaling up of work in priority sectors such as water, food security, agriculture, sustainable cities, oceans, etc."

There was a brief mention of the August consultation in Rio de Janeiro. As it had been held under Chatham House Rule, there was not much detail, but it was noted that "the proposal on sustainable development goals—as proposed by Guatemala and Colombia—came under discussion but the need for further discussion was quite evident." Although the eighteenth meeting of the Bureau on November 8 did not touch on the SDGs, at the nineteenth Bureau meeting on December 14 (just ahead of the Second Intersessional Meeting), the SDGs proposal was highlighted again in the discussions on the compilation document: "To address the implementation gaps, a development agenda with a mechanism for measuring progress have been suggested, which in turn is related to the idea of SDGs, their relation to MDGs and a post-2015 development framework."

Another key event in this time period was the sixty-fourth annual Department of Public Information/Non-Governmental Organization Conference, "Sustainable Societies, Responsive Citizens," held in Bonn, Germany, on September 3–5 and chaired by Felix Dodds. Since the meeting in Solo, Dodds had emerged as one of the most resolute champions of the SDGs, and the proposal got center stage at the conference. These conferences were premier platforms for bringing together representatives of civil society from around the world. In 2011, it focused on the role of civil society in creating and maintaining sustainable communities and developing responsive citizens. That year it had an unprecedented number of participants: more than 2,200 from more than 100 countries, representing hundreds of organizations. This event provided a global sounding board for the SDGs.

The conference issued a final declaration that included a section on Rio+20 and called on governments to adopt the SDGs "to achieve the goals of Rio+20 in an ambitious, time-bound and accountable manner." The declaration framed the SDGs "in accordance with human rights, the principle of common but differentiated responsibilities, and respective capabilities" and detailed a list of "aspirational goals," together with "sub-goals, reasons and clarifications relating to each." It outlined sixteen goals that ranged from sustainable consumption and production to clean energy to basic health. The intense discussions that culminated in a call for the SDGs were key in getting many constituencies from all over the world to include the SDGs in their submissions on the Zero Draft to the UNCSD Secretariat in UNDESA that led the compilation process behind the scenes.

Getting the SDGs into the Zero Draft

On November 1, 2011, my team and I spent the whole day rooted in front of computers looking at the UNCSD website as the submissions from governments and constituencies on the content of the negotiation draft slowly came in and were uploaded by the Secretariat. We tallied every mention of the SDGs. "Enough" support had to be manifested for the SDGs to get them included in the Zero Draft, but what was the exact bar?

As the morning wore on, there was a steady trickle of support, but it was not overwhelming. We downloaded each submission, scoured it for any reference of the SDGs, and filled out a matrix tallying our progress. I kept contacting the Executive Coordination team and was assured that progress was good. But our anguish was palpable. Then the submission from the Caribbean Community (CARICOM) came in. CARICOM represents fifteen member states. It was a stunning endorsement. By the end of the day, among the countries that included the SDGs or an equivalently worded concept in their submissions were Algeria, Botswana, Brazil, Canada, Costa Rica, Croatia, Ecuador, Ghana, Japan, Indonesia, Liechtenstein (among the most full-throated and detailed submission on the SDGs), Mexico, Moldova, New Zealand, the United States, Paraguay, Peru, the Philippines, Sri Lanka, Switzerland, Thailand, and

Turkey. Others that endorsed the SDGs were ICLEI (Local Governments for Sustainability), the Stakeholder Forum, and UNEP. Language barriers impeded our evaluation of China's submission.

The language of the US submission reflected the argument we had put forward from the beginning. It was of particular significance coming from a country that had sometimes seemed recalcitrant. The United States stated that the SDGs, "if structured correctly, could be a useful means to assess progress, catalyze action, and enhance integration among all three pillars of sustainable development. . . . We believe the concept of sustainable development goals is worthy of consideration at Rio+20, and that the discussions at Rio+20 can inform ongoing and future deliberations about the Millennium Development Goals (MDGs) as we approach 2015."

We carefully scrutinized Brazil's submission, given that up to that point we were still not sure to what degree the host country was truly (beyond diplomatic camaraderie) willing to seriously back our proposal. We were pleased to see clear support of the SDGs. We devoted considerable time to understanding the process that was laid out in the Brazilian submission.

> Based on an inclusive green economy, instead of complex negotiations seeking to establish restrictive and binding goals, objectives infused with a spirit of guidance and addressing a wide range of issues could be established, similarly to the Millennium Goals, in areas where there is already a high degree of convergence of opinions. . . . This instrument could clearly indicate the macro-objectives that are being sought. . . . Thus, while an inclusive green economy program would establish a group of concrete initiatives focused on national and international cooperation instruments, guiding political commitments would identify the priority goals for sustainable development. Those objectives, in turn, would guide the policies and actions of countries, international organizations, multilateral development banks, and other public and private actors, inducing the adoption of more sustainable behaviors with an established horizon—for example, 2030. The strategic areas of those commitments could be defined at first, setting in motion a broad participatory process, from which the effective objectives would gradually emerge. Issues such as urban development, health, and water would reinforce the Millennium Development Goals while incorporating much broader aspects of sustainable development.

The submission went on to say that the SDGs "need to contain concrete objectives that are quantifiable and verifiable . . . [that] could subsequently be transformed into indicators to monitor achievement." The submission underscored the need to base the SDGs on existing documents or agreements and stated that they should not replace but complement the MDGs. The submission clearly stated that "The goals should be universal in nature, targeting developed and developing countries in equal measure." This was beyond what we were hoping for.

In the early hours of the afternoon, after yet another anguished outreach to colleagues in the Executive Coordination team, we were finally informed that the SDGs "were in." Enough support had been evidenced. This was the decisive moment. What had been deemed impossible just months earlier was fast becoming a reality. The small team leading work on the SDGs proposal at the ministry was overjoyed.

We learned years later that the Executive Coordination team undertook a rigorous tally of submissions and of the issue areas or concepts that were mentioned (see Appendix 6). A total of sixty-two "initiatives/concepts" were counted. In terms of the number of submissions that mentioned these "initiatives/concepts" the SDGs came in fourth, after broad concepts like "Participation," "Adaptation," and "Accountability." One hundred seventy submissions mentioned the SDGs, including 37 from member states, 102 from major groups, and 26 from UN organizations and IGOs. The level of interest was assigned the highest ranking: "excellent." Tellingly, "Green Growth" came in only thirteenth and merited a classification of "high" interest while the "Green Economy Roadmap" was ranked eighteenth and only as having "strong" interest. The Sustainable Development Council, one of the main initiatives under the IFSD pillar, was ranked nineteenth. The SDGs carried the day as the top-ranked concrete initiative. At the time, we were not aware of this internal tally and had no idea just how much support the SDGs proposal had garnered. We only knew that it had been "enough."

We were keenly aware of all the countries that had not mentioned the SDGs at all or that had strongly—and in our minds pointedly—advocated for the MDGs. They were quite numerous. India's submission worried us enormously. It stated unequivocally that it did "not support defining and aiming for quantitative targets or goals towards sustainable development. Since the Principles of Rio guide us—foremost amongst which is the principle of CBDR, we need to be mindful of whom we are setting targets for. CBDR exhorts developed countries to take on commitments first. This principle must be upheld in any implementation focused outcome on sustainable development, as opposed to MDGs. The context of MDGs and SDGs (Sustainable Development Goals) are disparate."

Nonetheless, on that first day of November, we celebrated. The SDGs were slated to be part of the negotiating text and were therefore formally a part of Rio+20 preparations. Although the road ahead was challenging, we had achieved an essential, historic first step against seemingly insurmountable odds. Our strategy of working outside the formal system and advancing a bottom-up approach of progressive support and ownership had paid off. Dozens of governments and hundreds of constituencies were invested in the SDGs. Together we were developing a framework to help reshape the world's understanding of development. But the work was just beginning. The next six months required shifting into an even higher gear.

Notes

1. The General Assembly organizes its works in one plenary and six committees. The plenary approves the resolutions and decisions of all committees and takes action directly on many others. The committees are specialized to deal with the various issues of the core UN agenda: First Committee, Disarmament and International Security; Second Committee, Economic and Financial (also Environmental issues); Third Committee, Social, Humanitarian and Cultural; Fourth Committee, Special Political and Decolonization; Fifth Committee, Administrative and Budgetary; Sixth Committee, Legal.

2. At the United Nations, when delegates meet for consultations, it is understood that they represent the positions of their respective countries. Thus we refer to "Egypt" instead of "Delegates from Egypt."

3. Means of Implementation (MoI) is a standard phrase used in international negotiations that refers to the finance, technology, and capacity building needed to deliver on commitments or agreements. It often becomes the decisive issue in a negotiation as many governments are loath to sign up to goals or actions unless they are assured that the requisite—additional—resources will be available.

4. The Secretariat, according to the UN Charter, is one of its main organs. Within the Secretariat, the Department of Economic and Social Affairs (DESA) coordinates social and economic issues for the work programs of main organs, such as the Economic and Social Council (ECOSOC). Many major conferences depend on the ECOSOC and therefore DESA plays an important role in supporting many processes, including fora related to sustainable development at the UN.

5. UNEP (2019).

6. The Preparatory Committee of the UN Conference on Sustainable Development (UNCSD), the formal name for Rio+20, had two co-chairs. In the first meeting in 2010, Ambassador John Ashe of Antigua and Barbuda was designated as one of the co-chairs. The other was Ambassador Park In-kook of the Republic of Korea (RoK), who served from 2010 through December 2011, when he was replaced by Ambassador Kim Sook, also of RoK.

7. The UNCSD Bureau was in charge of organizing the work, content, and implementation of the agenda for Rio+20 based on the structure and focus defined in UN Resolution A/RES/64/236.

4

Getting the World to Understand the SDGs

Getting the Sustainable Development Goals (SDGs) into the Zero Draft was a historic achievement, but we knew that it was just a vital first step to get to a common, shared understanding of what our proposal was about. We needed to address the major concerns that many constituencies and delegates had been raising. This chapter is bookended by the two most important international consultations on the SDGs that we orchestrated, which also gave rise to the "friends of the SDGs." The first was held in Bogotá in November 2011, and the second was in Tarrytown, New York, in January 2012. Creating these opportunities for dialogue proved essential in getting the needed traction around the SDGs.

Bringing the World to Bogotá

After the Economic Commission for Latin America and the Caribbean (ECLAC) meeting in September 2011, we decided the time was ripe for the first international consultation on the SDGs in Bogotá. We drew up an extensive wish list of all the countries and organizations we wanted to invite and started to canvass. We needed to have representation along the whole spectrum: from those who had expressed some support for the proposal to those that were skeptical or openly opposed to it. We reached out to civil society organizations because from the very beginning, we wanted them at the table. Governments had to negotiate and endorse, but the reality of a new development agenda meant we needed to create broad and deep ownership. We knew that higher ambition and effective implementation would depend on actors outside the sphere of government.

As we drew up lists of potential invitees, we faced a significant quandary. We had no financing, and if we were not able to provide financing to delegates from developing countries, our meeting would be largely limited to delegates from developed countries and representatives from the respective embassies of developing countries in Bogotá. We needed to have those who would be actually participating in the negotiations at the table. Building on the signals of support we had received from many in the European Union, we sent out feelers to a few embassies to inquire about the possibility of providing financing for broader participation in the consultation. Together with Alicia Lozano, a team member financed by the UN Development Programme (UNDP), we met with Maurice van Beers, a diplomat at the embassy of the Netherlands. He became a stalwart champion and committed to securing the necessary funding. Shortly thereafter he confirmed his government's support. The consultation was on. We had wanted to hold the consultations well ahead of the November 1 milestone for Zero Draft submissions, but as the days went by, that date seemed increasingly out of reach. We aimed for the earliest possible date at that point: November 4–5, 2011.

We were dejected that we had not been able to organize the consultation in October, when it could have influenced the submissions for the Zero Draft. At that point we were receiving encouraging signals from colleagues in the Executive Coordination team of the UN Conference on Sustainable Development (UNCSD) and other friends who were close to the process in New York, but Colombia had received no clear indication from Brazil of the degree to which they supported the idea. The endless flow of emails and consultations that I engaged in with a vast number of countries still signaled fervent opposition to the SDGs from many. Thus, as we made preparations throughout October, we viewed the November consultation as a potential plan B. In case the SDGs did not make it into the initial negotiating text, the consultations offered the possibility of generating enough momentum to figure out another way forward. Moreover, these consultations, the second ones after the initial dialogue in New York in May 2011, would give us a clearer sense of the political economy beyond the Latin American and Caribbean region. It would enable us to hone our proposal and our defense, validate allies, and better understand the opposition. Just in case the SDGs did become a formal reality in the negotiations, it was critical to have a first international discussion as soon as possible to continue to build the proposal.

The entire ministry was mobilized. We pored over every single detail of the consultation, from the agenda to the delegates' welcome at the airport to the menus for the two days, to the vast image of the globe that dominated the plenary room. As we say in Spanish, we threw the house out the window and spared no effort. We wanted the meeting to be seared into participants' memories.

As it turned out, we got confirmation that the SDGs were in the Zero Draft and formally a part of the Rio+20 negotiations just three days before Colombia hosted the first international Informal Consultation on the Sustainable Development Goals (SDGs). We were invigorated. There was no need to activate our plan B; the SDGs concept had overcome the initial derision and rejection and, despite myriad obstacles, was a reality in the process. We wanted to take stock of the state of play of the concept across delegations and constituencies: the areas of convergence, the red lines, the horizon for increasing ambition. Above all, we wanted everyone to feel that the SDGs were theirs to craft and define, that Colombia was merely the facilitator of a new, brave agenda.

The consultation took place in the Colombian Ministry of Foreign Affairs, in the imposing Salon Simon Bolívar from where the Liberator had dispatched affairs of state as president of the Great Colombia (1821–1830). The venue was ideal, spacious, and historic—Colombia's first seat of government after independence. For two full productive days, we gathered fifty-eight delegates from twenty-nine countries from all regions in the world. From the Executive Coordination team, Liz Thompson and Henry de Cazotte joined us, as did three representatives from the UN Environment Programme (UNEP) and representatives from UNDP Colombia. ECLAC was present. Local Governments for Sustainability, the Stakeholder Forum, and Oxfam represented civil society. A huge screen contained an iconic photo of the planet from space to remind us of what was at stake. In those early days, our efforts were geared at building a positive narrative about the potential of the SDGs, defanging the concept, so to speak. There was growing awareness that Rio+20 loomed ahead with an agenda that, as we saw it, had nothing of relevance or import to the wider world beyond the UN spheres of influence. So we emphasized all the positive (and nonthreatening) contributions the SDGs could make in terms of policy coherence, partnerships and coordination, and innovation.

A significant amount of time was taken up on Millennium Development Goals (MDGs)–related discussions with a special focus on the need to ensure that MDGs implementation through 2015 would not be undermined by any other process, that they should be amply supported, and that the two frameworks would need to be complementary. In the minds of many, acceptance of the SDGs was not an exclusive proposition: the assumption was that the MDGs could still be rolled over in 2015. This assumption played out later in the negotiations with vehement opposition to the word "single" when describing the process to craft the post-2015 regime (see Chapters 7 and 9).

The seeds of future major breakthroughs were already present in these discussions. Concepts that we had been tirelessly advocating for throughout the year were now the focus of exchanges. Critically, it was the first international discussion about a universal agenda, one that was "relevant for all countries": an acknowledgment that there were some development issues that needed to be addressed by every country and others that needed to be tackled jointly. This marked a decisive step in walking away from the prevailing paradigm that divided the world into developed and developing countries, with the latter bearing the responsibility for action and the former—somewhat grudgingly in many cases—for supporting it.

These were also the first discussions about how to reconcile the universal dimension of the SDGs with the fact that they would need to be tailored to specific national circumstances, that is, one size does not fit all. This was an issue around which much ink and many slide presentations and discussions would focus in the ensuing months. This was inherently linked to the notion that the SDGs should be voluntary—the prevailing view—and to attendant concerns that governments might lack ambition in defining their own targets and simply enable a race to the bottom.

The status quo is always hard to shatter; many G77 and China member countries insisted on the need to "build on existing agreements and principles," which was a standard formula for covertly referring to common but differentiated responsibilities (CBDR). This remained one of the most outstanding hurdles until the last days of the negotiations in Rio. Indeed, even many stalwart advocates for the SDGs thought that CBDR would ultimately prove to be an insurmountable obstacle.

Another key area of discussion was around implementation. There was recognition that effective implementation includes not just financial resources but also institutional and governance capacities at a national level, as well as issues such as absorptive capacity for new technologies, dissemination of best practices, and inclusion of key stakeholders ranging from youth to the private sector. Developing countries were concerned that this new framework could create new responsibilities and demands they would be hard pressed to fulfill. However, it was broadly agreed that implementing such an agenda would not depend only on governments, and therefore the active engagement and owner-ship of the agenda by the private sector and international finance insti-tutions were also crucial.

Importantly, the consultations laid out expectations for an outcome at Rio+20: to launch an SDGs process to actually define and agree on the framework. From the outset we were obsessed with the need to ensure a pathway after and beyond Rio+20 that would effectively define and structure this new development paradigm. There was no agreement on the process, but the fact that this requirement resonated with many was already incredibly encouraging. By now we knew there was no way that the full new framework could be defined by the time of the summit, and therefore it was imperative to establish a process to do so.

The consultation was held under the Chatham House Rule, but the discussions were so informed and rich that we got authorization from participants to prepare a chairperson's summary, which was ultimately circulated as "Insights from the Informal Consultations on the SDGs Proposal" (see Appendix 7).

After the meeting adjourned, and after the requisite group photo was taken, I shepherded some of the delegates into the minister's pri-vate meeting rooms. I wanted those delegates who had most strongly supported the SDGs to come together into an informal group that I could call on as we continued to prepare for Rio+20. The preceding months had been intense and lonely. I needed to confirm interest in funding for future consultations, which were sure to be needed. This core group—which I came to call "the secret friends of the SDGs"—slowly came together over the next months. Even after Rio+20, during the Open Working Group discussions, we continued to meet regularly to strategize on how to achieve a high level of ambition and common sense. Sometimes, when the negotiations were particularly challenging, it was a space for collective catharsis. This group's commitment to the process was repeatedly put to the test over the next six months.

At the Starting Gate

On December 15–16, 2011, the UNCSD Secretariat convened the Sec-ond Intersessional Meeting of the UNCSD in New York. The agenda focused on providing information on the process and describing the contours of the Zero Draft (which was only to be released in January 2012). At the meeting, Ambassador Kim Sook of the Republic of Korea was elected as co-chair following the departure of Ambassador

Park In-kook, joining Ambassador John Ashe of Antigua and Barbuda. Together, co-chairs Kim and Ashe would lead the Rio+20 preparatory process in coordination with Brazil as the Rio+20 host, with the decisive support of the Secretariat. The December 2011 meeting was framed as an opportunity for delegations to discuss their expectations and priorities for the process. Many of the statements made by delegations covered issues and terrain that were already well known, reflecting views and positions that spilled over from other fora and negotiations. The greatest buzz was around the SDGs proposal.

During the intersessional meeting, the Under-Secretary-General of UN Department of Economic and Social Affairs (DESA) and Secretary-General of the UNCSD Sha Zukang described the challenges and conundrums the international system was experiencing ahead of Rio+20. He stressed that "we need to decide how ambitious we want to be at Rio" and that "this is a hugely important Conference." He added, "At stake is no less than the effectiveness of multilateralism in addressing humanity's common future . . . and that depends on the political will and the level of ambition you set for the Conference." He reminded delegates of "emerging challenges" and said, "In addition to the challenges of 1992, new issues have come to the forefront—food insecurity, volatility in energy prices, global economic uncertainty, and high unemployment." Indeed, these were the reasons Colombia was so adamant on the need for a new, integrated development framework beyond the minimalism of the MDGs.

Referring to the submissions of November 1, 2011, Sha Zukang noted that

> One of the most interesting—and I dare say unanticipated—developments is the broad interest in measuring progress through a set of sustainable development goals. . . . The references to the SDGs refer to the need to make them global and universal—applicable to developed and developing countries alike, though in accordance with common but differentiated responsibilities and respective capabilities. There has also been an emphasis on defining goals that address all three pillars of sustainable development. Most have insisted that the list of goals be short and that they be politically engaging, as are the MDGs. Indeed, one issue raised in many submissions is exactly how such SDGs would relate to the MDGs and the ongoing discussions on what comes next after 2015.[1]

In his statement, Sha summed up some of the main tenets and proposals of the submissions. Many mentioned a range of priority areas, including sustainable energy for all, water and oceans, food security and sustainable agriculture, sustainable cities, green jobs, employment and social inclusion, disaster risk reduction and resilience, biodiversity, and forests. Sha asked, "How should these sectoral priorities and related actions be reflected in the zero draft? Should each have associated SDGs? Should they be encompassed in a 'framework for action'? How would the actions reflect a serious advance on current approaches and orientations?" The SDGs already seemed to be permeating the entire agenda.

The fact that the Secretary-General of the UNCSD had not just mentioned the SDGs but afforded them primacy thrilled us. We were not surprised that he tied the reference to their universality to the CBDR principle. This was par for the course. For us, there was a sense of redemption. Our SDGs proposal had only slowly worked its way into Sha Zukang's agenda and priorities. Since early 2011 we had tried to secure meetings with him, to no avail. Our first meeting had taken place in New York earlier in the year, and he had listened to the proposal but remained noncommittal. After the November 1 submissions, Sha clearly recognized that this was a concept with the potential to deliver a resounding outcome at Rio+20. At the time we did not know that in the Executive Coordination team's tally of the November submissions, the SDGs initiative had emerged among the highest priorities across all submissions (see Appendix 6).

Thereafter, we often met with Sha Zukang when we went to New York. We would go to his office to share our views of the negotiations, the trends, and our strategy to position the SDGs and tackle the many voices of dissent and opposition. In the multilateral system, there is the belief that member states can make it on their own without having the UN bureaucracy involved. Those who understand the system know that it is critical to have the Secretariat on board to deliver meaningful change. For us, getting Sha Zukang's support was decisive.

Still, at this point, despite the seemingly solid pathway that the SDGs appeared to be on, we knew that for many governments, UN agencies, important philanthropies and nongovernmental organizations, the SDGs were still marginal to the process. For them, the deliverables of Rio+20 were locked in by UN Resolution A/64/236 and limited to the pillars of green economy and the International Framework for Sustainable Development. Moreover, many thought that if they went forward, the SDGs would simply be a niche and ancillary tool. At this stage, a significant number of delegates expected the concept to fizzle out and fade away during the arduous negotiations that still lay ahead.

The Informal Colombian Track

The December 2011 meeting was remarkable for the entire Colombian delegation. Delegates from all regions plus representatives from many constituencies reached out to the Colombian delegation to ask about the SDGs: what they meant, what we had in mind, what our vision was. The permanent representative to the Colombian Mission to the UN, Néstor Osorio, said he had never been so sought after. There was incredible energy around us. Obviously, many raised the well-known concerns about whether the SDGs would undermine the MDGs, distract from efforts to eradicate poverty, and create conditionalities for developing countries. But overall, there was a sense of expectation and anticipation. The major stakeholder groups and other civil society and private sector actors were vehemently and vocally supportive. This was an agenda that resonated with them and with which they could engage.

The delegations that had come together at the conclusion of the consultations in Bogotá started to meet and orchestrate their support. The "secret friends of the SDGs," as I lightly referred to them, was never a formal group but a grouping that came together thanks to deep ties of trust and camaraderie and underpinned by a shared vision (for simplicity, I henceforth refer to this loose grouping as the friends). At the December 2011 meeting in New York, the friends were very active. The mission of Sweden hosted a lunch on December 14, 2011, with eighteen delegations from all regions as well as civil society and UN organizations. The following day, the United Kingdom's mission hosted a breakfast for donor countries to ensure support for the consultative process. This set in motion the kind of consultations and events that the friends hosted during all the meetings in New York.

Given that the December 2011 Intersessional Meeting was only two days long, and that the compilation text of the November submissions was more than 6,000 pages long, the UNCSD Secretariat encouraged member states to hold side events to brief others on issues of importance to them or on specific initiatives. Colombia needed no encouragement. As soon as we had received informal confirmation that the SDGs were part of the Zero Draft in early November, we planned a major side event in New York to present the SDGs proposal to as many delegates as possible. We had no idea who would show up, but in a move that was part hope, part defiance, we booked one of the biggest negotiation rooms in the UN.

Given the myriad discussions, consultations, and exchanges of the previous four months, it had become clear to us that a new position paper was needed that focused more clearly on the process ahead and the deliverables. There was incipient support for the concept, but that would mean nothing if the process to develop the SDGs was not robust. I prepared a new concept note and spoke with Guatemala for their endorsement once again. At the same time, the Peruvian delegation reached out to us. President Ollanta Humala had become a strong supporter of the SDGs, and the Peruvian delegation in New York expressed its interest in cosponsoring the new proposal. Through the end of the process in Rio+20, Peru remained a keen supporter of the SDGs.

When consultations ended that day, I went back to The Pod hotel and drafted a new version of the proposal and emailed it to colleagues in the missions of Guatemala and Peru, who shortly thereafter confirmed that they were in. Another country!

This new text built on the preceding ones, but in addition to describing the SDGs concept once again, it focused on the process going forward and the deliverables from Rio (see Appendix 8). We had started to ask a question that would haunt us through the culmination of the negotiations in June: "What about Rio+1? What happens the day after Rio? What process will take the concept forward to make it a reality?" The (now) tripartite proposal stated that there should be "agreement on the process to finalize the SDGs framework" and proposed a subsequent timeline that would culminate in its adoption by the UN General Assembly. This was the first time that a process for taking the SDGs forward was outlined. Ensuring that this was delivered became our obsession. We feared that unless an innovative process was agreed to at Rio+20, the SDGs proposal would become mired and politicized, never delivering on its potential for real transformation.

It is important to understand that these position papers were not academic exercises but an essential negotiating tool. Each one was crafted to respond to a specific political and negotiation context and built on the preceding one. By the end of the process, we issued a total of four (see Appendixes 3, 5, 8, and 22). They had to deliver on several fronts and pave the way for increasing support. Thus the aims were to (1) create and consolidate milestones in the discussions so that there were referents in the process and a sense of forward momentum; (2) create trust by laying out the central concerns underlying the differing positions so that everyone felt (this was a very emotional process) that they were heard and their position respected; (3) identify and characterize the core issues so that (a) the discussions could become more focused and concrete—and easier to manage—and (b) the process could be more readily steered toward securing an arena of consensus. For this paper, we starkly shifted the focus on defining a concrete way forward after Rio to define and negotiate the SDGs framework. These papers played a central role in shaping the narrative around the negotiations and the actual architecture of the negotiations. The issues identified in them were in fact the central tenets of the discussions. They became a tangible referent for everyone.

The next day, we hosted our side event. The vast room began to fill up as we waited near the podium with the other two cosponsors, Guatemala and Peru. We watched nervously as delegates picked up the new text and started to discuss it. The noise level progressively increased as the room filled up. We could not believe that so many countries had come. In the end, the intergovernmental consultation was attended by 114 countries.[2] This was the last meeting at the UN before the formal negotiation process was due to start in late January, and we were amazed and encouraged by how far we had come. However, we also knew that the hardest part still lay ahead. We had set ourselves to deliver three key outcomes at Rio+20: (1) get agreement on a robust concept of the SDGs; (2) get agreement on a process to actually develop the SDGs; and (3) get agreement on—at a minimum—a preliminary, indicative, illustrative, descriptive list of thematic areas for the SDGs.

A Country Behind the Proposal

The SDGs undertaking, although led by the Ministry of Foreign Affairs, had support across the Colombian government, especially from President Juan Manuel Santos. After being initially consulted on the idea in February 2011, he enthusiastically embraced it. Thereafter, he was regularly briefed by Minister María Ángela Holguín, and he included strong advocacy for the SDGs idea in many of his bilateral meetings. On January 18, 2012, we were convened to the Palácio de Nariño, the presidential residence, together with Minister Holguín, Minister of Environment and Natural Resources Frank Pearl, and Climate Change Director Andrea Guerrero.

We gave President Santos a detailed briefing on the SDGs proposal and our progress to date. He was enthusiastic and supportive, appreciative of the enormous transformative potential of the idea. He gave the two ministries clear mandates: Minister Pearl was asked to try on the SDGs for size and develop a suite of national SDGs on water, energy, food security, cities, and oceans. This was to be a concrete deliverable that Colombia would take to Rio+20 to showcase what was possible. The Foreign Affairs team was instructed to continue to position the SDGs and make them the key outcome of Rio+20 no matter what. In his words, this was to be our overriding priority. We discussed the convergence of the SDGs and the climate change agendas and the need for highest ambition on both fronts.

We walked away from our meeting exhilarated and empowered. Our president confirmed that he understood the dimensions of what we were attempting to do on both the post-2015 process and climate and gave us his unconditional backing. It was this kind of leadership that made it possible for Colombia to spearhead a new global agenda.

In fact, at the national level we were equally active. We sought the involvement of all sectors and constituencies as the effective implementation of the bold agenda we were envisioning required the broadest ownership possible, with decisive political buy-in and technical support. The negotiation process could not remain a distant issue managed by the Ministry of Foreign Affairs. Thus, in parallel to our international efforts, we undertook a range of consultations to make as many Colombians as possible aware of the idea and garner their input. The national consultations we started to undertake in 2011, which continued through 2014, with government, academia, civil society, and the UN system in Colombia helped us better understand and shape the national position on the SDGs. Led by Alicia Lozano, a course was created for the diplomatic academy that was made widely available throughout our embassies so that Colombian diplomats around the world were up to date on the proposal and could help position it. In January 2012, the minister of Foreign Affairs created a high-level advisory group.

Starting in September 2011, my team and I designed a demanding schedule of meetings around the country with regional and thematic perspectives. The process was open, transparent, and inclusive: from the outset, we knew that successful implementation of the SDGs depended on the degree of engagement and commitment from stakeholders on the ground, where SDGs progress would matter most.

This work was primarily led by Carolina Aguirre, Alicia Lozano, and Ángela Rivera. From September to November 2011, we held an initial series of *conversatorios*, open convenings with civil society that were designed as conversations, a two-way communication process to inform and receive inputs and recommendations. In October 2011, conversatorios were held in three representative regions of Colombia (Barranquilla on the Caribbean coast; Cali in the southwest; and Medellín in the northwest). Convened at various universities, our goal was to actively engage not just academia but youth. The team from the ministry that participated in these included youth representatives. Specific stakeholder groups were also targeted. Meetings were organized with a representative group of leading business people with the support of the UN Global Compact. A platform was established in the Ministry of Environment and Sustainable Development's website to receive inputs from the public.

Civil society organizations and academics participated in line with their expertise under the umbrella of the Colombian Confederation of Non-Governmental Organizations. In the end, 630 organizations and 1,200 individuals representing environmental organizations, the private sector, labor unions, professional associations, foundations, academia, activists, LGBTQI, youth, and the elderly participated at some stage of the process. Bilateral and multilateral institutions, chambers of commerce, and banks were also involved in our national consultations. Their participation brought to our attention a wide range of visions and perceptions regarding the diversity of realities across the country, and this dose of reality and pragmatism helped us shape the SDGs idea.

Active engagement from ministries and specialized government agencies was promoted from the outset. A broad mix of government agencies were involved, including on agriculture, biodiversity, communications and technology, education, energy and mines, environment, gender, health, public-private partnerships, science, social protection, and the treasury. We specifically targeted the national statistics agency and the National Planning Department, which is charged with defining and advancing public and economic policy across all dimensions of development. As the proposal gained traction, we began to work ever more closely with this department as our vision spanned the whole of government. We also involved local and regional authorities.

To build ownership and to try on the SDGs for size (as it were), following initial meetings to update government representatives on the SDGs process, a detailed questionnaire was sent out in August 2011 asking for concrete inputs for defining and framing the new agenda. We continued to receive recommendations on the SDGs framework in the run-up to Rio+20 and then during the Open Working Group sessions that followed, and we delineated the specific goals from 2012 to 2015. We asked each sector to define priority global targets for their fields, with a focus on their transformation potential across all dimensions of development. Incredibly rich and unexpected processes were triggered in many ministries. Working across sectors and together with the Ministry of Environment and Sustainable Development, we drafted thematic SDGs proposals that fully integrated the dimensions on cities, energy, food security, and oceans. Each agency and ministry designated a focal point to engage in the SDGs process through the end. The deep sense of ownership by all sectors that had already started to align themselves with this ambitious and targeted agenda was certainly one of the reasons Colombia was able to quite seamlessly incorporate the SDGs in its National Development Plan 2014–2018, well before the SDGs were adopted through General Assembly Resolution A/RES/70/1 in September 2015. Colombia was the first country to incorporate the SDGs in its main social, economic, and environmental strategies, setting an example for many other countries that followed.

Tarrytown: Kicking Off the Process

On the margins of the many formal and bilateral meetings in New York during those hectic days, the friends met frequently and discussed how to maintain momentum and create spaces for dialogue to sort through the many contentious issues that swirled around the SDGs. There were vast undercurrents of resistance and a growing number of issues and questions that fed into a cacophony of opposition. It was imperative to be able to (1) surface and frame the main issues and concerns; and (2) generate informed discussions where these could be sensibly analyzed and discussed outside of the relentless politics of the upcoming negotiations. I was convinced that a second international consultation was needed, building on the one in Bogotá in November 2011. This consultation would need to be held in New York so that more delegates and representatives from civil society and the UN could come.

The friends agreed that it was essential to have a substantive discussion on the SDGs proposal before the start of the negotiations, which were scheduled for New York at the end of January 2012. We knew well that the negotiations provided no room or time for sensible, informed discussions and that positions would get locked along negotiating blocks from the very beginning. Then it would be much more difficult to advance the conversations that were needed to unpack and mature the SDGs concept in a participatory way that built up the necessary ownership and transparency. Without this, the SDGs faced a significant risk of becoming yet another placeholder for hardened positions that spilled over from one negotiation to another. A comprehensive discussion with all the key parties in the room, especially those who opposed the concept, was essential. Time was short, and several colleagues said that it would be nearly impossible to organize an international event of the requisite magnitude by the end of January.

While in New York in December 2011, we had no time to discuss the details of such a gathering. By the time everyone flew back to their capitals, it was already after mid-December 2011. That meant that we had just one week to pull this off—December 19–23—before everyone disappeared for the holidays. One week to structure, organize, fund, and send out invitations to a major international conference. Because it was also the last week of the 2011 UN General Assembly, delegates and permanent missions were scrambling to wrap up the year and their deliberations, many delegates had already left New York, and everyone was winding down as the end of the year approached. Delegates and friends involved in the Rio+20 process were engaged in the UN Framework Convention on Climate Change (UNFCCC) negotiations, so many had not been home in weeks, having come to New York straight from Durban, South Africa, where the climate conference had just been held. In a nutshell, it was mission impossible.

And yet. Colleagues in New York suggested a marvelous venue just outside the city, the Tarrytown Estate. Friends from the governments of the Netherlands and Norway offered to fund the event. We decided to hold the consultation just before the next formal meeting on the Rio+20 process, scheduled in New York for January 25–27, 2012, by the co-chairs to get agreement on the Zero Draft as a basis for the negotiations. Marit von Zommeren of the Netherlands mission undertook to contact the conference venue and negotiate the package. We drew up wish lists of all the delegations we would want to participate based on geographic representation and to ensure a good balance along the political spectrum in terms of how they viewed the proposal. We drew up lists of those who might need some financial support, as we were all keen to ensure strong representation of the Global South. Then we assigned tasks across the friends and we began to canvass specific delegations to attend the event.

By December 23, for all practical purposes the last day of the year, we had secured a venue (conference and hotel) and a growing list of delegates who were willing to contemplate the possibility of coming in a few days early ahead of the upcoming UNCSD meeting (with funding where needed) to participate. News of the upcoming conference spread quickly across the UN, and we got early confirmation that Secretary-General Ban Ki-moon would send a representative, as would other UN agencies. We started outreach to many nonstate constituencies as we were firmly of the view that although an intergovernmental process was required, civil society always had the right to a seat and voice at the table.

As we advanced in the preparations, a delegate from Switzerland suggested that it would be good to have a few background papers to spur the discussion. As part of ongoing work with the World Resources Institute (WRI), a global think tank, Switzerland commissioned three briefing papers. The papers were especially useful in highlighting the importance of initiatives such as the SDGs. They also dealt with the relation between the MDGs and the SDGs that were of concern for many delegations, and they reiterated the fundamental need to have a result-oriented forward-looking Rio+20 outcome. I spent hours on calls with Peter Hazlewood of WRI, who led the drafting team to ensure that the papers were framed as the highly political documents they were and not merely as an academic exercise. Every word and phrase was reviewed with a sharp political lens.

The new year brought the long-awaited negotiation text. On January 10, 2012, the co-chairs of the UNCSD submitted the Zero Draft of the conference's negotiation document, titled *The Future We Want*, "for consideration by Member States and other stakeholders." The SDGs were included in Chapter V, "Accelerating and Measuring Progress." From that moment, the SDGs proposal, now formally endorsed by Colombia, Guatemala, and Peru, was officially a part of the negotiations.

Throughout the first weeks of January 2012, the hectic preparatory process for the Tarrytown retreat continued. Over the course of one month—which included the year-end holidays—an international conference was pulled together from scratch (thanks especially to the unflagging support of the Netherlands and Norway). This was a constant juggling act until the end as now, suddenly, many governments wanted more than one delegate to participate; the conference was seen by many as a critical event to attend. As the meeting date neared, the list of participants was changing on an almost hourly basis.

The two-day second international consultation orchestrated by Colombia began on January 23, but delegates were invited to arrive on the day before to network and gather for dinner.[3] Ample time was built into the agenda because we knew that hallway and coffee break discussions were essential components of the consultations. I chaired the meeting around a huge rectangular table that seated eighty. The fact that everyone could see each other created a sense of purpose and openness.

The discussions were intense, often contentious, and surfaced the many diverse takes on the MDGs, the MDG+ option, and the SDGs. There were difficult conversations around universality and differentiation, about the unfinished business of the MDGs, and the need to "prioritize people."

Again, given the richness of the discussions and how much they contributed to collectively maturing the SDGs concept, I got agreement to issue a Chair's Summary (see Appendix 9). These summaries of major consultations were a key component of the genesis of the SDGs. The retreat's summary signaled that the process was inclusive and consultative, that the proponents were listening, and that there was an open invitation to cocreate and evolve the concept. The more contentious the issues were, the more we insisted on creating spaces for airing differences and understanding where everyone was coming from. It is good to recall that at this juncture in the process, those actively supporting the SDGs across governments were still a minority, and that stark divisions remained within many governments.

At Tarrytown, the foundations for a future agreement were first laid out, generating a basic understanding that made it feasible to tackle the many contentious, outstanding issues over the coming months. The agenda for the "Retreat on SDGs, Rio+20 and the Post-2015 Development Agenda" stated that the objective was "to forge a collective vision on SDGs, and to build consensus on the way forward in the context of Rio+20 and the post-2015 development agenda." The agenda focused on three core issues that remained the basic tenets of the negotiations through to the final negotiations in Rio de Janeiro in June 2012:

• *Why:* Clarifying the nature and purpose of the SDGs, their relationship to the MDGs, and their contribution to framing the post-2015 development agenda. (As noted earlier, the Rio+20 process and the MDGs were separate processes, the latter zealously guarded by the MDGs constituencies);

• *What:* Defining a feasible and strategic Rio+20 outcome on SDGs, which focused essentially on the architecture and characteristics of the SDGs; the idea was to jump-start initial conversations around the SDGs to make the concept more tangible for many delegations and constituencies; and,

• *How:* Identifying a roadmap for further developing the SDGs both before and after Rio+20 and in relation to the post-2015 development agenda process. From the outset the need to agree to a process to actually define the SDGs framework after Rio was an obsession for Colombia.

At the outset of the meeting, Rio+20 was acknowledged as a milestone event that presented the international community with a unique opportunity to strive for a high level of ambition and ensure a clear and robust outcome in the form of a renewed and actionable sustainable development agenda. This was critical because it was a subtle way of confirming that the two items formally agreed to in the UN resolution were insufficient and that there was a need for something truly historic and, above all, relevant to the wider world. The offer on the table from Colombia and its small group of allies was the SDGs framework. This framing helped create ownership around the need for ambition. In the months ahead, when discussions stalled or became particularly acrimonious, I would often say, "If you don't like the SDGs, that's fine. But please then propose something else."

The main area of contention and concern remained the relationship to the MDGs. This endured as the greatest divide in positions long after 2012, surfacing again and again under various guises. At its most basic, there was a concern that a universal agenda would imply a shift away from the MDGs' focus on poverty eradication.

Thus, a first order of business for the retreat was to assure delegates from both the industrialized and the developing world that the primacy of the MDGs through 2015 would not be undermined by the SDGs proposal. The MDGs were acknowledged as "unfinished business," and the three years that remained in their timeframe were characterized as ones of redoubled efforts to achieve them. For most, it also inherently reaffirmed that their preferred way forward, the option of simply rolling them over after 2015—the MDG+ option—remained firmly on the table. This status quo was comfortable for developed and developing countries.

Thus, in the Chair's Summary, as well as in briefing papers and side events, Colombia endlessly reiterated that there was a clear understanding that the formulation of SDGs would not divert or in any way undermine the focus of the international community on achieving the MDGs by 2015 and that "the SDGs should build upon and complement the MDGs, and reflect lessons from MDG implementation."

The truly revolutionary aspect of the SDGs was that they were posited as a universal agenda, and this was the focus of considerable discussion at Tarrytown. This raised a host of issues and concerns that were ultimately laid to rest only when the final SDGs framework was adopted. It was at the core of the paradigm shift that the SDGs entailed. A total rethink of what "development" means.

Yet this called for ensuring that the primacy of poverty eradication be maintained, an issue around which there was absolute support. From the beginning we ensured that the strong consensus around this was acknowledged and underscored to create a shared understanding around which other areas of consensus might be safely explored. There was consensus on little else. We were proposing a single set of international development goals relevant for all countries with sustainable development and poverty eradication as the overarching focus, an agenda of shared responsibilities, wherein each country could find itself along a spectrum of development issues.

In addition to the fact that this undermined a firmly held position by many delegations in G77 and China of the primacy of the CBDR principle, it raised real questions about how such an agenda could possibly be implemented. No one knew how to even talk about development in the context of developed countries. Issues that cut across many countries, including developed ones, such as child malnutrition, had always been studied and discussed almost exclusively in reference to developing countries. Moreover, if this was a global framework, how could it be tailored to the specific context and different needs of individual countries?

From the beginning, Colombia stated that this would have to be a voluntary framework—like the MDGs—and that each country could adapt it to their specific circumstances. To many this was more proof of how unworkable the proposal was. There were confounding tensions around this: many feared the framework would give rise to all manner of conditionalities, and there were also fears that a voluntary mechanism would translate into uneven implementation and cherry-picking by governments—a race to the bottom, according to many. Thus, for us it was critical to get a sensible, robust conversation going as early as possible around differentiated implementation.

At Tarrytown, by framing these discussions as part of "guiding principles," it was possible to surface the salient issues and map out the potential arena for consensus without having governments—or more precisely, individual delegates—get locked into specific positions early in the game. Thus, the Chair's Summary explicitly paired the "universal relevance of the SDGs" with the allowance for the differing priorities and capacities of countries and regions. Voluntary application was iterated across the text. Another concern with the proposal was that it would mushroom into an unmanageable list of goals. There was broad consensus that what had made the MDGs so captivating was their simplicity. Thus, the fact that SDGs should be few, easy to understand, as well as "time-bound and measurable, with targets and indicators" was highlighted. In fact, these characterizations eventually made it into the final Rio+20 outcome document (see Appendix 27).

In addition to setting out the basic landscape for negotiating the SDGs concept, at Tarrytown the discussion on the "guiding characteristics" that we led also helped bring up emerging broad areas of consensus around the SDGs. By framing these issues as "characteristics," we were able to objectify the SDGs, gradually moving away from a very abstract and therefore threatening concept. It bred familiarity and ownership. By framing these as "guiding," we abided by the long-standing aphorism that "nothing is agreed until everything is agreed" and created space for substantive discussions about core issues. In fact, in the following months of negotiations, the referent of "guiding principles" proved to be a decisive tool in enabling the negotiations in the G77 and China to advance and ultimately gain broad acceptance and endorsement of the SDGs concept.

For Colombia, an integrated framework was at the very heart of the proposal. This was extensively discussed in Tarrytown. We considered that one of the inherent weaknesses in advancing something called "sustainable development" was the simple fact that there was no recognition or comprehensive management of trade-offs and synergies across policies, investments, plans, and actions—between sectors. A core part of our quest was to make the integration of impacts and dividends across sectors and dimensions central to the logic and structure of the new framework and of the negotiations.

For us, a new development structure that simply created more narrow sectoral targets would have been an outcome as dangerous and limited as MDG+. For example, we sought—eventually with considerable success—to proscribe the word "pillar" and get everyone to talk of "dimensions," a term that better captured the deeply interconnected nature of human social and economic endeavor and its relationship to planetary systems. We aimed to create an integrated framework that would encompass drivers and multipliers as well as enablers across all goals—thus we steered the discussion to issues of technology transfer and capacity building, including managing information and data. We were adamant that this had to be a science-based process.

At Tarrytown we had the first substantive discussions about the process for defining the post-2015 framework. Crucially, we emerged from the retreat with the beginning of a confirmation that the two processes that had previously been assumed as wholly separate—the MDGs and Rio+20—could now be envisioned as one. Thus, by late January 2012 we had achieved two major successes. First, against all odds, we had placed an entirely new item on the agenda for Rio+20; second, we had managed to start to bring together two separate processes—the post-2015 (MDGs) process and the Rio process. In the UN, such alchemy is not easily achieved—witness the fact that even today the sustainable development agenda and the climate change agenda remain stubbornly separate, with separate constituencies, summits, and processes. (Indeed, as we write, we hope that soon they will become aligned and then merged.)

We were able to kick off a substantive conversation about the fact that this had to be a decisively participatory process, led by governments and with active engagement by all constituencies. Colombia envisioned a single unified process that, while centered around government consultations, created active conduits for inputs from stakeholders, as well as expert scientific advice. Many governments were profoundly uncomfortable with this and preferred a strictly intergovernmental process. From the outset, Colombia insisted that if the new agenda was going to be truly relevant and actionable, everyone had to have a seat at the table so that they would be invested in its eventual implementation.

In Tarrytown, this was both figuratively and literally true. Civil society was at the table in November 2011 in Bogotá when we convened the first international consultation on SDGs. In Tarrytown, representatives from the nongovernmental sector included Development Alternative (India), Oxfam (UK), Stockholm Environment Institute (Sweden), and WRI (US). From the outset, we laid the groundwork and parameters for the later negotiations around what would become the Open Working Group. From the UN, in addition to colleagues from the UNCSD Secretariat, the Executive Coordination team, UNDP, and UNEP, the Secretary-General sent Janos Pasztor as his representative.

We wanted to shift mindsets about what a successful endpoint of the negotiations could be around the SDGs. Crucially, the core issues of contention were now in the open and the initial morass of concerns and views and assumptions about the SDGs had been given a thorough run-through. The inchoate opposition to the SDGs had now evolved into concrete concerns that could be more sensibly addressed and discussed. The neat outline of issues, as described in the Chair's Summary, belied how complex the discussions had been and the starkly different views on what the SDGs entailed as well as the process for defining them beyond Rio+20. The discussions "reflect differing levels of ambition for Rio as well as different understandings of the required process for defining the SDGs."

Importantly, at Tarrytown we became aware of plans in the UN for the process after 2015. Representatives of UNDESA and UNDP informed us that the Secretary-General had already established a UN task team to support the process and develop a roadmap for the post-2015 development agenda process. We were informed of his intention to convene another high-level panel after Rio+20. This was not well received by all delegations, some of which affirmed that the new framework had to result from an intergovernmental process. The discussion presaged the contentious negotiations we would have to define the process after Rio+20 and the surprising debacle that surfaced in June in Rio de Janeiro that almost derailed the process we were leading.

The Tarrytown retreat was truly a watershed moment because it enabled delegates and other stakeholders to enter the formal Rio+20 negotiations with a clearer understanding of the contours of what Colombia, Peru, and Guatemala were proposing. Key stakeholders had the opportunity to understand and hone their positions and perspectives, which, even when these were in opposition to the concept, enabled more substantive discussions to follow. Well aware that what we were proposing was a paradigm shift, we needed to avoid the dead-end of knee-jerk opposition to the SDGs without a clear framing of concerns or options. Advancing the concept meant making sure that we were enabling as many delegates as possible to think it through for themselves.

For us, the consultations were key as they allowed us to understand the full political economy of the SDGs, the baseline, as it were. Overall, it signaled clearly to all delegations and constituencies that the proponents of the SDGs wanted to build the concept in a fully participatory manner, with no hidden agenda. Given that the debacle at the Copenhagen climate conference was still fresh in every negotiator's mind (see Chapter 2), such a signal was essential to ensure the successful evolution of the process. Tarrytown laid out the blueprint for the coming negotiations. This was exactly what was needed for the Initial Discussions on the "Zero Draft" of the Outcome Document for UNCSD that started the next day.

Embarking on the Zero Draft Negotiations

On January 25–27, 2012, the co-chairs and Bureau of the UNCSD Preparatory Committee convened a meeting to get agreement on the Zero Draft as a basis for the negotiations and to begin discussions on the first two sections: the Preamble/Stage Setting and Renewing Political Commitment. These highly political sections would frame the playing field, so it was important to get a first reading of the room. Further written comments were to be provided by the end of February on the other three sections, which were equally political but with stronger technical underpinnings. Initial agreement on using the Zero Draft for the forthcoming negotiations was essential because it was an attempt by the UNCSD Secretariat to distill the over 6,000 pages of comments and inputs they had received by the November 1, 2011, deadline into a functional negotiation draft of around 20 pages (see Appendix 10). Comments on this first draft would enable the Secretariat, which worked tirelessly backstage throughout the process, to further hone the negotiation text ahead of the first negotiations of the outcome document in March 2012.

The discussions we had had in Tarrytown proved vitally important to the Zero Draft meeting. They had enabled the delegates that had attended to better understand and think through their positions. Even though opposition to the SDGs had grown firmer across a significant number of delegates, everyone's arguments were framed more cogently. This ensured that we could at least bring up the main concerns and engage in substantive, thoughtful discussions. The reference to "delegates" rather than "delegations" here is intentional—as was observed time and again throughout the process, there were deep internal divisions in most countries, with some officials or ministries in favor of an SDGs framework and others bitterly against it.

During the three-day consultation, there were frequent meetings of the G77 and China to start to define the group's positions vis-à-vis the vast range of issues in the Zero Draft. We faced a situation that would become our bane in the coming months: there were so many topics to cover that the time allocated to the SDGs was insufficient to work through and understand the conflicting positions and find a degree of consensus in the G77 and China. There was insufficient time to discuss the SDGs informally and formally—exactly as we had foreseen when the consultations in Tarrytown were convened.

In the G77 and China, the divisions were deep. Many countries looked askance at the proposal, convinced that it would undermine the MDGs, curtail international aid, and create new conditionalities and unfunded responsibilities for developing countries. If developed countries were mostly responsible for the sorry state of the planet, if they had not fulfilled their commitments on financial flows, why should developing countries willingly take on more responsibilities? Many delegates were deeply concerned about the implications of this wide-ranging proposal. If they signed on to a new framework with new goals that would be challenging to implement, what would be the reaction back home? What would they be held accountable for signing on to? The majority of African countries were adamant that the SDGs could not replace the MDGs. India voiced significant concerns with the idea. Several Latin American and Arab countries that considered CBDR to be a linchpin of international architecture were adamantly opposed to a universal agenda. Yet a few delegates started to focus on the characteristics of the SDGs. Some countries focused on how to build on the MDGs process, calling for an MDGs review that would highlight gaps and new opportunities. From the outset, China said that they should be voluntary.

One option to come up during these early consultations that evinced enthusiasm among some delegates was to advance both frameworks in parallel with the implicit assumption that the MDGs would continue to dictate cooperation engagement with developing countries while the SDGs would somehow be focused on issues deemed more pertinent to developed countries. The latter issues would include consumption and production patterns and, above all, financial and technical support for other nations. During one long period in the process, a leading Brazilian delegate proposed two sets of goals, "one for rich countries and one for poor countries." To us this made no sense at many levels. Although the MDGs had served the notable purpose of focusing priorities on poverty eradication, the framework had also established a division between poverty and sustainable development and established a narrow set of targets. The MDGs had perpetuated an artificial separation among nations and did not consider, for example, the structural underpinnings of poverty. The reasons establishing this dual track would undermine the SDGs proposal were legion. But this idea of two sets of goals—one for rich countries and one for poor countries—persisted and resurfaced well past the Rio+20 Summit.

Another issue implicitly linked to the MDGs versus SDGs discussions was CBDR. Although CBDR was touted as a framing tenet of the G77 and China's position—mention of the SDGs had to be framed under this principle—in reality across the group there were a range of more nuanced positions. For some the principle was sacrosanct, reflecting a sense of historic injustices and imbalances; for others it was the pièce de résistance in an arsenal of negotiation tactics, a holdout issue that could be bargained with when the final negotiation package would become clearer in the final hours of the process. In reality, the principle had been undermined at the UNFCCC COP 10 in Copenhagen, where Brazil, South Africa, India, and China (the so-called BASIC countries) had announced voluntary mitigation targets, but it was resurrected time and again in many multilateral negotiations. For many in these negotiations, it made sense: given the potential scope of the SDGs idea, CBDR provided needed guardrails around this new agenda. Thus, within the group there were different understandings of the centrality of this concept and thus differing expectations regarding negotiation tactics, something that contributed to the fierce tensions that played out in Rio de Janeiro in June 2012 (see Chapter 8).

Given the fact that these Initial Discussions in late January 2012 were focused only on the first two sections of the Zero Draft, along with Guatemala we had decided to host an additional informal discussion in New York so that delegations—and delegates—that had not been at the Tarrytown meeting could benefit from the discussions. The event was widely attended, evidence that heartened us as it meant that the proposal was gaining more traction and relevance.

By this point, we were trying to push for as much definition of the SDGs as possible so that a core framework would already get sign-off from heads of state at the high-profile summit. We knew the road ahead was difficult, but at that point, having recently gotten the SDGs into the Zero Draft, we were far too sanguine about the process that lay ahead. We did not then comprehend or anticipate the depths of opposition and division around the SDGs concept and the resistance we would still encounter in the months ahead.

In our ongoing conversations with the Executive Coordination team, we had been advised to tone down the insistence on "overarching" themes. Already, in parallel to the endless discussions of the dynamics between MDGs and SDGs, constituencies and stakeholder groups had begun to advocate for specific goals or targets. This gave credence to some who warned that the SDGs were too ambitious and would become an unwieldy morass of thematic goals across a vast range of issues. To counter these fears, we laid out different options that stood a chance of ensuring a concrete outcome at Rio+20.

Our preference at this Zero Draft stage was to get agreement on a suite of core issues as an "indicative, illustrative, and descriptive" list that could then be developed after Rio+20 to get the process going and help shape it. We referred to "test-driving" a few issues: energy for example, around which the Secretary-General had launched the multistakeholder platform on Sustainable Energy for All. For several delegations from countries with significant fossil fuel production, this was a nonstarter, and in informal discussions we were told that there would never be consensus on a goal on energy. It was also feared this would prejudge the outcome of the endless climate change negotiations. The discussions went from broad concepts to the nitty-gritty of specific issues, all signaling that agreement on a final framework would be fraught. Precisely for this reason, we wanted to get delegations to think beyond just the concept of the SDGs to the process. Without the latter, all efforts would come to naught. We had no faith in the ability of a formal highly politicized UN intergovernmental setting (in other words, a process like Rio+20 itself) to deliver a functional metric.

In our interventions—the last ones we were to make in formal and plenary settings as Colombia, because after that the G77 and China coordinators took the lead on behalf of all members[4]—we reiterated the key tenets of our position and sought to incorporate responses to the issues that had been raised in Tarrytown. We reaffirmed that poverty should be the overarching objective and that the SDGs would build on the MDGs process, but we also acknowledged as clearly and transparently as possible that there were areas of disagreement, including on details of the process to elaborate the SDGs and how this could be reflected in the final Rio+20 outcome.

We remained committed to gradually building consensus around our proposal, but as the consultations ended, for the first time we had a clear understanding of just how difficult the process would be in the lead-up to Rio+20. Not just because of the controversies around an idea that was in fact a paradigm shift, but because we were competing for time and attention in an unwieldy negotiation that aimed to find consensus language around a fairly comprehensive suite of development issues: the first part of Section V of the Zero Draft, which included the SDGs, also covered fifteen—then twenty-six—separate thematic issues. This was proof, if any was needed, of how urgently the world needed a comprehensive metric rather than more negotiated language. But back then, it remained a massive hurdle.

We took great comfort in a few outcomes from that week that we held onto as evidence that there was a pathway forward. In the closing session, Brazil mentioned the SDGs as an outcome of Rio+20. Then the Republic of Korea suggested including a mandate for the SDGs in the preamble of the Rio+20 outcome document. This was a huge breakthrough, as Korean Ambassador Kim Sook was one of the co-chairs of the process. Finally, Sha Zukang once again referred to the SDGs in his statement. However, echoing the prevailing position of delegations such as France, he linked the SDGs to the delivery of a "green economy," a concept mired in controversy. This was a new front we would have to tackle in the coming months, ensuring that the SDGs steered clear of the green economy discussions and text.

Regardless, together with the friends and my team, we were energized. More and more constituencies and delegations were requesting meetings. In an otherwise bureaucratic and highly politicized discussion, the SDGs started to stand out for many as a shining, concrete option that could "save" Rio+20. Néstor Osorio, Colombia's ambassador to the UN, was galvanized. Different stakeholders were asking for meetings to better understand what we were proposing. As Néstor told us at one point, "This is surreal. Even Nobel Prize winners want to talk to us." Intergovernmental discussions may have been fraught, but across stakeholder groups—scholars, scientists, advocates, youth, UN major groups, the private sector—there was increasing excitement around the SDGs idea.

Notes

1. Statement by Sha Zukang, 2011.

2. We tasked a staff member from the permanent mission to count the delegations present.

3. I arrived two days early with Heidi Botero from my team. I remember wandering the imposing grounds covered in fresh snow, holding on to over eighty name cards and wondering whether or how the SDGs would ultimately see the light of day.

4. When countries belong to a formal negotiation group, they do not speak out independently in formal negotiation sessions. The respective group designates a coordinator or lead negotiator who speaks and negotiates on behalf of the group. To enable this, there are internal coordination sessions in the groups throughout the negotiations to arrive at common or consensus positions that the coordinator then takes to the negotiation space. If or when negotiations evolve beyond the agreed position of the group, it is necessary for the group to reconvene and undertake internal negotiations until a new position on a specific topic or issue is arrived at. Appendix 2 explains the basics of negotiations at the UN.

5

Positioning the SDGs

The political economy of the negotiations was complex, with a rich cast of countries, people, and positions. In this chapter we describe the preparatory events that marked the beginning of the formal negotiation process and provide insights into its workings. Key players are introduced, and the dynamics of the negotiation explored.

Aligning the Global South

Up until the first discussion of the Zero Draft at the end of January 2012, Colombia had been marketing the Sustainable Development Goals (SDGs) on its own with the support of Guatemala, Peru, and other friends. This provided a freedom of action that had been key for positioning the SDGs across governments and regions, UN agencies, and an array of constituencies. This also enabled us to gradually build up a critical mass of support, based on a carefully curated process of transparent and informed discussions and consultations. Vast numbers of people were now invested in the SDGs, and there was a growing sense of ownership across many groups. However, we had not yet formally presented the proposal to the negotiation group we belonged to, which would actually lead the entire negotiation process for Colombia: the G77 and China.

Throughout 2011, our goal had been to garner the needed support to get the SDGs formally into the Rio+20 process. A parallel goal had been to get other countries to endorse the idea as we did not want this to be exclusively "the Colombian proposal." We were delighted when Guatemala endorsed the second concept note in August 2011 but frustrated that a few weeks later at the Economic Commission for Latin America and the Caribbean (ECLAC) meeting, we were unable to get the Latin American and Caribbean region to formally endorse the proposal. This was due to regional dynamics that had little to do with the merits of the SDGs idea.

When Peru came on board in December 2011, we had renewed hopes for broader formal support, given that many delegates had evinced support at different moments. Within days of the Tarrytown retreat, on January 31, 2012, the Latin American and Caribbean Environment Ministers Forum was held in Quito. Colombian Minister of Environment and Sustainable Development Frank Pearl was tasked with giving endorsement from the region another try. We were hopeful that the substantive consultations to date had nudged enough governments along to get the endorsement.

However, as had happened at ECLAC in September 2011, although the region acknowledged the proposal, no full endorsement was forthcoming. The final declaration merely noted that in the preparatory process for Rio+20, it could be useful for "the themes of the sustainable development objectives [to be] defined in the framework of proposals for new development models, taking into account their characteristics of universal scope and national application, comprehensiveness and complementarity, having as a referent the Millennium Development Goals (MDGs), without prejudice to their implementation." Thus, we entered the negotiations with no regional consensus and a proposal endorsed by only three Latin American countries.

A completely new chapter of negotiations for Rio+20 was beginning. Strict rules, procedures, and hierarchies would henceforth dictate the process (see Appendix 2). What might be called the "warrior operation" of that first year of the SDGs journey, the remarkable journey of informal diplomacy, had to make way for the rigid and rigorous parameters of international negotiations at the UN. As a developing country, Colombia's formal negotiation group was the G77 and China. The time had come to formally present the proposal to the group and ask for their support. This was a pivotal moment. How we did it mattered enormously. We needed to send the strongest possible signal of the proposal's importance for Colombia, to draw a line in the sand, so to speak.

Therefore, a two-pronged political strategy was put in place that reflected our approach to a bottom-up diplomatic modus operandi: first, the presentation would be made at high political level on the part of

Colombia;[1] second, the initial presentation would be made directly to the delegates of the Second Committee, who were going to be responsible for leading negotiations on the Zero Draft, rather than the permanent representatives (equivalent to ambassadors) to the UN.

Through the Colombian UN mission in New York, we asked Algeria (which in 2012 was the chair of the G77 and China) to convene a meeting of the G77 and China members of the Second Committee to discuss the SDGs. At the meeting, Patti laid out the proposal, underscoring its importance as one wholly created by the Global South. She recalled the top-down origins of the MDGs and, while praising everything they had helped achieve and reiterating Colombia's firm commitment to full implementation by 2015, she noted that the problems and challenges our countries faced were too complex to be addressed only through the MDGs. It was time that the Global South took the lead in defining the international sustainable development agenda, one in which all countries had responsibilities for action. The fact that this presentation was made by a vice minister impressed on the delegates the importance that Colombia attached to the idea. For many, it was a bracing moment.

Although we knew that there were deep divisions in the room, the interventions were constructive and at worst noncommittal coming right after the Tarrytown consultations. Many of the delegates had come to our international consultations and had a clearer understanding of the SDGs proposal. Many had sharpened their opposition to the idea, but we considered that a positive development as at least now the arguments were clearer and we could engage them constructively. In any case, no one was going to show their hand that early. Algeria concluded the meeting by assuring Colombia that the G77 and China would take the negotiations of the SDGs forward. We had succeeded in signaling that the Colombian government was behind this proposal and that it was our highest priority for Rio+20.

In addition to the decisive presentation to the G77 and China, we programmed meetings with all the main regional groups of the Global South. One of the toughest meetings was with the ambassadors at the headquarters of the African Group, which encompasses fifty-four countries. It was key to brief this group as many had deep concerns that the SDGs would fatally undermine MDGs-based cooperation in Africa. The meeting was intense. We were grilled on the potential fallout from the SDGs idea. We explained how the SDGs could actually improve the level and degree of cooperation, helping align support around nationally defined priorities that could allow them to actually tackle more structural issues. What we were proposing would shift engagement with

Africa from donor-led aid to comprehensive development assistance. Admittedly, the reception was lukewarm, but it gave us an opportunity to directly respond to many of the concerns they raised. And it gave us an opportunity to explain why Colombia, as a developing country, saw this as an agenda not of conditionalities but of transformation.

The meeting with the Caribbean Community (CARICOM) was memorable given the strong and unconditional support they continued to express. CARICOM countries were early advocates of the SDGs and had clearly expressed this in their submission for the Zero Draft. As small island developing states (SIDS), they knew firsthand that development impacts and opportunities spill across sectors. The Caribbean support would later play a key role in convincing many African nations of the merits of the SDGs, given the special relationship at the UN between CARICOM and the African Group. Convinced that the active participation of every stakeholder was vital, we held a series of bilateral meetings. But a new chapter on the SDGs journey was beginning. Henceforth, although to the end Colombia continued to hold side events and informal meetings, all negotiations were now under the aegis of the G77 and China.

As is the norm for any negotiation, the G77 and China designates "coordinators" or "facilitators" from among its ranks, selecting the most seasoned delegates to lead on various tracks and issues. A few days after our official briefing, Algeria announced that the lead negotiator for the SDGs would be Farrukh Khan from Pakistan, one of the group's most experienced negotiators, with a deep knowledge of countries' positions and a well-honed capacity to steer negotiations. He had also been part of the UN Conference on Sustainable Development (UNCSD) Bureau from the start.

This appointment, although we did not know it at the time, proved to be instrumental in enabling the successful adoption of the SDGs in Rio+20. At the time though, Khan was unconvinced of the SDGs proposal and had to be pressured into accepting the role by Abdelghari (Abdel) Merabet, the Algerian delegate to the Second Commission who would be leading the negotiations on Rio+20 on behalf of the group. As Khan later wrote, "The SDGs seemed like yet another half-baked, crazy idea for us to pour hours and hours into before discarding it. I was worried that after nearly a decade of work, countries had finally figured out the MDGs, and now, we were about to change the rules of the game on them again. True, we were getting close to the expiry date but nowhere close to achieving the goals. Logically, we should have extended and boosted efforts around them."[2]

Indeed, when he was appointed, we had deep misgivings. Khan was an incisive and experienced negotiator I knew well from the climate change negotiations, but I was aware that he was widely dismissive of the SDGs. His position echoed concerns shared by many, and he wondered how such a proposal would be met in Pakistan. There was a palpable tension between the potential of international policy and domestic realities. However, as the negotiations got underway and especially as delegates started to discuss the idea, building on the extensive consultations that Colombia had hosted, Khan started to reconsider. A decisive shift took place in the first rounds of negotiations as he came around to appreciate how critical the SDGs were for the kind of disruptions and transformations he knew were needed. The concept of the green economy remained elusive. By the time of the third round of negotiations in April, he had become what I called a "fellow conspirator for the greater good," working to uphold the core principles of the group but also finding ways through the convoluted negotiations to ensure not just the adoption of the SDGs concept but the launch of a radically different process after Rio+20. One highlight that spoke to the long journey we had all traveled on was when Khan was invited to one of the friends' strategizing sessions. Somehow, this signaled the closing of a circle around the most ambitious outcome possible in Rio+20.

Players: A Partial Who's Who of the Negotiations

At the start of this chapter of the negotiations, there were vastly differing positions with regard to the SDGs, not just between governments but within governments. Surprisingly, the position was often defined at the individual level. Over time I got to know the varying attitudes to the SDGs proposal across and within many delegations. As noted earlier, a country's position sometimes depended on what delegate attended a meeting. The informal network of connections and friends I gradually built up over the course of the process thus served me well to understand governments' positions and navigate the often labyrinthine decisionmaking processes within them.[3]

One rule that held across many delegations was that in general, most Ministries of Environment were more open to the SDGs, whereas ministries or agencies in charge of cooperation and aid were more firmly wedded to the MDGs and more firmly opposed to the SDGs idea. Ministries of Foreign Affairs were a mixed bag, although most of the friends were career diplomats. Among these, the Netherlands (Kitty van der Heijden), Mexico (Damaso Luna), Norway (Marianne Loe), Peru

(Victor Muñoz), Switzerland (Franz Perrez), and Sweden (Anders Wallberg and Annika Markovic) played a decisive role throughout the Rio+20 process and in later shaping the evolution of the SDGs in the Open Working Group established after Rio+20. The Netherlands helped fund the first SDGs consultation in Bogotá in November 2011, and along with Norway, the Tarrytown consultation. From the side of the Ministries of Environment, the support of the UK Department of Environment, Food, and Rural Affairs (DEFRA) throughout the process was decisive and encompassed not just the lead negotiator (Chris Whaley) but even the minister (Caroline Spelman).

The European Union, which in many ways was a lead counterpart to the G77 and China, was no exception to the prevalent divide in positions. In the years before Rio+20, there had already been discussions led by those who saw a need to build the MDGs to incorporate economic and environmental dimensions. However, given that across industrialized countries the agenda was dominated by the development community, efforts to broaden the scope of the MDGs had not prospered. Thus, when the SDGs proposal appeared, it was largely embraced by environment agencies while those from the development arena opposed it. In a way, the SDGs fell into divisions that already existed. Here, too, the position of the respective Ministries of Foreign Affairs varied. Interestingly, two of the EU presidencies during the SDGs process were dedicated supporters. Poland, which held the presidency during the latter half of 2011, encouraged Colombia to persevere in what was then still a quixotic undertaking over the summer of 2011. On behalf of the EU, Poland was one of the countries that sought me out during the meeting in Solo, Indonesia. Denmark took on the presidency in 2012 and, as an astute and dedicated supporter of the SDGs, played a hugely influential role. I met several times with Minister Ida Auken, who was personally committed to ensuring that the most robust SDGs proposal possible would see the light of day. Similarly, I met throughout the negotiations with EU Environment Commissioner Janez Potočnik, candidly discussing the state of play of the process and jointly strategizing on how to advance different tracks of the SDGs discussion.

However, many from the development community from industrialized nations and the European Union were convinced that the SDGs idea was too ambitious and unwieldy and would collapse on its own in the course of the negotiations. Many of these representatives initially rejected the universal dimension of the SDGs proposal as they considered that their countries had already met development objectives and thus this agenda was not relevant to them. Down to the last days in

Rio, they were convinced that the onerous SDGs proposal was doomed to failure. Salient among these was the administration of UK Prime Minister David Cameron, which advocated for a concept called the "Golden Thread" that dovetailed nicely with an MDG+ vision of the future. Fortunately, as a result of this conviction, the SDGs negotiations were led by DEFRA until almost the end of the negotiations in Rio, and they were keen supporters of the SDGs. (Thus, the shift in the United Kingdom's position once in Rio de Janeiro speaks to the tensions in governments with regard to the SDGs proposal.) For their part, the delegations of the Netherlands and Sweden were staunch supporters of the SDGs and saw this as an all-important outcome of Rio+20. Colleagues from these three countries worked indefatigably to frame, position, and advance the proposal. But they had to navigate complex waters in the European Union as not all countries embraced the SDGs. France, for example, opposed the SDGs as a stand-alone area and insisted to the end that the SDGs could only be countenanced under the Green Economy pillar.

For many European delegations, the Tarrytown consultation was decisive because it confirmed that this was a serious proposal that was now on the table. Those who had been advocating for a more inclusive focus beyond the MDGs saw the SDGs as an opportunity to embrace a more comprehensive approach to sustainability. Sweden, for example, worked hard to convince other Nordics and Europeans of the merits of the proposal. At the level of the EU, however, divisions were exacerbated by its siloed architecture, which made it more complicated to advance consensus across issues that were addressed by different commissions—especially the Environment and the Development Cooperation Commissions. In addition to this, in the EU there were diverse working groups, each with a thematic or sectoral focus, with only a few dealing with cross-cutting issues. Because the proposed SDGs agenda was so comprehensive, there was not a good fit with the existing EU structure. EU Environment Commissioner Janez Potočnik endeavored to coordinate across agendas, but it was challenging to arrive at proposals and positions as issues were being addressed—including gender, peace and security, and governance—that were outside of the mandate of the Environment Commission. Throughout the negotiations, there was an undercurrent of tension regarding which ministry would lead, with different configurations in different countries. This often spilled over into the negotiations.

The United States experienced widely differing views across government agencies, informed by a commitment to the MDGs and by concerns that any instrument or agreement that required approval in Congress was essentially a nonstarter. As in many other developed countries, the idea that there would be a universal agenda that applied equally to them was met with skepticism. Many at the White House and the US Agency for International Development were concerned about watering down the MDGs and about the implications of a new metric. I met with many delegates across agencies in the months leading up to Rio+20 and came away with a mixed bag. At the consultation the United States hosted during the preparatory process, "Rio+20: Bridging Connection Technologies and Sustainable Development" in Palo Alto, California, at Stanford University, I met with Kerri-Ann Jones, the assistant secretary of state for the Bureau for Oceans and International Environmental and Scientific Affairs, who reaffirmed that the MDGs were a priority for the United States. This echoed the position of Ambassador Susan Rice, then US permanent representative to the UN, who remained committed to an aid-based vision of development and to tackling the MDGs' "unfinished business."

However, there were also more progressive voices that grasped the potential of the SDGs and how well it aligned with US support for science-based instruments and approaches that enabled more robust engagement by the private sector. Core to this cohort, John Matuszak and Elizabeth Cousens from the US State Department patiently and persistently advocated for the SDGs.[4] They brought a sharp understanding of the complexity of development issues. Cousens played a key role in the government in generating more receptivity to the SDGs. Matuszak led the technical negotiations for the State Department from the outset—he had been at the first SDGs consultation in Bogotá in November 2011—and as a stalwart supporter of the Group on Earth Observations and an advocate of natural capital accounting, he understood well the power of metrics. These divisions across a ministry merely reflected the deep divisions within and across governments and agencies writ large with regard to the MDGs-SDGs issue.

In April 2012, a major shift took place at the start of the Second Informal Informal consultations. Todd Stern, President Obama's special envoy for climate change, was designated to lead the Rio+20 negotiations. I knew him from the UN Framework Convention on Climate Change (UNFCCC) negotiations, and he asked to meet with me. Coming into a mature process, he wanted to get the state of play from colleagues he knew and trusted. I impressed on him the critical importance of getting agreement on the concept and characterization of the SDGs and of settling on a science-based process and entity after Rio+20 to actually develop the framework. With years of experience in the climate change negotiations, Stern unlocked a new understanding of what was at stake for the United States and how the Rio+20 process could positively affect other strategic interests and play out across other fora, especially the UNFCCC negotiations. The US delegation went on to play a major role in the final days and hours of the negotiations in Rio.

Other key delegations experienced internal tensions that played out in the process. Chief among these was Brazil, given their important role as host country of Rio+20 and bearers of the Rio legacy. Brazil's position regarding the SDGs proved to be complicated and waxed and waned during the long and convoluted process. Ultimately, Brazil played a key role in delivering the SDGs as part of the Rio+20 outcome as by then they recognized that the SDGs were the most compelling and substantive component of the conference. However, the path to Rio+20 reflected an occasional ambivalence toward the concept that had its roots in at least two issues.

First, as was the case with many governments, there was not a uniform or common position on the SDGs. Reflecting the position of most Ministries of Environment, Brazilian Minister of Environment Isabella Texeira was strongly supportive of the SDGs. However, Itamaraty, the Brazilian minister of Foreign Affairs, had a far more complex relation to the SDGs. Brazil had a leading role in the UNFCCC negotiations where, together with other BASIC countries,[5] the principle of common but differentiated responsibilities (CBDR) was a mainstay of negotiation tactics and had spilled over to other regimes that addressed environmental issues and global public goods. At its core, CBDR emphasized structurally different responsibilities between developed and developing countries. Even though the principle was undermined in Copenhagen in 2009 when BASIC countries announced voluntary emission reductions, the tenet of differing responsibilities remained central to the process. A universal agenda, as called for by the SDGs, challenged the foundations of the CBDR principle. It was not surprising (although unwelcome) that at one phase in the process, a leading Brazilian diplomat advocated for the adoption of two sets of goals, "one for rich countries, and another one for poor countries." This was linked to the all-important agenda of sustainable consumption and production that was a priority for Brazil and others.

Second, the Brazilian presidency needed to maintain a degree of manageable distance from an idea that—until the end—was profoundly controversial and stood a high chance of not being accepted. As we heard in the hallways, several in the delegation considered it likely that the SDGs proposal would flounder. Thus, at opening or closing sessions of various key meetings when speaking as the host of Rio+20,

Brazil would mention the SDGs as an important outcome in Rio, while during the actual negotiations within the G77 and China where the issues around the proposal were so contentious, Brazil largely maintained a neutral role.

Another key player was China. China was in a unique position as it had played a decisive role in delivering on poverty reduction at the global level called for under MDG1 (eradicate extreme poverty and hunger). China was beginning to appreciate the environmental problems caused by breakneck economic growth and was thus more open to a broader, more integrated agenda. In the negotiations, in keeping with their negotiation strategy as a BASIC country, the SDGs were always framed in the context of CBDR, but China tacitly supported a Rio outcome with a strong SDGs component.

Such was not the case with India, which flatly opposed the SDGs from the beginning. In their submission for the Zero Draft on November 1, 2011, they clearly stated that they did "not support defining and aiming for quantitative targets or goals towards sustainable development." Invoking the principle of CBDR and underscoring that developed countries had to take the lead, they concluded that CBDR had to "be upheld in any implementation focused outcome on sustainable development, as opposed to MDGs. The context of MDGs and SDGs (Sustainable Development Goals) are disparate." India was profoundly influential in the negotiations, and its positions often help shape the scope of the discussions and define final outcomes.

Across the G77 and China, the entire gamut of positions was present in terms of governments and delegates. This is what made the negotiations in coordination meetings so difficult.[6] There were other blocs within the group that had an outsize influence on deliberations and decisions. The Bolivarian Alliance for the Peoples of Our America (ALBA) led by Bolivia, Ecuador, Nicaragua, and Venezuela, was a contesting force in the negotiations.[7] Highly disciplined and tenacious in their positions, their delegates often played a decisive role in shaping and framing discussions in the group. They largely stuck to hardline positions underpinned by an unswerving commitment to the primacy of the CBDR principle. Maintaining the strength of the Group of 77 and China was ALBA's overriding concern, and this was a key reason for their outright rejection of the country-led, technical working group that Colombia advocated for as a post-Rio+20 process until the last days of the negotiations (see Chapter 9).

Other blocs balanced out these positions, and within the Latin American and Caribbean region, the Caribbean SIDS played an outsize role in the negotiations. Their full support for the SDGs in their submission to the UNCSD Secretariat on the content of the Zero Draft was quite influential. Colombia and the CARICOM nations were close allies from the UNFCCC negotiations, where they shared similar positions. Like other SIDS, their high vulnerability to climate impacts led them to drive for the highest possible ambition across regimes. They had outstanding delegates, savvy and seasoned, and punched far above their geopolitical weight. Together with a group of other progressive countries in the G77 and China that included Colombia, they often banded together in negotiations. One of the lead negotiators was Selwin Hart from Barbados, who went on to play a leading role in Rio as facilitator of the SDGs negotiations.

The Arab group encompassed a wide range of views. Throughout the negotiations, Algeria was the chair of the G77 and China and did a solid job of navigating through the shoals of the widely divergent views within the group. Leadership for the presidency fell largely to Abdel Merabet, who successfully led an unwieldy and multifaceted process, managing not only relations across the group but also the politics between the group and the bureau. Merabet and others in the Algerian delegation were able to maintain a healthy neutrality that more than once kept the group from imploding, and they did an admirable job in tasking and delegating difficult negotiation tracks to seasoned and highly trusted colleagues. All in all, they ran a well-oiled machine. Within their own group, this called for dexterous balancing as it included governments like Saudi Arabia, which was known for its hardline positions across negotiations, and that of the United Arab Emirates (UAE), a progressive government that pushed for an ambitious SDGs outcome. Majid Hassan Al Suwaidi, who led the negotiations for the UAE, was a core and important friend. The Arab group also included Egypt, which played a vital bridging role, with a keen understanding of the group's variegated landscape and a quiet commitment to a strong outcome at Rio+20 across many tracks. From the outset, Egypt's Mohamed Khalil understood the potential of the SDGs proposal and often worked to broker better understanding across different constituencies. His support for the SDGs got many in the group to delve more deeply into the proposal and gradually support it.

The African group was a multifaceted cohort. Initially, it was largely united by its unrelenting support for the MDGs and pushed for an MDG+ outcome in the initial months of negotiations in 2012. African countries had benefited enormously from the support that flowed through the MDGs framework and were deeply concerned that the SDGs would knock the wind out of the MDGs long before these were more advanced in their implementation. Over time, nuances emerged in various countries' positions. As a member of the African group and the Arab group, Egypt had an influential role in helping many delegates more fully understand the SDGs and worked to bridge divisions, especially in the final days in Rio. Over the course of the negotiations, the least developed country (LDC) group played an increasingly important role. In 2012, thirty-three countries in the African group belonged to the LDC constituency, and as understanding of the SDGs proposal matured, a significant number came to view it as a way to ensure access to more coherent, comprehensive support.

Another decisive cohort were those countries that did not belong to any political negotiation group. This meant that they had considerable freedom to craft their own positions without having to first negotiate them in a group encompassing a diverse group of countries. They could bring them directly into the negotiations. While a country like Colombia could not intervene in a plenary or more formal settings where the G77 and China coordinator would speak on behalf of the group, "independent" countries could intervene at will. Thus, countries like Australia, the Republic of Korea, Mexico, Norway, Switzerland, and the United States could wield significant power in the negotiations.[8] They could bring in language that broadened the negotiation field and propose alternatives that laid out new pathways to consensus or to challenge the text. Critically for us, several of these countries, including Mexico, Norway, and Switzerland, were staunch members of the friends. Mexico (Damaso Luna) played a leading role in proposing text that got early language on what became the Open Working Group on the table. Switzerland (Franz Perrez) and Norway (Marianne Loe) held a steady rudder throughout the negotiations, keeping language and ambitious options on the table. Norway provided generous funding for many of the consultations that Colombia organized, making it possible to reach out to a significant number of countries and constituencies at critical junctures.

Throughout the negotiation process, Colombia and friends were permanently reaching out to other delegations through side events, consultations, dinners, lunches, and breakfasts to create opportunities for discussion, explaining the SDGs, and building trust. One suite of initiatives that stands out was promoted by Franz Perrez, ambassador of Switzerland. Concerns from developing countries that official development assistance (ODA) for the MDGs would be derailed or dropped as the SDGs gained ascendancy was a major hurdle for the negotiations. Perrez decided that because this was such a core issue, it had to be tackled directly and openly. He organized several dinners with different delegates from the Global South and the Global North. The objective was to create a safe space where donor countries could assure their colleagues that the SDGs process would not undermine commitment to the MDGs.

One memorable evening, after a heated discussion about developed countries' shortfalls in meeting their 1970 pledge for ODA at a minimum of 0.7 percent of gross national product,[9] Marianne Loe from Norway spoke up and described her government's commitment to keeping this pledge. Ositadinma Anaedu from Nigeria, who had been a leading voice in the discussions, stared at her for a few seconds. Then he slowly said, "Norway has always lived up to its commitments. I believe you." This permanent engagement through backroom channels proved decisive. Gradually many in the LDC group started to come around to the SDGs idea. The friends worked tirelessly on all fronts to tackle blockages in the negotiations, create spaces for sensible conversations, and above all, build trust in the concept and in the process.

February 2012: Staking the Battle Lines

February was an intense month for the SDGs cause, and it resulted in us further consolidating gains around the proposal. At the UN Environment Programme (UNEP) Governing Council/Global Ministerial Forum, held February 20–22 in Nairobi, the growing momentum around the SDGs was palpable. Everyone wanted to talk about the SDGs with our delegation. There were numerous bilateral meetings and dinners with ministers from developed and developing countries, the first of many meetings with EU Commissioner for Environment Janez Potočnik, and meetings with leading nongovernmental organizations. The tide had definitely turned. Far from being regarded as an outlier and latecomer to the Rio+20 process, the SDGs were taking center stage. The UNEP Governing Council also marked an important watershed for the European Union as consultations and discussions cemented the EU's support for the SDGs under the Danish presidency.

Colombia hosted two events in Nairobi. The first was held at the Colombian embassy the night before the formal meetings started. As it got underway, it quickly became standing room only. The energy in the room was unlike any we had experienced before. Everyone seemed to support the SDGs idea. If there was any opposition, it was muted. The second event was held two days later. It was memorable because after the initial presentation, a participant from an organization from the US Midwest excoriated the SDGs concept. Before Colombia could respond, Minister Caroline Spelman, secretary of the DEFRA (UK), who had simply walked into the event and taken one of the seats, asked for the floor and proceeded to deliver a ringing and pithy defense of the SDGs. It was a remarkable moment.

Another development in February 2012, one that went largely unnoticed at the time, was the release of the final report of the Secretary-General's High-level Panel on Global Sustainability, "Resilient People, Resilient Planet: A Future Worth Choosing."[10] This panel had been established in August 2010 and was co-chaired by the presidents of Finland and South Africa, with a view to providing inputs and guidance to the Rio+20 process. The report included many recommendations and called for the adoption of a "nexus approach" to address food, water, and energy security issues in an interlinked way. At the formal launch in March, UN Secretary-General Ban Ki-moon said he would explore the option of preparing a global sustainable development outlook report that would periodically assess progress toward goals of sustainable development and low-carbon prosperity. However, the panel had been mired in internal difficulties and operated entirely behind closed doors, an approach that ultimately contributed to the report's broad rejection by many member states who considered it a top-down and untransparent process. (For example, we only became aware of the existence of the panel and the report in January 2012.) The report had a hard landing, and its recommendations ultimately had no echo or effect on the negotiations, which was unfortunate because considerable energy, resources, and leadership by the UN had been invested.

February was also a critical month for the Rio+20 process. It gave negotiation groups and delegations time to prepare for the upcoming round of negotiations, called the "First Informal Informal Consultations and Third Intersessional Meeting," which were scheduled for March 19–27 in New York. It also gave time to the Secretariat to further hone the draft negotiation text.

Arduous negotiations took place in New York all February as delegations and negotiation groups reviewed, digested, and contested the Zero Draft. The G77 and China organized a steady stream of consultations, or "coordination meetings," with Second Commission delegates; these were facilitated by Merabet.

The modus operandi was standard: the Algerian mission would inform that consultations on the Zero Draft would be held on a given day, usually with short notice as it was assumed that only delegates based in New York would attend. Often the exact section(s) of the Zero Draft to be discussed were announced only the day before. Given the decided opposition by the majority of its members to the SDGs and the fact that this document aimed to define the playing field for the SDGs, I sought to participate in any and all meetings on the SDGs even though I was based in Bogotá.

There were deep and seemingly unbridgeable chasms between the outcome that Colombia sought with the support of a few delegations, and the majority position in the G77 and China. For many delegations, the tension between the MDGs and the SDGs was untenable, and there were early moves to flush out the SDGs entirely from the Zero Draft. If this failed, the fallback position was to underscore the importance of the MDGs and begrudgingly tack the SDGs to some future evolution of the MDGs.

Opponents raised serious concerns that the SDGs were going to become a millstone around the neck of developing countries: more conditionalities, more responsibilities, and more reporting in tandem with the apportionment of bilateral aid among a vast number of issues, with donors doing the picking and choosing. Moreover, few believed that developed countries would accept a universal agenda or, if they did, take it seriously. These concerns meant that the G77 and China would be eroding a principle that was sacred to many—CBDR—for nothing in return. In the view of many, the SDGs were nothing short of gratuitous self-immolation. The negotiations in the group were long and acrimonious.

On March 5, the G77 and China shared its version of the Zero Draft, laying out its position on every single issue and paragraph (see Appendix 11). In effect, the group presented their own version of the Zero Draft. This proposal contained language that spoke to the core of the group's concerns and reflected long-standing positions from negotiations in other arenas. It was a strong hand to play just two weeks before the First Informal Informal Consultations, and it set the tone for the fractious negotiations in the coming months.

These initial negotiations in the group were also a foretaste of the struggles that would rage over the following months. The entirety of the original Zero Draft language on the SDGs was eliminated (see strike-outs in Appendix 11). In its place, several paragraphs extolled the merits of the MDGs and essentially subsumed and tied any possible SDGs outcome to the further evolution of the MDGs. The discussions were so fraught that we took the radical and unheard of step of demanding the inclusion of language ascribed only to Colombia in the group's text, a clear and visible break with the group and a break with long-standing protocol that laid bare our isolation.

In fact, the first round of substantive negotiations throughout February 2012 defined and honed our strategy for advancing our negotiation positions working in the G77 and China and with other countries. As there was so little time for substantive discussions, we would endeavor to clearly stake out our position at the outset of each G77 and China consultation. Then we would listen to the positions, taking note of the political geography that emerged. We would argue for the outcome text Colombia wanted—with varying degrees of support from other delegations. Friends in the group would often try to rally to support our positions, but we were utterly outnumbered. When the opposition was too strong within the group, we would take our concerns and position to the friends, where through rich and substantive discussions, we would pick apart the concerns and issues that were raised and strategize on text to get the language we wanted into the rapidly evolving negotiations. This often led to the proposal of language by an "independent" country that made it into the Zero Draft during the negotiations and thus broadened the negotiation playing field. It was hard and lonely going even with the support of our friends.

At the end of this first round of negotiations in the G77 and China, we had a better sense of the negotiation landscape ahead and which battles to pick and which to leave to others. There were so many issues to contend with that we decided early on to focus our efforts within the group on getting basic agreement on concepts and process, knowing that in the melee of the plenary negotiations, other delegations with more leeway would broaden the negotiation space.

We knew that CBDR would remain a mainstay of the discussions, a bargaining chip until there was more clarity, toward the end of the process, of the overall outcome package. But we worried that for some, CBDR was truly sacrosanct and that it would exacerbate resistance to a proposal that called for a universal agenda, one with equal responsibilities across all countries. Given that there was no possibility of changing the group's prevailing position, and a head-on battle against CBDR would undermine our ability to advance on other critical fronts, we acquiesced, knowing that other delegations and negotiation groups would oppose it in the plenary.

After the initial round of prenegotiation consultations and meetings in New York in February, back in Bogotá we assessed the situation. In private, several countries in the G77 and China had confirmed the value of the idea. In public, those same countries were noncommittal. Key countries that played a larger role in the G77 and China, particularly the BASIC countries, were either largely silent or strongly opposed.

We went through the roster. China? Appeared comfortable with a universal metric as long as it is voluntary and developed through an intergovernmental process. India? Flatly opposed, with long-standing concerns about fallout for the climate change negotiations and the imposition of conditions. South Africa? Seemingly in line with the over-riding African position to support only MDGs. Brazil? Largely neutral in the G77 and China, avoiding getting caught up in the tense discussions on the SDGs. As we analyzed the various groups, we decided that we needed to ensure the support of the majority of the BASIC countries given their size and importance in the multilateral system and in the G77 and China.

In our assessment, Brazil was supportive because the SDGs would mean delivering a concrete outcome at Rio+20. China was raising no sub-stantive issues. Engaging with South Africa would require deep band-width to hold consultations across the African group. We decided we needed to first talk directly to the Indian government, widely renowned for the ability of its diplomats and the rigor of their negotiation positions.

Thus, on March 13, 2012, we set off on a trip to India to personally explain to high-level government authorities in the Ministry of Foreign Affairs the merits and logic of the SDGs and dispense with the many concerns and reservations raised during the consultations.[11] In the end, India understood the strengths of the proposal and its unique contribu-tion to both the sustainability and equity dimensions of development. The discussions helped Colombia further mature the proposal. India committed to support it.

Two months later, in the midst of acrimonious negotiations in the G77 and China in preparation for the final round of consultations in New York before heading to Rio de Janeiro, we got proof of India's commitment. The group had painstakingly come up with consensus lan-guage on the importance and utility of SDGs when a delegate from Nigeria, a country that carries significant weight in its region and who had participated only marginally in the drawn-out negotiations, informed the group that this language would never be accepted by his government. There was a moment of silence, and many delegates began to talk all at once, breaking protocol. Several delegates were nodding. The hard-won gains of previous months threatened to evaporate.

The moment was broken by Vivek Wadekar, the Indian delegate. He pulled out the text from the preceding round of the group's negotiations and proceeded to read out the exact text that had been already agreed to. He affirmed that the group operates on the principle that what has been agreed must be respected. He was so categorical that silence ensued. The discussion moved on and the text held. When the meeting ended, I approached Wadekar and thanked him for his determined support.

He looked at me with a smile and said, "India said we would support this proposal, and we keep our word."

As this anecdote illustrates, the process was very fluid and demanded that we invest continuously in helping delegates, especially from our group, better understand the proposal and its many facets. Between March and June 2012, I traveled to New York six times, thrice for G77 and China meetings that were often convened with scant advance notice. The group's coordination meetings had moving agendas, and it was never entirely clear when the SDGs would be discussed. In the Colombian mission in New York our delegate for the Second Commission, David Rodriguez, received a constant stream of guidance from Bogotá to navigate negotiations. It was essential that our position—which remained marginal on many fronts—be reflected or at least considered and that every opportunity for nurturing and advancing consensus was capitalized.

In fact, the negotiations in the G77 and China were so complicated that the network we had studiously built up during our year-long undertaking of informal diplomacy now served us well. Throughout the next months, all our efforts were centered in backroom consultations and informal diplomacy as well as determined outreach across constituencies and civil society groups. I kept up a drumbeat of momentum around the SDGs through innumerable side events that we hosted and were invited to and meetings with UN agencies and stakeholder groups. There were memorable *encerronas*—meetings of virulent and quite high-level opposers of the SDGs that I was invited to alone in the expectation that I could be browbeaten into accepting that the SDGs were an untenable proposition. The Colombian permanent mission was increasingly pulled into the process, and our ambassador had to allocate time to respond to the growing number of requests around the SDGs. My resolute team in Bogotá helped generate a seemingly endless flow of presentations, briefings, and talking points.

During the negotiation sessions, the friends met on a daily basis, convening in the hallways and the Vienna Café. We started the practice of holding at least one friends' consultation during each Intersessional Meeting. We would meet at the permanent mission of one of the friends' delegations, where we would take stock of the negotiations and define critical ways forward. We took turns organizing these meetings, which were safe spaces to share the dynamics of the discussions in the different negotiation groups and strategize on how to position issues or language. The friends' meetings were also cathartic, an opportunity for mutual encouragement, fortitude, and inspiration when the going got rough. There was remarkably little substantive divergence in our positions regarding the SDGs concept. Where we differed, it mostly related to tone or scope. With regard to the core outcome we were after, we were all on the same page. We have said that it took a village to make the SDGs a reality. The friends were a vital part of that.

Notes

1. Occasionally, Patti, in her duties as vice minister, would participate in meetings and lobby for the SDGs idea to represent and make explicit the full governmental support behind the proposal, from both the minister of Foreign Affairs and the president of Colombia.

2. Khan (2016).

3. The core group of friends included Yeshey Dorji, Bhutan; Jimena Leiva, Guatemala; Damaso Luna, Mexico; Kitty van der Heijden, Netherlands; Marianne Loe, Norway; Victor Muñoz, Peru; Anders Wallberg and Annika Markovic, Sweden; Franz Perrez, Switzerland; Majid Hassan Al Suwaidi, United Arab Emirates; Chris Whaley, United Kingdom.

4. John Matuszak was division chief of Sustainable Development and Multilateral Affairs, Office of Environmental Policy, Bureau of Oceans and International Environmental and Scientific Affairs, US Department of State. At the time, Elizabeth Cousens was chief of staff to Ambassador Susan Rice at the US permanent mission to the UN and later led the US delegation in the Open Working Group negotiations.

5. BASIC refers to a group of large emerging nations (Brazil, South Africa, India, and China) established in the context of the UNFCCC negotiations.

6. In principle, for every negotiation, there are daily G77 and China coordination meetings, as a first order of business in the morning and on specific negotiation tracks—to strategize on the various negotiation items. The plenary meetings take stock across the different negotiation tracks to gauge progress, identify priority concerns and issues, define strategies, and deal with operational issues. At these meetings, diverging positions across the 134 members surface constantly and call for nimble diplomatic efforts on the part of the group's presidency to either find consensus language and positions or define pathways for advancing toward a collective endgame. Coordinators are assigned to lead the different negotiation tracks in a given process, and they set up thematic coordination meetings, which usually meet in the evening and often into the late hours. See Appendix 2 for more information about negotiation at the UN.

7. At the time, ALBA (Bolivarian Alliance for the Peoples of Our America—Alianza Bolivariana para los Pueblos de Nuestra America) was composed of Antigua and Barbuda, Bolivia, Cuba, Dominica, Grenada, Nicaragua, Saint Kitts and Nevis, Saint Lucia, Saint Vincent and the Grenadines, Suriname, and Venezuela. It was started in 2004 by Venezuela and Cuba.

8. Australia, Canada, Japan, New Zealand, Norway, the Republic of Korea, Switzerland, and the United States participate in JUSCANZ (a name derived from the combination of its founding members: Japan, the United States, Canada, Australia, and New Zealand), an informal coalition of countries largely from one of the five UN regional groups, the Western European and Others group. A combination of some of these countries participate in the Umbrella group. Other groups include the

Environmental Integrity group, which includes Switzerland, the Republic of Korea, Mexico, and Norway. However, during the Rio+20 process, these groups did not play distinct roles.

9. The 0.7 percent pledge refers to official development assistance (ODA). It originated in UN General Assembly Resolution 25/2626 of October 24, 1970, paragraph 43: "Each economically advanced country will progressively increase its official development assistance to the developing countries and will exert its best efforts to reach a minimum net amount of 0.7% of its gross national product."

10. UNSG (2012).

11. In Delhi we met with a wide array of government officials and spent long hours in deep and substantive conversations. We met with Madhusudan Ganapathi, secretary for the Western Hemisphere, and with the under-secretary for Economic and Social Affairs, T. S. Tirumurti, and under-secretary for Political Affairs, Pavan Kappor, as well as J. M. Mauskar, who had been a longtime head of delegation for the UNFCCC negotiations.

6

A Tortuous Process

Chapters 6 and 7 cover the same phase of the process, from February 2012 through to the third and last negotiation in New York before delegates went to the Rio+20 Conference. Chapter 6 describes the process and Chapter 7 delves into the actual negotiations with a detailed analysis of the evolution of the Zero Draft's section on the Sustainable Development Goals (SDGs).

The Zero Draft: Basis for the Negotiations

The structure of the Zero Draft defined the dynamics and rhythm of the entire negotiations that followed (see Figure 6.1). The draft was organized into five sections, which were further divided into fifteen subsections.[1] Section V on Framework for Action and Follow-up, which included the SDGs, also covered thematic areas and cross-sectoral issues, which included all the main development areas around which there were strongly held views and conflicting positions. The SDGs were sandwiched between "priority/key/thematic/cross-sectoral issues and areas" and "Means of Implementation (finance, access to and transfer of technology, capacity building)." Fully 51 percent (66 out of 128) of the paragraphs fell under Section V.

Figure 6.1 Table of Contents, Working Draft, *The Future We Want*

138-a

UNITED NATIONS

January 10, 2012

THE FUTURE WE WANT [1]

TABLE OF CONTENTS **Paras**

[1] Submitted by the co-Chairs on behalf of the Bureau in accordance with the decision in Prepcom 2 to present the zero-draft of the outcome document for consideration by Member States and other stakeholders no later than early January 2012.

This positioning of the SDGs in the longest section proved to be detrimental for their negotiation as they were wedged between two subsections that were of high priority for most delegations. On one hand, the negotiations around Means of Implementation, which included finance, were among the most charged. On the other hand, priority issues encompassed a massive suite of core development issues that delegations were deeply invested in, as many were part of other arduous negotiations and fora. In the initial Zero Draft released in January, there were only fifteen thematic issues.[2] By the time we got to Rio de Janeiro, the list of priority issues had grown to twenty-six.[3] The scope for substantive discussions on Section V was almost completely taken up by the highly politicized negotiations around these issues, many with well-defined and long-standing positions that were rolled over from other negotiations from past years. If anything, these discussions were a stark reminder of why the world so desperately needed a nonpoliticized, sensible framework to tackle these challenges.

For the SDGs' cause, this arrangement in an already crowded Section V created enormous hurdles. When the negotiations started, the SDGs were still marginal. For many, the SDGs were essentially a stone in the shoe, a minor side event that had to be dispensed with, preferably with minimal effort. Given that the SDGs were a tiny fraction of the Zero Draft—initially just 7 paragraphs out of 128—the text-based negotiation format gravely limited the time allotted to the SDGs in the formal negotiations and in G77 and China coordination meetings. The first four sections of the Zero Draft—two of which framed the negotiations and two of which focused on the formal pillars of the outcome document (Sections III and IV)—captured significant time and attention. These were, after all, the main outcome areas that had been formally agreed to since 2009 and, along with Means of Implementation (MoI), were considered by most delegates the priority negotiation tracks. Many expected that the SDGs appendage would inevitably wither and die.

The negotiation architecture was complex and became more convoluted over the following months. From the outset, each of the subsections that constituted the Zero Draft was negotiated separately, with facilitators assigned to each. Negotiation groups like the European Union and the G77 and China assigned lead coordinators for each negotiation track. As the negotiations got underway and the sections and issues spiraled into layers of complex positions, facilitators began to be assigned to tackle specific issues or subsections in what were called splinter groups. By the time we got to Rio in June 2012, there were fourteen of these splinter groups, each negotiating specific tracks. Even though the two co-chairs for the process were leading parallel sessions, during the intersessional meetings over the coming months the demand for negotiation time became increasingly challenging. It should be recalled that in parallel to the formal negotiations in plenary, the different negotiation groups, such as the G77 and China and the EU, were always meeting, at least once a day, trying to find consensus language and positions across their many member states.

First Round of Informal Informal Negotiations

Building from the Zero Draft, over the course of the initial ten-day negotiation session, formally known as the First Informal Informal (March 19–23, 2012) and Third Intersessional Meeting (March 26–27, 2012), language solidified.[4] The G77 and China had already put forward a new text, rejecting the entirety of the Zero Draft. Other proposals were put forward, the result of six weeks of deliberations that delegations had undertaken since the last meeting in New York in January 2012. By the end of this first negotiation session, the proposed language had become an explosion of paragraphs, many of which consisted of strings of bracketed (unapproved) text that were almost illegible.[5]

After a week of negotiations, the first full reading of the SDGs section concluded on March 23, a Friday afternoon. Although discussions in the G77 and China had been contentious and difficult, many other parties were increasingly supportive of the proposal, as were many constituencies and stakeholder groups. There was considerable anticipation, matched by confusion given how convoluted the negotiation text had become. Yet the fact that so many delegations had participated in the Tarrytown consultations and in other events and meetings we hosted or participated in contributed to more substantive discussions. Given the time constraints during the negotiations, we decided that another consultation was imperative so that more delegations could benefit from informed discussions. That weekend, in the middle of the negotiations, Colombia hosted yet another informal consultation.

We were obsessed with enabling negotiators to be able to sensibly and rationally discuss and explore the various facets of the decisions we faced. This included characterizing the SDGs, defining their relation to the MDGs and the post-2015 agenda, and agreeing to a process after Rio+20 to develop them. We were desperate to get conversations going in the G77 and China that were not tightly wound around language. We needed to pull delegates back from the words to concentrate on the substance. We wanted positive cross-pollination across negotiation groups, especially the EU and the G77 and China, with positive reinforcement from delegates from "independent" countries who were also among our friends.

Thus, on Saturday, March 24, 2012, with the generous support of the Ford Foundation, we hosted a consultation. In the morning, only representatives from G77 and China were invited to take the pulse of the room and the negotiations over the main outstanding issues in the discussions. We wanted to build trust and a shared sense of purpose. We invited Brazil to give initial remarks to underscore their leadership and tie them explicitly to the proposal. Brazil was supportive of the proposal but did not actively engage in the substantive discussions that ensued. In the afternoon, all governments were invited, and again Brazil was asked to provide opening remarks.

Importantly, this time we invited ambassadors and not just the delegates from the Second Committee who had led the discussions on the SDGs for their respective missions. We wanted to engage more senior levels in the missions so as to create interest in the SDGs proposal outside of the usual cohort of delegates, and thus greater engagement and ultimately accountability for the course of the negotiations. We went over issues that were well known to some but not to the many diplomats who were not in the Second Committee.

Coming after a week of an incredibly frustrating exercise of live dictation—the constant stream of additions to the Zero Draft hardly classified as negotiation—delegates welcomed the opportunity to dig into the issues. There were no breakthroughs (none had been expected), but the meeting created goodwill and confirmed to many that the SDGs were a sensible proposal that needed to be crafted in a sensible way. It also signaled once again that Colombia aimed to co-create the proposal and had no hidden agenda or interests. Given where we were, that counted as a success.

In addition to this, Colombia participated in side events and consultations throughout the ten days. The friends were also indefatigable in hosting events and informal consultations. I spent lunch breaks and evenings meeting with civil society representatives who flocked to the Colombian delegation, excited with the potential of the SDGs idea.

The first round of negotiations concluded on March 27, 2012, on a bitter note, however. The sessions had been exhausting and frustrating. The consolidated negotiation text on March 27 was a morass of brackets and alternative text (see Appendix 12). Because there were several parallel negotiating groups working on the Zero Draft, it was difficult to have a good understanding of how the process was advancing. Most worryingly, the time allotted to the various items was increasingly insufficient for substantive discussions as the text spiraled out of control.

Lead negotiators from the formal negotiation groups, where a degree of consensus had been painstakingly crafted, were unable or unwilling to budge from their positions. Each negotiation group or country (for those that did not negotiate in one of the established groups, such as Mexico, Switzerland, or Norway) was intent on making sure their exact language was reflected while often bracketing others' proposals. Issues mushroomed in tandem with different approaches for tackling each one. The Zero Draft had started out life with 65 paragraphs but was now more than 200 pages with around 400 additional paragraphs in Section V alone.[6]

The status of the SDGs at the end of this first round of negotiations was uncertain, but several delegations were strongly supportive. Those supporters provided clear language to shape the section into a sensible narrative that would frame the idea and ensure a robust way forward. Within the G77 and China, progress was minimal, but at least there seemed to be nascent consensus on the existence of the SDGs, and on the three-part architecture in the Zero Draft: (1) vision of the SDGs, (2) guiding principles, and (3) a process for developing them. Mindful of the genesis of the MDGs, we emphasized that the SDGs must be country-driven and inclusive. But the road ahead was daunting. Our priorities were in stark opposition to what the majority of the G77 and China group wanted, particularly with regard to the relationship between the SDGs and the MDGs, the inclusion of a list of indicative thematic issues the SDGs would focus on, and the establishment and nature of a process after Rio. Long hours of negotiation lay ahead to ensure that what was ultimately agreed to was truly a new paradigm and not just the same old thing with a bit of varnish.

Second Round of Informal Informal Negotiations

Despite the frustration that had permeated the first round of consultations as text and brackets proliferated on screens in the meeting rooms, the Second Informal Informal consultations on the Zero Draft (April 23–May 4, 2012) should have gotten off to a hopeful start with the issuance by the co-chairs of a new draft consolidated outcome document that pointed to potential areas of consensus. However, a few days before the start of the negotiations, the EU released a proposal for a set of five "goals, targets and actions in priority areas" under a "green economy roadmap" based on a non-paper prepared for their

Informal Environmental Council. This proposal created an uproar in the G77 and China.

Evidently, the intent of the EU was to raise the ambition in the negotiations and, by spelling out a suite of goals and targets, demonstrate what a future SDGs framework could look like. At a minimum, it was supposed to be an instructive exercise. In reality, the situation illustrated the tense and difficult state of the negotiations. At the first G77 and China coordination meeting during the Second Informal Informal consultations, the EU proposal was decried as proof that the EU had a secret hidden agenda and wanted to impose a specific set of priorities.

The fact that one of the goals in their proposal was on energy—even though all it did was reiterate the three goals widely accepted under the Sustainable Energy for All initiative—was interpreted by some in the G77 and China as further proof that this was a backdoor effort to negotiate climate change issues under a different guise. Similarly, there was a backlash against a goal on "resource efficiency, in particular waste" even though it was based on the 10 Year Framework on Programmes of Sustainable Consumption and Production around which there was strong consensus and which echoed agreed language from the Johannesburg Plan of Implementation. This was pointed out during the group's meeting by a few delegates, to no avail. Moreover, by framing these goals in a document that referred to a green economy roadmap, many in the G77 and China inferred that the EU was stealthily laying the ground for derailing the SDGs section and moving all reference to the SDGs to the green economy section.

For Colombia, this was an unforeseen and serious setback. Getting agreement on an "indicative, illustrative" set of thematic areas the SDGs might focus on was one of our three objectives for Rio+20. I was in constant contact across delegations and groups on all SDGs matters, so I understood the EU's constructive intent vis-à-vis the proposal. My efforts to explain this during the G77 and China's consultation either seemed not to be heard or started to raise suspicions that shenanigans were afoot. As soon as the meeting ended, I went to look for EU delegates to explain the situation. They were dumbfounded. It took a while for them to understand the gravity of the situation and how the proposal had been read by a significant majority of the G77 and China. For the EU, the situation was tricky. This was not simply a proposal put forward in good faith for the consideration of delegates in New York but one that had been signed off at high levels in Brussels.

The following days, we devoted inordinate amounts of time to managing the noise and dust raised by the proposal. Friends stepped up and provided safe spaces for discussing how to defuse the situation. When Janez Potočnik, the EU commissioner for environment, arrived in New York, we met and I sought to explain how the proposal had been received in the G77 and China. I made the case for withdrawing it as well as the targets that EU delegates had introduced to the negotiations of the respective thematic areas. The EU finally withdrew their proposal for "transitional targets." But this episode cemented the opposition by many to any kind of "indicative" list of priority areas for the SDGs.

Nonetheless, the EU succeeded in helping shape the contours of the future negotiation on the actual framework. Ultimately their proposal did achieve part of what they had aimed to do in terms of raising the overall ambition of the discussions. Their proposal presaged what the SDGs would become: "It should be underlined that the goals and targets do not represent a legally binding engagement; rather they provide aspiration for the world to focus on and try to achieve progress in the area of the transition to an inclusive, green economy. This progress should be measured with appropriate indicators."

Even with this debacle and the hurdles in advancing the compromise text, by the end of the first week of the Second Informal Informal negotiations, the concept of the SDGs was sufficiently advanced that we were fairly certain that the concept would be an integral part of the Rio+20 outcome, in one way or another. Our overriding concern now was to ensure that the outcome also included the process to actually develop and define the SDGs framework. That discussion was intense, even within the friends as several of them supported the option of having the UN Secretary-General lead the process, an option largely favored by the EU.

A key modality we had adopted for influencing and steering the negotiations was through the concept notes that we issued. The first two—one alone and the other with Guatemala—put SDGs on the map. The third one with Guatemala and Peru helped frame the start of the negotiations. In the middle of the second round of informal informal negotiations with scant progress being made, we felt that something was needed to jolt the process. We decided to issue a new concept note, one that outlined the requirements for the post-Rio process.

Over the weekend (April 28–29, 2012), I prepared a new concept note. I consulted among friends to explore who could endorse it. Peru once again confirmed. In a new development that was deeply significant, the United Arab Emirates also signaled that they would join. The endorsement of the paper not just by Latin American countries but also by an Arab country marked a watershed moment. It was a proud sign of the reach the SDGs had achieved. The note would have been remark-able just for that. For Colombia, it was a development that we had worked on for a long time because we needed to evidence strong inter-regional support. In the G77 and China, the announcement of the new concept note drew gasps when it was introduced by the UAE delegate, on May 3, 2012, the next-to-last day of the negotiations (see Appendix 22). Abdel had to call for a break immediately after the announcement as the room erupted into multilingual cacophony. It was a pivotal moment because this meant that three countries from two regions were staking out a position that ran counter to that of the majority of G77 and China with regard to the post-Rio process.[7] It was a wonderfully redeem-ing moment in an otherwise fraught process.

Positions around the post-Rio process were hardening, especially in the G77 and China. Given that some of the starkest opposition to the evidence-based process Colombia was proposing was within the ALBA (Bolivarian Alliance for the Peoples of Our America) countries, parallel discussions were being held across the Latin American and Caribbean constituencies, where the divisions were stark. We reached out to Chile, who held the pro tempore secretariat of the Community of Latin Ameri-can and Caribbean States (CELAC); Chile proposed to convene a meet-ing to try to unite the region. Chile asked if we would be willing to have Brazil be the lead on the SDGs proposal henceforth. We immediately confirmed. More than anything, we wanted the region united behind an ambitious and sensible outcome.

Throughout the months of negotiations leading up to this point, Brazil had expressed support for the SDGs but had not come out as a decided champion in the actual negotiations and had not supported Colombia in difficult moments in the G77 and China. The general understanding was that they wanted to maintain a degree of neutrality as hosts of the conference. Thus, when Chile posed the question to us, we saw it as a pathway to getting Brazil to fully and expressly back the pro-posal and thus get some of the more recalcitrant G77 and China mem-bers to do so, too. We hoped that this would break the impasse around the format of the post-Rio process. Chile convened a CELAC meeting with heads of delegation where, after a long discussion, several coun-tries (including Venezuela) broadly expressed support for the SDGs pro-posal (but not for a process to develop them), but only if led by Brazil. Brazil affirmed that for President Dilma Rousseff, a key result for Rio+20 would be to launch an SDGs process. Colombia agreed to the proposition, and we exchanged a round of goodwill declarations. Every-one in the room seemed to want to help move the process along.

However, at the negotiation table at the conclusion of the ten-day intersessional on May 4, 2012, the results were dire. The Zero Draft consisted of 420 paragraphs, of which 399 remained in brackets.[8] This meant that only twenty-one paragraphs had been approved *ad referendum*—that is, subject to agreement by others in line with the overriding negotiation principle that "nothing is agreed until everything is agreed." Many of the paragraphs remained strings of alternative bracketed text. Agreement on text made at one session was undermined at the next as the brackets proliferated. Facilitators' attempt to put forward consensus language was marginalized as text imploded under the weight of new changes. None of the SDGs-related paragraphs had been agreed. Indeed, even the title of the subsection was still bracketed. On May 4, the co-chairs issued a new attempt at more consolidated text (see Appendix 15). There was some improvement over the draft of May 2, but not enough. Extensive language that was not based on consensus meant that long hours of negotiation lay ahead.

The prospect of getting to Rio de Janeiro with this unwieldy draft and just a few remaining days for negotiations, with a heads of state summit looming, was problematic. Brazilian President Dilma Rousseff had high stakes in hosting an unequivocally successful conference. Thus, on May 4, 2012, the co-chairs informed delegates that an additional negotiating session in New York would be held, squeezed into the tiny window remaining before the formal start of Rio+20. What was in fact an emergency session was scheduled from May 29 to June 2, 2012. The final intersessional was programmed to start on June 13 in Rio de Janeiro, right before the launch of the summit.

Elsewhere, the SDGs were making headway. In parallel to the negotiations, from April 23–25, 2012, the Swedish government hosted Stockholm+40—Partnership Forum for Sustainable Development, a meeting that issued "The Stockholm Call for Action." It was a celebration of the fortieth anniversary of the first major UN conference on sustainable development in 1972 and was well attended with over forty ministers and deputy ministers, leaders from the private sector, and hundreds of stakeholders from civil society and academia. Colombian Minister for Environment and Sustainable Development Frank Pearl also participated and was deluged with queries about the SDGs and expressions of support. In addition to King Carl XVI Gustaf of Sweden and Swedish Prime Minister Fredrik Reinfeldt, Wen Jiabao, premier of the State Council of the People's Republic of China also attended.

The call for action detailed thirteen "Main Messages from Stockholm to Rio and Beyond," one of which expressly supported the SDGs:

3. A common direction is needed for sustainability efforts. Building on the positive experience of the Millennium Development Goals (MDGs), which have focused the international development agenda on progress and results in well-defined areas, the proposal for Sustainable Development Goals by the Governments of Colombia, Guatemala and Peru was welcomed as very valuable in this context. Such goals should be universal, serve as a valid development instrument for all countries, integrate common social, economic and environmental challenges in a balanced way and contribute to poverty eradication. Based on the review of the MDGs, an integrated framework should constitute the post-2015 agenda.

This was a welcome accolade and a confirmation of the unwavering support of the Swedish government, whose delegates were stalwart members of the friends. We took as a positive sign the fact that a very senior Chinese official was among the participants issuing the call to action. After the meeting, colleagues from the Swedish Ministry of Foreign Affairs congregated a group of key participants, including leading countries in the G77 and China, in a small room where they spent considerable time reviewing the pros and cons of the SDGs proposal and discussing how it could be operationalized. Such were the determined efforts of the friends that paved the way for the eventual adoption of the SDGs.

Third Round of Informal Informal Negotiations

On May 22, 2012, ahead of the third round of informal informal consultations on the Zero Draft, a new eighty-page draft outcome document was issued by the co-chairs. This reflected the unflagging work by the Secretariat in meticulously tracking all the negotiation fronts and identifying potential consensus text. It was a valiant effort to cut through the morass of brackets and shine a light on possible compromise language. This was critical because as the third round got underway, we were less than three weeks away from the start of the UNCSD and were nowhere near a version of the Zero Draft that could result in a viable Rio+20 outcome.

In the afternoon opening session on May 29, 2012, UN Secretary-General Ban Ki-moon urged resolution of the final text. Among the key outcomes necessary for Rio+20, he included a process to define the SDGs. This endorsement clearly highlighted just how critical the process was.

Although progress was painstakingly slow in the negotiation sessions, the new draft compromise text succeeded in shifting gears across all fronts. Negotiating positions remained rather rigid but delegates were acutely aware of the ticking clock and the fact that whatever we ended up with on June 2 would be what we would have to contend with in Rio de Janeiro. The draft compromise text was a referent that helped delegates keep a sense of what the final package could look like.

Nonetheless, the time allotted to discussing the SDGs was increasingly inadequate as both the G77 and China presidency and the co-chairs had to parcel out negotiating time across the two working groups and around fourteen issue-specific splinter groups that were negotiating different parts of the draft outcome in parallel.

On the SDGs front, divisions remained stark, with marked differences especially between the G77 and China's position and that of many other delegations. The Western group of countries had proposed detailed changes to the draft compromise text, while the G77 and China requested deletion of all paragraphs except the first and put forward alternative text for the others. As had been the case in the long preceding months, a first paragraph that ensured that the SDGs would not undermine the MDGs remained the only area of clear agreement.

It would take many more pages to describe the difficult and grim negotiations that were taking place behind the scenes. Colombia remained firm with regard to the three core outcomes it was seeking in Rio: agreement on a separate, robust SDGs framework; a listing of indicative thematic areas to kickstart the process; and an open, government-led, expert-driven process to define the SDGs. Yet two of these three were anathema to many delegations in the G77 and China. The friends were playing an increasingly vital role, valiantly staking out key positions in their respective groups and in the negotiations—especially those countries that were not part of a formal negotiation group—but the pace of progress was frustrating. In the preceding negotiation session, for example, Mexico had introduced what many of us considered a critical third option for the process to define the SDGs, yet it failed to be included in this round (see Chapter 9).

As mentioned earlier, by now there had been another decisive development: the evolution of the lead G77 and China coordinator for the SDGs, Farrukh Khan. Although he initially questioned the need for a suite of SDGs, with his long experience as a diplomat and a development expert, Khan was now convinced of the importance of this paradigm shift. He had also been a member of the Green Climate Fund (GCF) Transitional Committee and was convinced that it was the best model to ensure the development of a robust SDGs framework.[9] He was, however, treading on a minefield. Many of the most vocal G77 and

China members still questioned many of the proposed characteristics of the SDGs and were adamant that any future framework had to be under the common but differentiated responsibility (CBDR) principle and negotiated in a traditional UN setting rather than set up like the one that had created the GCF. Any effort toward consensus on these issues could be viewed as an utter betrayal by many. As group coordinator, Khan ultimately only had trust for currency.

By the end of the five days of marathon negotiations, the draft compilation text had evolved but was not trending toward speedy resolution of outstanding conflicts. The draft outcome text that had started out the third round of informal informal consultations with 401 paragraphs was now down to only 259 bracketed paragraphs. There was some comfort to be had from the fact that there were now seventy paragraphs agreed *ad referendum*.[10] In the closing session, UNCSD Secretary Sha Zukang reiterated that a process for SDGs development would be one of the key deliverables of the conference. Similarly, Brazil stated that for President Rousseff, one of the key results of Rio+20 was to launch a process to develop the SDGs. Given how difficult the negotiations were at that point, such clear political support was welcome. Yet, given the stark divisions over the options for delivering the SDGs, many worried that politics would win and whatever option had the majority's endorsement would carry the day.

This emergency five-day negotiation session concluded on June 2 at 5 p.m. The co-chairs issued a consolidated text of *The Future We Want*, a final effort to get us all to Rio de Janeiro with a text that could be tackled in the few negotiation days that remained (see Appendix 18). The section on the SDGs had one paragraph on the importance of the MDGs that everyone agreed to, but the other paragraphs remained heavily bracketed. With this, we concluded the New York round of negotiations; our next meeting would be in Rio de Janeiro.

Notes

1. The sections of the Zero Draft were labeled as follows: I. Preamble/Stage Setting; II. Renewing Political Commitment; III. Green Economy in the Context of Sustainable Development and Poverty Eradication; IV. International Framework for Sustainable Development; and V. Framework for Action and Follow-up.

2. These issues were food security; water; energy; cities; green jobs–social inclusion; oceans and seas; SIDS; natural disasters; climate change; forests and biodiversity; land degradation and desertification; mountains; chemicals and waste; sustainable consumption and production; education; gender equality.

3. These were poverty eradication; sustainable agriculture, food security, and nutrition; water and sanitation; energy; sustainable tourism; sustainable transport;

sustainable cities and human settlements; health and population; promoting full and productive employment, decent work for all, and social protections; oceans and seas; small island developing states; least developed countries; landlocked least developed countries; Africa; regional efforts; disaster risk reduction; climate change; forests; biodiversity; desertification, land degradation, and drought; mountains; chemicals and waste; sustainable consumption and production; mining; education; and gender equality and women's empowerment.

4. This was the first round of formal negotiations as part of the Rio+20 process to ultimately agree to a final Rio+20 outcome document. However, as explained in Appendix 2, the characterization of negotiations at the UN reflects the nature of specific negotiations. In general, the more "informal" a negotiation is, the more substantive it is, as the "informality" provides space for actual discussions, whereas more formal or plenary sessions are usually arenas for more political and often predefined interventions. Thus, the fact that these negotiations were (formally) designated as "informal informal" indicated that their main objective was to establish a forum to actually negotiate the Rio+20 outcome document.

5. When text is being negotiated, it is a fluid and complex process. The key is to differentiate between text that has been approved by consensus (or not) and the source of the text. Text that is proposed by one or more parties is registered in brackets; these are only removed when/if the text is approved by all parties. With particularly complex negotiations like this one, some parts of very lengthy text are put in bold letters simply to make the various edits easier to read. The country or group that proposed the text is annotated at the end of each insert. See Appendix 2 for further information.

6. "Summary of the UNCSD Informal Informal Consultations and Third Intersessional Meeting," 2012.

7. A new government had just entered office in Guatemala and was defining priorities. For this reason, Guatemala did not formally endorse the concept paper.

8. "Summary of the UNCSD Informal Informal Consultations 23 April–4 May 2012," 2012.

9. See Chapter 9 for more details on this proposal.

10. "Summary of the Third Round of UNCSD Informal Informal Consultations," 2012, and see Appendix 2 explanation of ad referendum.

7

Evolution of the Negotiation Text

Chapters 6 and 7 cover the same timeframe of the SDGs negotiations process, from February 2012 through to the third and last negotiation in New York before delegates headed out to Rio de Janeiro for the actual Rio+20 conference. In Chapter 6 we described the negotiation process with an emphasis on the evolution of key ideas. Here we delve into the negotiations in more detail, providing an in-depth analysis of the evolution of the Zero Draft's section on the Sustainable Development Goals (SDGs).

Core Issues of the SDGs Negotiations

Over the course of the three rounds of informal informal negotiations in New York, the section on the SDGs in the Zero Draft veered among a diversity of widely differing options but was largely centered around a suite of core issues:

- The relation of the SDGs to the Millennium Development Goals (MDGs)
- Agreement on an "indicative" list of thematic areas that the SDGs development process could consider
- Establishing indicators and targets for 2030 prior to the goals' adoption
- The nature of the process for developing the SDGs

• The need for either a report or information that would be "global, integrated and science based."

The issue of whether the SDGs framework would be under the principle of common but differentiated responsibilities (CBDR) was also an area of contention to the end.

This basic architecture for the negotiations had been laid out in the initial Zero Draft prepared by the Secretariat and issued by the co-chairs, in Chapter V, subsection B "Accelerating and Measuring Progress (SDGs, GDP and others)":[1]

• Paragraph 105 recognized the importance of measuring "progress towards sustainable development and agree[d] to launch an inclusive process to devise by 2015: a set of global Sustainable Development Goals that reflect an integrated and balanced treatment of the three dimensions of sustainable development, are consistent with the principles of Agenda 21, and are universal and applicable to all countries but allowing for differentiated approaches among countries." It also called for "a mechanism for periodic follow-up and reporting on progress made toward their achievement."
• Paragraph 106 requested the UN Secretary-General to coordinate the process alluded to in paragraph 105.
• Paragraph 107 proposed some of the "priority areas" the SDGs could include.
• Paragraph 108 affirmed that the SDGs "should complement and strengthen the MDGs" and decisively linked the two processes together by proposing to "establish . . . a set of goals in 2015 which are part of the post-2015 UN Development Agenda."
• Paragraph 109 called for establishing indicators and targets to 2030 for the goals to be adopted.
• Paragraph 110 confirmed that countries' capacity for monitoring the SDGs should be strengthened and called for promoting a global partnership.

As discussed in prior chapters, the period between the issuance of the Zero Draft in January 2012 and the start of the negotiations in March 2012 was used by delegations and negotiation groups to digest the co-chairs' proposed text and prepare. The G77 and China embarked on an intense round of consultations in February. Before the negotiations even started in mid-March, in its opening gambit on March 5, 2012, the group put forward its own version, effectively rejecting the entirety of the draft proposed (as discussed in Chapter 5, see Appendix 11). It was a strong hand to play at the outset of the negotiations, and this set the tone for the fractious process that played out over the following months.

The group's proposal started out by reaffirming and detailing the merits of the MDGs and underscoring the "relevance of all the outcomes of all major UN conferences and summits . . . including the MDGs" and "reiterating our determination to ensure the timely and full implementation of these outcomes and commitments."

The closest the text came to acknowledging the possibility of an SDGs framework was this:

> We recognize that goals can be useful for pursuing sustainable development, taking into account the need for an integrated approach incorporating economic, social and environmental dimensions and recognizing their interlinkages and avoiding dealing with them in separate or parallel tracks. In this regard, Sustainable Development Goals *built upon the MDGs* [emphasis added], could be a driver for implementation and mainstreaming of sustainable development as well as of integration of its three dimensions. (Agreed ad ref).

This language hedged bets for the MDG+ option and sought to constrain the future SDGs framework. The following paragraph recognized "the importance and utility of a set of SDGs" but made this dependent on "fully respect[ing] Rio Principles in particular CBDR, build[ing] upon commitments already made, respect[ing] international law and contribut[ing] to the full implementation of the outcomes of all major summits in the economic, social and environmental field taking into account that these goals should ensure a holistic coherence with the goals set in Agenda 21 and JPOI [Johannesburg Plan of Implementation]." This coded language was anathema to developed countries because it not only underscored CBDR but obliquely linked acceptance of the SDGs by the group to the fulfillment of commitments made at "all major summits," including on financing for development.

The G77 and China's submission included a list of "guiding principles and characteristics." This list had evolved during hours and hours of painstaking internal consultations in February. Although many bullets had been the object of intense discussions, this list gave many members the assurance that key tenets of the group's traditional positions, for example, regarding CBDR as a framing principle and Means of Implementation for developing countries, were explicitly included. These discussions had proven important to getting several countries to discuss the SDGs, as they served to frame and condition the proposal and capitalized on the international consultations Colombia had engineered. Many of these bullet points included language considered particularly unpalatable by developed countries, and thus this text set the stage for intense discussions that took up a good deal of the limited negotiation time. Six points were central to understanding the group's overriding concerns, in addition to the two points that made explicit mention of CBDR:

- Build on and complement the MDGs and renew and strengthen commitment toward their achievement;
- Take into account different national realities, capacities, and development priorities;
- Contribute to the monitoring of fulfillment of developed countries' international commitments, especially those related to financial resources, technology transfer, and capacity building;
- Include Means of Implementation for developing countries, including under each goal;
- Do not place additional restrictions or burdens on developing countries or dilute responsibilities of developed countries;
- Respect policy space and national development priorities of each country, in particular avoiding the establishment of mechanisms for monitoring national policies.

These guiding principles evidenced deep concern across the group that the SDGs would impose more responsibilities and obligations on developing countries without commensurate support in terms of financing, technology transfer, and capacity building. Thus, a key early requirement was that each goal would detail the Means of Implementation that would be made available for its implementation. There were also concerns over whether the SDGs could become a Trojan horse and lead to undue pressures and influence over countries' policy framework and priority setting. Once in plenary, this long list degenerated into an inexorable exercise of additions and edits. At one point, the list grew from the original fifteen bullet points to twenty-seven "principles and characteristics," most of them containing several brackets reflecting enduring disagreements.

The G77 and China's version of the Zero Draft concluded with two alternative paragraphs on the process for defining the SDGs in the follow-up to Rio+20, both of which called for establishing an "ad-hoc Open-ended Working Group" under the General Assembly, which would present a report with recommendations to either the General Assembly's sixty-seventh (2012–2013) or sixty-eighth (2013–2014) session.

The initial round of negotiations in the G77 and China was so fraught that Colombia took the unprecedented decision of insisting on including language that was not supported by any other member state. This was a public break with the group, but we were distraught by how badly the consultations had gone and determined that such a stark and politically untenable move was necessary to ensure that the draft outcome text included a clear mention of the SDGs.

The first paragraph proposed by Colombia stated, "We therefore agree to undertake the establishment of a single set of Sustainable Development Goals consistent with Agenda 21 and JPOI in full compliance with the Rio Principles, in particular CBDR." In a vain effort to make our language more acceptable to the group, we included language on the CBDR principle that everyone knew we did not support in this context. We were signaling a willingness to meet other delegations halfway. However, our language was widely rejected as the majority could countenance an SDGs framework only in the MDGs regime at this point in the negotiations. With this in mind, our second paragraph simply stated that "the SDGs should complement and strengthen the MDGs in the development agenda for the post-2015 period." Insistence on including our two paragraphs was contrary to all established norms, and Colombia emerged from the first round of internal negotiations battered and regarded by many in the group as a renegade. We remained undeterred, convinced that eventually a critical mass of delegations would understand the urgency and importance of agreeing to a robust SDGs framework.

First Round of Informal Informal Negotiations

During February, all other delegations and groups were equally industrious, and by the time the First Informal Informal meeting got underway on March 19, 2012, a considerable amount of new language had been proposed. On SDGs, this included a new preambular paragraph, with three differing versions, and two competing proposals for restructuring the whole section. Paragraph 105 exploded into eleven different paragraphs. Over the course of the ten-day meeting, language metastasized. By the end of the meeting, many of these strings of bracketed text were almost illegible. For an illustration of how challenging and undecipherable the text had become, see Box 7.1. (See Appendix 2 to navigate text such as this.)

Box 7.1   Illustration of How Confusing Bracketed Text Can
Become at the Height of Negotiations

One of the paragraphs from the draft negotiation text on March 27 at
6 p.m. read: [[**105 bis. a)/ We agree to advance**—EU] [a set of—EU
delete] global [**and coherent**—EU] Sustainable Development Goals /
considering sustainable development goals—US, Canada] that—
Norway delete] [**could be incorporated into any post-2015 framework and—US, Canada**] [reflect] [an integrated and/**a—Switzerland**]
[balanced treatment of / **complement and strengthen the development agenda for the post-2015 period, full encompass—EU [and—
Switzerland] / integrate—New Zealand**] [the three dimensions of
sustainable development, [**in a balanced and synergistic way—EU**]
[**are developed with consideration of cross-cutting themes—
Australia, Canada**] [**are gender responsive, Iceland**] [**reaffirm the
Rio principles—Liechtenstein**] [are/and—**Japan**/ and be—**Norway**]
[consistent with the [**Rio—Norway**] principles of [**the 1992 Rio Declaration—EU**] Agenda 21 [—Japan delete], **and the Johannesburg
Plan of Implementation,—EU**] [**are based on and ensure the full
and equal enjoyment of human rights/protection and promotion of
human rights, democracy, the rule of law and good governance,
gender equality and women's empowerment—Liechtenstein**] and
[are b) **be—Norway**] [universal and—New Zealand delete] applicable to all countries/ **nationally-defined and relevant and universally applicable or accepted—US, Canada**] [but/while—**Norway**
allow[ing for differentiated approaches among countries—US delete/
different paths to achievement—New Zealand, Republic of Korea]
[**enabling all countries to translate it into national commitment to
policy coherence for sustainability through appropriate legislative
mechanisms—Liechtenstein; Switzerland reserves**].

The original Zero Draft's opening paragraph on the SDGs (paragraph 105) gave way to all manner of variations as delegations grappled
with the new concept. The language attempted to tackle a vast array of
issues including links to the Rio legacy; the placement of the SDGs
within the two agreed agenda items for the Conference; the need for
balance and integration across the economic, social, and environmental
pillars of sustainable development; and underpinnings of human rights
and gender equality. The G77 and China proposed five paragraphs

underscoring the importance of the MDGs and seeking to ensure continued commitment to their full implementation. One of the paragraphs that begrudgingly acknowledged that "there could be a need to formulate sustainable development goals" went on to emphasize that "they must neither be used as a pretext for avoiding international commitments towards meeting MDGs targets nor pose new conditionalities for accessing development assistance."

The original paragraph 107, which focused on the priority areas the SDGs could encompass,[2] was joined by four more paragraphs variously proposed by different delegations. In addition to the eight issue areas originally proposed by the Secretariat, member states now had proposed twenty-three more themes. From the outset, the G77 and China opposed the inclusion of any list and bracketed all the proposals. In the group, Colombia insisted on the importance of putting forward a "descriptive, indicative, illustrative list," but to no avail. The same held for paragraph 108 on the relationship to the MDGs. The G77 and China maintained its request to delete the entire segment because it preferred to maintain the detailed text and the several paragraphs proposed under paragraph 105 that extolled the MDGs and sought to protect them from any perceived threat.

Through several new paragraphs, delegations brought in language on the process to develop the SDGs—rushing to counteract the simple formula proposed in the original version that the process "be led by the Secretary-General." Four of the paragraphs numbered 106 called for actions by the Secretary-General to variously launch a process, "provide all necessary support," or provide proposals for measuring and reporting on progress. The option of having the president of the General Assembly and the president of UN Economic and Social Council "develop a meaningful framework" was also put forward. Some requested that the process be undertaken in conjunction with an MDGs review.

The new language under 108 also reflected how delegations were starting to think through the overall process. Although heavily bracketed, language explicitly integrating the SDGs to be agreed to in Rio+20 with the post-MDGs agenda (now called the post-2015 agenda) was appearing. Mexico, in particular, under the leadership of Damaso Luna, put forward robust language that helped frame these discussions for the next round. Mexico called for an explicit linkage between the two agendas and for "set[ting] off a process for a single post 2015 framework in order to further develop the SDGs." We welcomed this language because it reflected the proposal we had put forward earlier in the paper issued with Guatemala and Peru. Echoing a priority position of Colombia, Mexico recommended that "the General Assembly . . . establish a Group of Experts."

Although alternative text was proposed to paragraph 109 that called for measuring the goals with "appropriate indicators . . . and targets," the G77 and China rejected the entire passage. In other words, the group rejected establishing any kind of monitoring process for whatever emerged from Rio+20. Connected to this question, paragraph 110 of the Zero Draft included a proposal to have the Secretary-General "promote a global partnership" to strengthen the capacity of countries to collect and analyze data and information to support monitoring of progress toward the SDGs. A few delegations put forward new language on this point, but the G77 and China and the EU asked for its deletion or bracketing. For their part, the delegations of Canada, New Zealand, and the United States requested that the whole section be "reserved" pending the evolution of the negotiations. In red lettering, the co-chairs bravely maintained the initial Zero Draft text, a stark reminder of how complex the negotiations had quickly become.

By the end of the first round of negotiations on March 27, 2012, the text in the SDGs section had mushroomed from five paragraphs into thirty-four assemblages of language that could barely be characterized as paragraphs. There was no clear structure to the section, so Switzerland, the Republic of Korea, and New Zealand idealistically proposed a structure consisting of four paragraphs. The G77 and China proposed a different, three-tiered structure. The tense and complex negotiations in the group throughout February had merely presaged what the process would be like. The Zero Draft had burgeoned from 19 pages to more than 200.[3]

Second Round of Informal Informal Negotiations

In the aftermath of the first round of informal informal negotiations, the co-chairs issued a draft consolidated outcome document dated March 28, 2012, and which was released on April 9 (see Appendix 13). This draft attempted to cut through the pages of unmanageable text, give structure to the various sections, and propose potential consensus language. This text was henceforth identified as CST (co-chair's suggested text) in the draft negotiating texts. This effort by the co-chairs came at a critical time as the many consultations undertaken between the negotiation rounds—in the G77 and China, across negotiation groups, with friends—did not bode well for whittling down more than

200 pages of text into a semblance of coherent narrative. This CST was a best effort to craft consensus language based on the preceding round of discussions, and it gave delegations and groups something to mull over between negotiation sessions.

In an attempt to expedite the process, the co-chairs also adjusted the format to create more negotiation time for the process. For the Second Informal Informal consultations on the Zero Draft (April 23–May 4, 2012), rather than a single negotiation track, two working groups were created that met in parallel during the consultations:

- Working Group 1 under co-chair John W. Ashe of Antigua and Barbuda was tasked with Sections III (Green Economy), and V (Framework for Action and Follow-up); and
- Working Group 2 under co-chair Kim Sook of the Republic of Korea was focused on Section I (Common Vision), II (Renewing Political Commitment), III (Green Economy), and IV (International Framework for Sustainable Development).

The paragraph-by-paragraph discussions continued, but they now included the CST options, which helped narrow the scope of the exchanges. For the SDGs negotiations, the CST text of March 28 ultimately played an important role in shaping the architecture of the section and augured the structure of the final outcome document agreed in June. Getting there was still going to require many more hours of arduous negotiations. The many paragraphs on the MDGs were whittled down to a single, introductory text and four related paragraphs that spoke to what the SDGs could accomplish and their overriding characteristics. The long list of "guiding characteristics and principles," over which so many vehement hours had been spent, were proposed to be excised entirely. We quietly welcomed this because it contained so many issues that were a bane for delegations outside the group. Deleting this list would narrow the field to what was truly essential for the SDGs section and enable precious and scarce time to be better allocated. Discussions on this list had played a foundational role in kickstarting the discussions in the G77 and China, but at this stage in the game, less would be better.

Discussions on including a potential list of thematic areas that the SDGs could focus on floundered from the start of this second round of negotiations. As noted in the preceding chapter, the EU presented a proposal to include five "goals, targets and actions in priority areas" that they had defined under a "green economy roadmap" based on a nonpaper prepared for the EU's Informal Environmental Council. This proposal was seen by the majority of G77 and China delegations as an obvious attempt to impose the EU's agenda and priorities and prejudge the outcome of the negotiations. It was met with an outcry at the first coordination meeting of the G77 and China as the Second Informal Informal negotiation got underway. These concerns were exacerbated by EU delegates' efforts to include specific language in the negotiation tracks of the thematic areas. Even though the EU was in fact attempting to raise the negotiations to a higher level by already showing how a few key areas could be framed, the effort backfired badly.

Largely as a result of this debacle, the paragraphs detailing specific thematic areas that the SDGs could encompass were replaced by an anodyne paragraph merely signaling consideration of the areas under negotiation in Chapter V, Section A. This was a blow to us and many other delegations who considered that an indicative list was essential to sketch out the overall direction of the SDGs. The outcome of the Rio process was so uncertain with regard to the SDGs that such a list would have provided comfort that a basic direction could already be framed. An "indicative, tentative, descriptive" list prejudged nothing but could have set the guardrails for a future process.

The intent of the CST text was evidently not wholesale adoption by the parties but to signal where consensus could be possible across the Zero Draft. It became a key referent that delegations could turn to in attempts to break out of entrenched positions. The co-chairs' effort paid off. At the end of the first week of negotiations, by April 27, 2012, the overall Zero Draft was down to a relatively more manageable 156 pages, from over 270. The co-chairs continued to propose consensus text, which was now called the new co-chairs' suggested text (NCST).

A week later, the SDGs negotiation text remained quite unwieldy with twenty paragraphs, of which eleven were variations on paragraph 105. These encompassed everything from characterizations of the SDGs, linkages to the JPOI, relation to the MDGs, proposed lists of thematic areas that the SDGs should consider, and the exhaustive list of "principles and characteristics," which remained heavily contested. Four paragraphs variously set out different and mutually exclusive processes to develop the SDGs framework after Rio. Paragraphs also remained calling for an indicative list of priority areas (CST 107) and on the need for indicators and targets to measure the SDGs (CST 109). The section consisted of six pages of assiduously bracketed text.

Two days later, on May 4, 2012, after two weeks of negotiations, NCST text was presented to delegates (see Appendix 15). It proposed pared-down language with only fifteen paragraphs—but, indicative of the time constraints everyone was operating under, made proposed changes only through paragraph 107. The document reads, "stopped here at 4pm, May 4." It was received with caution; by now it was clear that the negotiation format was deeply flawed given the vast scope of the Zero Draft and that it would be impossible to get to a viable outcome text in Rio if we proceeded in the same way. Even though an extra negotiation session was announced, squeezed into the five weeks until we were due to go to Rio, we knew that we were running out of time.

Under the NCST, the various options for structuring the section, which were mutually exclusive, were deleted. All things being relative, a real breakthrough was achieved with the first consensus agreement on a paragraph that, unsurprisingly, reiterated the importance of the MDGs and the need to support their full implementation. NCST 105 read, "We underscore that the MDGs are a useful tool in focusing achievement of specific development gains as part of a broad development vision and framework for the development activities of the United Nations, for national priority setting and for mobilization of stakeholders and resources towards common goals. We therefore remain firmly committed to their full and timely achievement." This remained the lone paragraph agreed to by consensus until the end of the process.

The long list of principles and characteristics, which the co-chairs had tried to eliminate in their earlier CST text, remained. The various options for defining a process after Rio remained. Two paragraphs pointed to different "indicative thematic areas that could help guide the process." The variations of paragraph 109 continued to call for a "global sustainable development assessment."

As the meeting drew to a close, there was a curious combination of despondency and determination. The two negotiation rounds had been exhausting. Many positions were increasingly entrenched. At the same time, the efforts by the Secretariat and the co-chairs to propose possible consensus language created a sense of minimal guardrails for keeping the process on track, even if barely.

Third Round of Informal Informal Negotiations

Ahead of the third, eleventh-hour round of negotiations to craft a draft outcome text that could be finalized and adopted in Rio+20 by heads of state, the co-chairs prepared another outcome text for the entirety of the

Zero Draft issued on May 22, 2012 (see Appendix 16). Although progress was painstakingly slow once the negotiations got underway on May 29, this draft compromise text succeeded in shifting gears across all fronts. A key innovation was to change the numbered paragraphs—some of which had metastasized into numerous options (105, 105 bis, 105 bis 1, 105 ter, 105 quint)—for succinct descriptors and a number, for example, SDG1, SDG2, and SDG3. The SDGs section had nine paragraphs.

Several of the paragraphs proposed by the co-chairs aptly and largely foreshadowed the outcome text that would ultimately be agreed to in Rio. In addition to the first paragraph that had already secured agreement (former 105), some of the others included

- SDG2 stated the agreement "to develop a set of global sustainable development goals" that was built on the MDGs and would be incorporated into the UN Development Agenda beyond 2015;
- SDG3 proposed that the goals be "consistent with the Rio principles and contribute to advance the implementation of Agenda 21 and JPOI"; and
- SDG4 proposed that the SDGs should be action-oriented and limited in number.

Notably, the long list of principles and characteristics, on which so much time had been spent, disappeared. As a signal of both pragmatism and exhaustion on the part of delegates—we knew it would be impossible to find a consensus language—this time, it was effectively deleted. The same pragmatism started to manifest across the board. By eliminating the long list of principles and characteristics and calling for the new framework to be "consistent with the Rio principles," the draft text offered a pathway to avoid direct reference to CBDR. The other paragraphs, however, focused on four areas that remained highly controversial and charged.

- SDG5 proposed a series of thematic areas that the "goals should address"—a proposition that had always been rejected by the G77 and China, an opposition that grew more determined after the debacle with the EU's nonpaper at the Second Informal Informal.
- SDG6 called for the Secretary-General to establish and lead the process to develop the SDGs framework after Rio+20, a process that would be "country-driven" and "guided by the General Assembly." Only a subset of delegations supported this option. The G77 and China remained wedded to a process under the

General Assembly (UNGA). A few delegations, like Colombia, continued to hold out for an independent, technical, evidence-based process.

- SDG7 called for measuring the SDGs by an "agreed and appropriate set of indicators and assessed on the basis of specific targets."
- SDG8 recognized the need for "an integrated, scientifically-credible global sustainable development report" and called on the UN Secretary-General to "make proposals for such a report."

By May 31, the first full reading of the SDGs section was completed with no compromise language agreed to beyond that first, lone paragraph. However, relative progress had been made. Delegations had focused on the May 22, 2012, draft and dropped demands to incorporate or focus on previous iterations of the Zero Draft. Instead of nine paragraphs, there were now thirteen—a result of the fact that the G77 and China in a final play to maintain a strong hand going into the upcoming final negotiations in Rio de Janeiro, had requested deletion of all the paragraphs except SDG1 and proposed alternative text in four succinct paragraphs. The original nine paragraphs were heavily edited and fecund with brackets. And yet, on the whole, the SDGs section was starting to hint at what the endgame might look like as we left New York (see Appendix 17).

Broadly, paragraphs proposed by the G77 and China reflected language that had been argued over the preceding months. There was nothing here that additional negotiation time could not work through except for the fact that CBDR remained prominent in the group's position. Indeed, the paragraphs "recognizing the importance and utility of a set of sustainable development goals" (SDG2/G77) and "recognizing that the goals should address and be focused on priority areas for the achievement of sustainable development . . . and be action-oriented, concise . . . universally applicable to all countries while taking into account different national realities, capacities and development priorities and not limiting the national policy space" (SDG4+5/G77) simply reengineered language we had spent months poring over and that was contained in the co-chairs' May 22 draft. With regard to a global sustainable development report, the G77 and China focused instead on the need for "information on sustainable development," and instead of calling on the Secretary-General to propose a way forward, reiterated its proposal for increased support for regional economic commissions.

Despite this progress, the four major outstanding, controversial issues at the outset of the Third Informal Informal remained outstanding and controversial at the end of the meeting. The G77 and China remained steadfast in its rejection of an "indicative" list of SDGs themes; the group insisted that in Rio de Janeiro the process to define the themes could be launched, but its outcome could not be prejudged. We spent long hours in consultations with the group arguing the case for the importance of an "illustrative and descriptive" list, to no avail. However, given that many other delegations in the Western group also wanted to include such a list, we remained hopeful. Indeed, seven delegations from the Western group and the EU continued to engage in fleshing out the list. The G77 and China rejected the option of creating a set of indicators and targets to measure progress, as well as the request to the UN Secretary-General to set up the process for creating a global sustainable development report. Finally, the group inserted once again a paragraph (SDG6 alt/G77) calling for the establishment of "an intergovernmental process on SDGs under the [General Assembly]."

From our perspective, these issues and differences were ultimately manageable. The major battles that had had to be waged in the earlier sessions were now seemingly resolved. There was no longer language insisting that the SDGs process had to be framed within the MDGs. Everyone committed to full achievement of the MDGs, but the SDGs were now embarking on their own process, building on the MDGs. Just how significant a paradigm shift this represented cannot be emphasized enough.

As the five-day extraordinary negotiation session closed on June 2, we were exhausted. The final battle over the nature of the process to define the SDGs after Rio still loomed ahead, and it promised to be grim.

As a parting gift, until we were to meet just ten days later in Rio de Janeiro, the co-chairs issued yet another draft consolidated text (see Appendix 18). The rapid succession of draft consensus text being put forward by the co-chairs speaks to the Secretariat's indefatigable and relentless work behind the scenes. These teams followed every negotiation track, itself a daunting task given that at one point there were up to fourteen "splinter groups" and that under Section V there were twenty-six complex thematic areas. The Secretariat team at UN Department of Economic and Social Affairs painstakingly mapped what consensus could look like. Based on this work, and the team's deep and rich experience in negotiations at the UN, they were able to present a constant rhythm of draft consensus text. Without a doubt, this was a major factor in enabling the negotiations to make progress. Without the focus and neutrality this language brought, it is doubtful that delegations would have been able to move away from entrenched positions and from the maze of bracketed language that became an unworkable labyrinth.

In the SDGs section, this new text laid out three initial paragraphs that captured all the preceding language. These proposals played on the fact that there were no substantive differences—except for the CBDR reference—in the various delegations' and groups' proposed language for the first paragraphs characterizing the SDGs and their context. These paragraphs would remain largely unchanged except for editorial tweaks. Tellingly, these paragraphs were presented to delegates without brackets even though they were not yet agreed to, that is, were not yet "agreed ad ref."

The remaining six paragraphs were in brackets and tackled the following still controversial issues:

- The possible inclusion of a list of indicative priority areas,
- The different options for undertaking a process to develop the SDGs framework,
- Measurement of the SDGs by indicators and targets, and
- The need for global, integrated, science-based information or reports.

With this draft, we headed to Rio de Janeiro.

Notes

1. As noted, this section included a paragraph on what came to be known as "beyond GDP." The negotiation of this paragraph falls outside of the remit of this book. Suffice it to say that it ultimately proved impossible to get agreement in Rio to "recognize the need for broader measures of progress to complement GDP, and in this request . . . to launch a programme of work in this area building on existing initiatives."

2. These areas were sustainable consumption and production patterns; oceans; food security and sustainable agriculture; sustainable energy for all; water access and efficiency; sustainable cities; green jobs, decent work, and social inclusion; and disaster risk reduction and resilience.

3. "Summary of the UNCSD Informal Informal Consultations and Third Inter-sessional Meeting" (2012).

8

Breakthrough in Rio

When delegates finally congregated in Rio de Janeiro in June 2012, despite months of consultations and negotiations, the negotiation text was still miles away from consensus. In this chapter, we take the reader through the complex negotiations and the stunning Brazilian diplomatic coup that in the end delivered a Rio+20 outcome that included the Sustainable Development Goals (SDGs) and the Open Working Group.

Backroom Negotiations

Delegates arrived in Rio de Janeiro geared up for days of nonstop negotiations. On our first day, June 13, we were greeted with a procedural change that simply spoke to how fraught the situation was and to the hopes of the Secretariat and the co-chairs that if the slight momentum from the last-minute emergency meeting in New York was maintained, we might achieve a breakthrough. Thus, although in principle the first three days formally corresponded to the Third Preparatory Committee for the UN Conference on Sustainable Development (Prep-Com III), its formal start was delayed. PrepCom co-chair Kim Sook informed us that we would continue to work informally under the same format as we had done in New York, with the two working groups and various splinter negotiation groups. Given how far we still had to go, wrestling the current text into a viable political document that heads of state could sign in just a week was a daunting task.

As delegates, we took a measure of comfort from the fact that if needed, there were an additional four days for negotiations after June 15. These were days slated by the Brazilian presidency for Dialogue Days—thematic roundtables that were to bring a large and representative group of stakeholders to discuss some of the key issues the Zero Draft was tackling. Negotiators were banking on these extra days to deliver a workable outcome document. The conference itself was slated to start on June 20 at the level of heads of state, but we all knew that as soon as heads of state and high-level representatives started to arrive, delegations would be stretched thin. Yet their arrival, under the traditional modus operandi for these kinds of negotiations, also signaled the possibility for a last-minute breakthrough. It was the practice for delegations to deliver as much agreement as possible across the negotiation tracks before the start of the high-level segment of a conference, but if intractable, highly political issues remained, these could be left to be resolved by ministers or heads of state. As negotiations got underway in Rio, as seasoned negotiators we all indulged in these mental calculations. We had not yet been disabused of this possibility.

Figure 8.1   The First SDGs Buttons Distributed in Rio

Note: Throughout the long preparatory process, Surendra Shrestha, of the UN Environment Programme (UNEP), provided unflagging support and encouragement to Colombia and the friends. For Rio, he mobilized support from the Asia-Europe Environment Forum to make buttons we handed out in Rio. Because these were the first SDGs buttons, we made sure to put "people" first to counter those who were attacking the SDGs as a covert and exclusive environmental agenda.

In Rio de Janeiro, we were greeted with good news for the SDGs. The PrepCom co-chairs designated Selwin Hart from Barbados, one of the most experienced negotiators, as facilitator of the splinter group on SDGs and Means of Implementation (MoI). He understood G77 and China dynamics intimately, had a comprehensive understanding of the SDGs landscape and the minefields of MoI, and was well respected by all groups. Farrukh Khan and I had worked closely with Hart in other negotiations, especially the UN Framework Convention on Climate Change (UNFCCC), and there was deep trust among us. From many difficult and tense negotiations in the UNFCCC, I knew Hart to be a staunch defender of progressive, ambitious outcomes. However, the fact that he was tasked with delivering on two negotiation tracks, one being MoI, meant that for the SDGs, negotiation time and Hart's bandwidth would be constrained.

MoI entailed getting agreement on the financial, technical, and capacity building support needed for developing countries to deliver across their commitments and was in many ways a backbone of negotiations in multilateral environmental agreements. This issue was closely tied to discussions around common but differentiated responsibilities (CBDR) and had repercussions across other issues as developing countries were loath to sign onto new agreements, commitments, or frameworks unless they were assured that additional resources would be made available. This included the SDGs. Thus, from the outset we knew that despite the limited negotiation space, the MoI negotiations would need extra time. There were, in fact, just two SDGs negotiation sessions in the first three days of negotiations in Rio de Janeiro. But these were decisive.

On June 13—our first day in Rio de Janeiro—Hart convened the SDGs splinter group. We had left New York with basic agreement on the opening paragraphs of the section, so we did not delve into this language. As we entered the home stretch, clear priorities emerged. Issues that were ultimately not critical to the final outcome and that would require further substantive discussions for which there was no time, started to fall by the wayside with tacit—albeit regretful—acquiescence on the part of the relevant delegations. For us, it was becoming increasingly clear that even though we had fought hard for it, the rejection by many delegations to include a list of indicative issue areas the SDGs could address was unrelenting. This discussion was given scant airtime. There was also minimal discussion on measuring SDGs given the G77 and China's staunch opposition to this language. The impasse over reporting on the SDGs remained: the group favored strengthening regional economic commissions, and other delegations wanted a global sustainable development report.

For many of us, the truly decisive issue—and one around which intractable differences remained—was the nature of the process after Rio to define the SDGs. There were two options formally on the table: (1) "under the UN General Assembly (UNGA)"—favored by the majority in the G77 and China, or (2) either established or "established and coordinated" by the UN Secretary-General. This was broadly understood to mean a high-level panel. Together with a few other delegations, we were holding out for a third option that had been variously tabled but was consistently pushed aside: a technical, science-based process (the details of this negotiation track are the focus of Chapter 9).

Other critical distinctions remained regarding the SDGs process in addition to the question of who would lead it and what its nature would be. Primary among these was the question of the relation between the SDGs- and the Millennium Development Goals (MDGs)–related post-2015 agenda process(es). This was embedded in the paragraph that the G77 and China consistently put forward when calling for a process under the UNGA. Although there was growing consensus that there should be a single process on the post-2015 agenda, a vocal suite of delegations in the G77 and China—as well as Turkey—were keen to maintain some degree of primacy and independence for the MDGs. The word "single" was a red line for many because it meant that there would not be two separate tracks for the future evolution of the MDGs and the SDGs. There would be a single framework for development. The language these delegations favored was, "The process needs to be coordinated and coherent with the processes considering the post-2015 development agenda" (SDG6 alt). In its most extreme manifestation, this would have meant that the MDGs process would continue unhindered beyond 2015—presumably under the aegis of a revision of the MDGs or what some called MDG+—while the SDGs process would evolve in a completely separate and distinct track. This late in the negotiations, what this language did was ensure that all options remained on the table as potential outcomes. Other issues related to whether the process should be intergovernmental or country-driven and the kind of technical support the process would receive.

At the end of the first round of discussions in Rio de Janeiro, it was clear that any progress would be hard-fought. An encouraging sign is that we were all working from the draft consensus text provided by the co-chairs on June 2 that was already considerably streamlined. Hart told delegates that he would undertake consultations with lead negotiators and interested parties and would then propose alternative text. Privately, he requested Khan as G77 coordinator, myself, and a few other delegates that had led on the SDGs negotiations to help find consensus language to bridge the sharp divides in the negotiations.

Hart had his hands full with the MoI track. During our second day in Rio de Janeiro, June 14, Hart dedicated his allotted time exclusively to this track and the SDGs group did not even meet. MoI discussions included a range of highly charged areas, and there remained deep polarization around issues regarding provision of finance, technology transfer, and international trade. Hart hosted two rounds of negotiations that day and proposed a compromise text. The primacy afforded to this issue area was warranted; in the afternoon, the G77 and China blocked further negotiations on the Green Economy track until progress was made on MoI.

For the next thirty hours or so, Khan and I spent most of our time in backroom diplomacy, engaged in consultations across delegations in what we called "the kitchen." There was a huge warehouse-like building where delegations had been issued offices—mostly small cubicle rooms, although some of the larger or wealthier delegations had what amounted to cubicle suites. Toward the back was a small café where we met to thrash out areas of consensus that could contribute to breaking the persistent logjams—this was the kitchen. The tension and stress were palpable. The conference venue was a two-hour bumper-to-bumper bus ride from Rio de Janeiro—where most were staying—and only if one got on one of the first buses before traffic really kicked in. This commute meant early mornings and late nights. The venue itself was vast, so walking between meetings was a marathon and walking to get food yet another hurdle that often simply could not be accommodated.

At that stage of the process, the only agreed text in the SDGs section was still a single paragraph that extolled the MDGs. The only other area of broad agreement was that this time—contrary to the MDGs' top-down UN-led process—the SDGs would result from a country-driven and/or intergovernmental process. Consultations in the G77 and China were intense, given the range of positions, especially on the process to develop the SDGs after Rio. The first session of the SDGs splinter group on June 13 had witnessed an increasingly bitter stalemate across entrenched positions as the endgame loomed, especially around the post-Rio process. As G77 and China coordinator speaking on behalf of a widely divergent group, Khan was navigating a complicated situation.

We knew there was a very narrow and closing window to get the third option back on the negotiation table for the most ambitious outcome possible while managing the tense stand-offs that had become a mainstay of the negotiations. The three of us—Hart as SDGs facilitator, Khan as G77 and China coordinator for the SDGs, and me—were united in wanting to advance the option that had been earlier sketched out by Mexico and detailed in the concept papers Colombia had distributed based on the model of the Green Climate Fund (see Appendixes 23 and 24). Khan had been an elected member of the committee as well as being a member of the Green Climate Fund Board and knew this format was uniquely suited for the challenging task ahead. Thus he and I engaged in nonstop consultations in the G77 and China and with friends and heads of other delegations including the United States and the European Union to sound out options for consensus language on the post-Rio SDGs process. Together with Hart, we had a good understanding of the playing field. However, this was a minefield for Khan as the majority of the group could not even countenance such an option. We spent hours in backrooms across the conference venue in consultations and drafting language that would achieve this aim.

By evening on June 14, just the second day into the negotiations in Rio, Khan and I had prepared a new proposal to put the outcome that we wanted back on the table: a science-based, open, and transparent body. The draft proposed establishing an "intergovernmental steering committee" to "oversee and guide" an "intergovernmental process on SDGs under UNGA." The reference to "under UNGA" acknowledged the stated preference of the majority of the group. What was critical was the overarching model. For the first time, we had spelled out (in as much detail as the negotiation process would allow) how the third option could be structured. There was now a pathway to the kind of SDGs development process we envisioned. This solution was as nonpolitical as we could make it, insofar as it was populated by individuals from governments. Truly participatory. Science-based. The contours of the future Open Working Group were finally visible. We were cautiously optimistic, based on our consultations, that this language had a chance of making it into the outcome at Rio.

These paragraphs laid the foundations for what became, over the course of the following days, characterized as the "open working group." Stepping up to the opportunity to decisively shift the balance of the negotiations, the SDGs facilitator used this text as a basis for the new draft consensus text he proposed to delegates. Although few realized it at the time, this was a watershed moment.

On June 15, the SDGs negotiations were convened for a second time to discuss the new draft language put forward by the SDGs facilitator (see Appendix 20). The mood was tense given the massive differences that remained, time constraints, and concerns over how the negotiations would be managed in the following days.

We had broad agreement on the opening paragraphs characterizing the SDGs except for the G77 and China's insistence on maintaining the reference to CBDR—a reference necessary to make the idea of a universal agenda palatable for many of the group's members. The fact that many of the delegates were also negotiators of the UNFCCC process, where CBDR was a key bargaining chip and even sacrosanct for several delegations, made the issue even more intractable. As the days passed ahead of the start of the actual summit, when heads of state would gather, higher level delegates began to arrive, swelling the numbers of the cohort that traditionally negotiated climate change. As our numbers rose, positions grew further entrenched. For many, giving up a reference to CBDR would set too dangerous a precedent and could undermine the group's position in other negotiations, especially those under the UNFCCC.

There was still no consensus on listing indicative issue areas for the SDGs to tackle. Hart, the SDGs facilitator, proposed alternative text that pointed to a possible compromise by proposing, instead of a short list of thematic areas, that the SDGs focus on "a limited number of the priority areas identified in section V.a of this document." Given that the issue areas being discussed under Section V.a covered basically all major areas of development, this was as inclusive as the language could get. However, agreement proved impossible. In addition to this, the issue of measuring the SDGs remained controversial, even though the new text proposed a way forward: a single crisp sentence that stated that "goals need to be assessed and accompanied by targets and indicators while taking into account different national circumstances, capacities and levels of development."

What astounded delegations in this new draft was the sharp break with the preceding rounds of negotiations, which had included only the two options favored by the respective majorities of the G77 and China and of the European Union for the process after Rio to develop the SDGs framework. Based on the text that Khan had submitted in his capacity as G77 and China coordinator, this option was now clearly favored, enriched as necessary to account for the positions of other countries. It was a format that could truly deliver a transformational outcome. The discussion on this item was one of the most intense we had had to date. Many delegations were indignant that a new option had appeared that could sideline the other two options, making the final playoff much more complicated. The facilitator did his best to find areas for compromise, but the session ultimately ended, as so many others had, inconclusively.

To say that a significant number of G77 and China members were irate at this turn of events would be an understatement. At the next consultation, the situation came to a head. Debates throughout the process had often been heated and acrimonious but always respectful. Now, a line had been crossed. A few delegates bitterly accused Khan of betraying the group in the discussions on the SDGs' definition process. Khan, who had been literally working around the clock for days, going from G77 and

China meetings to plenaries to consultations with delegations to the kitchen, was incensed. More than anyone in the room, he had worked to find positions that everyone could live with and craft strategies for strengthening the group's hand. He had sought an ambitious outcome while remaining faithful to the core positions of the majority of the group.

Khan resigned on the spot. The entire group knew what he had accomplished and considered him one of our most brilliant negotiators. Delegate after delegate took to the floor to reaffirm their support for his work and underscore appreciation for the challenging job he was tasked with, asking him to reconsider his resignation. Stalwart professional that he is, Khan finally agreed to stay on, but there was a lingering bitterness. The showdown strengthened his hand as it was clear that the majority of the group would ultimately support him, but it also struck a cautionary note given the increasingly emotionally charged positions.

As the three initial days of negotiation drew to a close, Khan moved away from seeking concessions, as did the EU and others. At that juncture and under the prevailing negotiation format, it was impossible to craft consensus language in the negotiation room that could stand a chance of being accepted across the various negotiation coalitions, in particular in the G77 and China. Rather than push for consensus language, Khan dug his heels in and refused to compromise on the still heavily bracketed text that was already on the table. The EU and others did as well. The divisions in the G77 and China were so wide that had Khan tried to negotiate on the floor, some members of the group would have openly questioned his authority to advance the text. Had the negotiations proceeded along the path they had been on for the prior six months, it is possible that our group would have actually split and broken down into small negotiation coalitions with widely distant positions such as the Bolivarian Alliance for the Peoples of Our America (ALBA); progressives like Colombia, Guatemala, and Peru; small island developing states; and others.

Such a rupture would have been highly detrimental for the credibility of the G77 and China as one of the major negotiating groups with real influence over UN outcomes. Under such a scenario, the outcome of Rio+20 would have been uncertain but likely (at best) a minimalist declaration of political intent. The levels of distrust and acrimony were at an all-time high. As a seasoned negotiator, Khan hardened the formal position to the point where no agreement was possible. This ensured that our group remained intact and opened the way for others to craft and propose another consolidated text.

Despite the minefield that the negotiations had become, the Colombian delegation was elated. Finally, the stars were aligning. Finally, there was a shot at getting a substantive, decisive outcome from Rio+20. The language we had fought for behind the scenes for months was now on the table. Privately, we celebrated Hart's leadership and tenacity knowing that he, like the Caribbean Community and many other progressive countries, wanted the most ambitious outcome possible.

The previous evening, on June 14, after the review of progress of the two working groups, rumors in the hallways had been confirmed by PrepCom co-chair Kim Sook: after the close of the PrepCom on June 15, the Brazilian government was going to take over coordination of the process through to the start of the actual conference on June 20. In the plenary on June 15, further information was provided. The thematic roundtables that our Brazilian host had planned, the Dialogue Days, were to proceed as planned, but as far as delegates were concerned, they were taking place in a separate universe, across the street from the conference venue, where civil society groups were meeting. As delegates we had all foreseen that the interim days between the PrepCom and the conference would be buffer negotiation time, but we had not anticipated that the conference host would take over and lead them. At this point in the increasingly high-stakes games, the prevailing sense over the announcement was one of anticipation. Antonio de Aguiar Patriota, Brazil's foreign minister, informed us that preconference informal consultations would begin at noon the next day, June 16.

We were also informed that after three days of intense negotiations, only 116 of 315 paragraphs had been agreed to *ad referendum*.[1] With that update, the informal negotiations (Third Informal Informal Consultation) that had started in New York were brought to a close, and co-chair John Ashe formally called to order PrepCom III, which was supposed to have started three days earlier. We went through the formal proceedings, duly electing new vice chairs and adopting an agenda. After a few more established procedures, the short-lived PrepCom III was formally closed.

Hardening Positions

On Saturday, June 16, 2012, exhausted delegates straggled across Rio, back to the conference center for the opening plenary of what amounted to a new and uncertain era, now led by the Brazilian presidency. Under increasing pressure from President Dilma Rousseff, the Brazilians had already signaled that they would not allow the negotiations to bleed into the high-level conference itself. Rousseff, widely famed for her quick temper, wanted to ensure that she would be able to host a flawless highest-level event. The Brazilian delegation was under the gun to deliver.

In the plenary, we were informed by Minister of Foreign Affairs Antonio Patriota that the Brazilian presidency would not continue paragraph-by-paragraph negotiations. In this new era of "preconference informal consultations," delegations would be given new draft consolidated text and were invited to identify concerns, consult around consensus language where needed, and share recommendations with the presidency. The Brazilian delegation also committed to undertaking further bilateral consultations across delegations to better understand what hurdles remained. This was a masterful move. The presidency was giving all delegations the opportunity to find consensus, demonstrating both inclusivity and transparency. At the same time, it validated their strategy of discrete, bilateral consultations to craft an outcome document that could be widely construed as being underpinned by extensive consultations.

Having experienced the fraught outcomes at the UNFCCC Conference of the Parties (COPs) in Copenhagen and Cancún, the Brazilians knew perfectly well that they had to ensure that nothing they did over the next few days could be characterized as a "take-it-or-leave-it" ploy. They had often heard many countries in the G77 and China bitterly recall the outcomes in those COPs and vehemently affirm that if they were faced with the adoption of a text crafted behind closed doors or not open to negotiations, they would rather walk away from the proceedings than accept such an outcome. At the same time, a fully transparent process with language crafted with full participation across all delegations—which was in effect what had been attempted since March—was simply not working. Over the next few days, Brazil demonstrated once again why its Ministry of Foreign Affairs was regarded as a paragon of international diplomacy.

In the plenary, our Brazilian hosts informed us that we would henceforth meet across at least six groups: international framework for sustainable development (IFSD), MoI, SDGs, Sections I and II, and green economy, each to be coordinated by a Brazilian delegate. We welcomed the fact that MoI and SDGs were relegated to separate tracks as the onus on the facilitator to deliver on both tracks in the preceding days had been daunting. For the next two days, there would be three rounds of daily negotiations across the newly established groups in the morning, afternoon, and evening. In the first indication of the unique dynamics that would drive the next days, our Brazilian hosts informed us that further meetings of each group would depend on how much progress was made—or not. The first session of the SDGs group was slated for the next day, on Sunday morning.

We took this as a clear signal of the importance conferred on a robust SDGs outcome by the Brazilians, especially because SDGs were included in the very first round of negotiation sessions. The SDGs group would be led by Raphael Azeredo, a canny but fair and seasoned negotiator we knew well from the UNFCCC negotiations. Ambassador Luiz Alberto Figueiredo, executive secretary of the Brazilian national commission for Rio+20, reiterated that the final text would need to be agreed to by June 18, 2012, as the Brazilian presidency had no intention of having heads of state tackle negotiation issues once the conference began on June 20. The first negotiation sessions were scheduled to start at 6 p.m. that very evening of June 16.

Even seasoned delegates were astounded at the audacity of these instructions. Brazilian diplomacy was rightly considered one of the most sophisticated and finely tuned in the world. But getting agreement on such a vast number of issues spread out over hundreds of paragraphs that had defied consensus over months in just over sixty hours, and with sufficient ownership on the part of all member states, called for suspending disbelief. It is fair to say that everyone was committed to getting Rio+20 to be as successful as possible, but no matter how we computed what remained to be resolved in the time that remained, we came up dry.

In a challenging start to this new round of negotiations, the new draft compromise text was made available only at 5:45 p.m. (see Appendix 21). The text was a masterful distillation of the vast array of positions and text that had accreted over months of negotiations, with periodic and heroic efforts at draft comprehensive outcome language issued by the co-chairs. It was a brilliant exercise that combined a deep and comprehensive understanding of the fault lines across the negotiations, sharp technical understanding of the issues, and a profound commitment to clearing the highest political bar possible across the negotiation tracks. It clearly laid out the endgame that Brazil was proposing. Areas where consensus had proved impossible and that were not essential for any delegation or group had been dropped. Bracketed text and paragraphs with options had been synthesized into judiciously crafted language that largely succeeded in balancing differing positions. This was no small feat. The paragraphs were once again numbered successively, signaling the shift in gears as we entered the final phase of the negotiations.

This comprehensive new negotiation text was based on the thorough and highly strategic follow-up and analysis of the negotiation undertaken by the team at the UN Department of Economic and Social Affairs (UNDESA), under the able and dynamic leadership of Nikhil Seth. Key members of his team, especially David O'Connor, had played a leading role behind the scenes in distilling the 6,000 pages of submissions made by parties and constituencies back in November 2011 into the Zero Draft that launched the negotiations in early 2012. Throughout the negotiations, they had tracked the evolution of the text and identified possible consensus language. To a large degree, they were the architects of the several co-chairs' draft texts that were periodically issued in an attempt to help delegates find consensus language. In the final days in Rio, based on a judicious analysis of the state of play across the tracks, they put together proposed text for a final Rio+20 outcome document. The Brazilian draft outcome text presented to delegations in the evening of June 16 was almost entirely (with some exceptions) taken from UNDESA's compilation table. The compilation table, which until the writing of this book had remained an internal document, was a two-column document (see Appendix 26). The left column kept track of the latest negotiation text across the tracks—a Herculean effort. The right column contained proposed consensus text.[2] The eventual successful outcome at Rio owes hugely to their work and contributions and to their unflagging efforts behind the scenes over the many months of negotiations.

Despite the extensive work that had gone into this new draft text, delegates were not prepared to embark on a new round of negotiations without first having had time to carefully review the text and undertake consultations across groups and delegations. The Brazilians were requested to convene another plenary for a general exchange of views, which started at 6 p.m. and proceeded uneventfully with delegations expressing support for the Brazilian presidency and outlining priority concerns after quickly analyzing the new text.

The Colombian delegation was jubilant. The Brazilians had clearly come down in favor of the third option for a post-Rio process, which was now the only one on the table. What had seemed almost impossible when we arrived in Rio de Janeiro was now within reach.

On Sunday morning, June 17, the SDGs group met to discuss the new Brazilian draft. The outline of the final Rio outcome document was stark and clear. The Brazilian play on the SDGs was captured in seven paragraphs, now numbered sequentially from 248 to 254—down from the fifteen we had been grappling with just thirteen hours earlier. While waiting for the session to begin, delegates huddled in small groups, talking quietly but animatedly. Those already sitting around the long rectangular arrangement that dominated the room, tried to surmise what the huddles were talking about and exchanged glances with each other. The tension was overwhelming. We were down to the wire. While most delegates recognized the skillful effort at consensus in the new consolidated text, everyone also knew that this was one of the last opportunities to get their issues, their language, and their preferences on the table and into the outcome document.

The Brazilian chair, Raphael Azeredo, who had been tasked to lead the SDGs negotiations, opened the session by echoing what his minister and Ambassador Figueiredo had said the night before. We were not going to negotiate the text before us. We were being given an opportunity to signal red lines, propose recommendations for bridging differences, and strengthen the language. Final consensus text had to be agreed to by the next day. Echoing what was being said by his Brazilian teammates across the different negotiation groups, Azeredo quietly intoned, "If you cannot resolve this, if you cannot make progress, you will leave us no choice." During the rest of the session and the final round the next day, every time discussions threatened to stall and get bogged down across negotiation tracks, this adjuration was repeated.

Our Brazilian host listened attentively as the main red lines quickly surfaced again. We went through a rote round of interventions; by now, any one of us could have spoken on behalf of another delegation and succinctly laid out their arguments. By now we also had a general sense of what the final trade-offs were likely to be. Savvy negotiators knew that this was one of the last opportunities to shape and frame the language before us.

The Brazilian text clearly laid out the final negotiation landscape: the two opening paragraphs on the MDGs and the SDGs (248 and 250, previously numbered SDG1 and SDG5) were retained from the draft of June 15 with minimal changes. The notable exception was that Brazil had included an explicit mention of CBDR in the paragraph contextualizing the SDGs (paragraph 249, previously SDG2). From a negotiator's standpoint, it made total sense. As a leading member of the G77 and China, Brazil had to play a strong hand at the outset and only consider deleting this reference as the cost of ultimate consensus. As expected, while the G77 and China insisted on the need to retain this explicit reference, other delegations adamantly opposed it. We all noted that several paragraphs already had language referring to the need to "take into account different national circumstances, capacities and levels of development," language that hearkened to the CBDR principle in the event that an explicit reference was ultimately removed.

The next five paragraphs were equally important for what they included and for what was effectively deleted.

Paragraph 250 (previously SDG3) characterized the SDGs as "action-oriented, concise, . . . limited in number" and maintained language to the effect that they should be "global in nature and universally applicable to all countries while taking into account different national realities, capacities and levels of development and respecting national policies and priorities." Opposition to the concept of a universal framework had waned over the preceding months, but there was still resistance in several delegations. This was a stark affirmation that Brazil supported this decisive interpretation of the new framework.

Despite months of opposition by many delegations (especially from the Global South) to explicit inclusion of targets and indicators, the short paragraph 253 "[recognized] that progress towards the achievement of the goals needs to be assessed and accompanied by targets and indicators." This was a core demand of many developed countries.

Paragraph 254 delivered on the balancing act by supporting the position of the G77 and China, deleting any reference to a periodic global sustainable development report and instead requesting that the regional economic commissions be supported to inform "this global effort."

Language on an "initial indicative list of priority issues the SDGs could address" was notably absent. We knew then that that was one battle we had lost. But all things considered, of the three main outcomes we had set ourselves for Rio—agreement on the concept of the SDGs, agreement on a transformative process to craft them, and agreement on a preliminary list of focus issues—the last one was definitely the least important. Despite insistence on the need for an explicit paragraph on this by several delegations, including the EU and Switzerland, on this issue the G77 and China's position prevailed.

Delegates' attention was riveted on paragraphs 251 and 252, on the process to take the SDGs framework forward after Rio+20. The draft outcome text issued by Brazil was the game changer. They had clearly thrown their gauntlet down in favor of the third option that the SDGs facilitator had put on the table just forty hours earlier even though many still opposed it. This text included just a single option that called for the establishment of "an inclusive and transparent intergovernmental process on SDGs that is open to all stakeholders with a view to developing global sustainable goals to be agreed by the United Nations General Assembly." Paragraph 252 echoed the language that had been proposed a few days earlier by Khan and asked the UN Secretary-General to establish an interagency technical support team and expert panels. It confirmed that "reports on progress of work will be made regularly to the General Assembly" (paragraph 252). It was exactly what Colombia had fought for all the preceding months. With many of the friends and Khan, we had spent the last days in Rio in backrooms explaining ad nauseum the merits of this option to as many delegates as possible. The paper we had circulated on the Transitional Committee as a model (see Appendixes 23 and 24) demonstrated that there was already a precedent for this option. Laying out how it could be structured had helped many delegates better understand this format. These efforts contributed to paving the way for this. But it took significant political courage on the part of Brazil to support this play.

Many G77 and China delegates were still incensed that an option that had appeared just two days earlier calling for a steering committee to be established was now the only one on the table; they insisted on having the process go forward under the UNGA. The tension was impossible to manage for the G77 and China's coordinator, so Khan simply listed toward the minimum common denominator and noted that from the group's perspective, the process had to be an intergovernmental process under the UNGA.

Throughout the intense discussions, when the divisions became stark, Azeredo would intone, "if you cannot resolve this, if you cannot make progress, you leave us no choice." At the end of the allotted two hours, the SDGs group broke up unhappily. There was bitterness in the air from delegations that felt that their preferred options and language had been sidelined. Everyone was anguished over what the final play would be as the Brazilian hosts kept insisting that the negotiations had to conclude the next day. We all felt that we needed much more time to arrive at a consensus text. Azeredo urged us to consult among ourselves and come to his delegation with resolution of any outstanding issues and to propose consensus language as needed. Given the state of play of the process, this was not remotely feasible. He said that the Brazilian team would do likewise, continuing its own consultations. As noted earlier, this was a masterful play by the Brazilians. Everyone was being given a chance to be heard and shape the final outcome. However, if we were unable to come up with language ourselves, the Brazilians were simply stepping up to fill the collective leadership gap. A narrative was being crafted for the endgame.

That Sunday afternoon, tensions in the G77 and China remained high, heightened after the morning session on the SDGs chaired by Brazil. One reason for this had to do with the overall process that was being led by Brazil. It was clear from the plenary discussion the preceding evening that getting consensus across the outstanding issues by the next day, Monday, June 18, was a massive task. If, as Brazil kept insisting, June 18 was the deadline to finalize the outcome document, surely there would have to be a sleight of hand to deliver it. There were dark rumblings among some delegations about what would happen if Brazil tried to "put a take-it-or-leave-it" text on the table. Despite Brazil's deadline, the hallways were rife with speculation about just how long the negotiations might actually drag on. The draft text that Brazil had presented was an important step toward consensus language, but there were still so many red lines.

The other reason for tension in the group was the glaring and enduring internal division regarding the process to define and develop the SDGs after Rio+20 concluded. For Colombia, at this point this was the only relevant outcome of the conference. The relentless work of the past one and a half years would come to naught if a robust process could not be agreed on. For months I had talked about Rio+1—the day after the Rio conference ended—and the need for an open rather than an open-ended process. We knew that unless a different kind of format under-pinned by a clearly defined process was locked in, the coming years would be spent not defining the SDGs but in rabid political battles over the format, and then on political declarations distant from the metric we envisioned. My anguish was shared by Khan.

The G77 and China coordination meeting on Sunday afternoon was thus a watershed in that for the first time, some of the key delegations that were most strongly opposed to the open working group option to take the SDGs forward signaled a willingness to consider it (see Chapter 9 for a detailed analysis of this meeting).

On the evening of June 17, the SDGs group met again, largely to review new text proposed by Brazil for paragraph 251 on the SDGs process. Although there was now somewhat greater acceptance of the option before us, some members of the G77 and China still insisted on the need for a process under the UNGA while other delegations questioned the viability of an intergovernmental process to deliver an SDGs frame-work. The new text proved to be historic: for the first time, the body that was to develop the SDGs framework was referred to as an open working group, and the number of representatives was set to thirty. Two other changes were noteworthy: the inclusion of "the scientific community and the UN system" in the process and the clarification that the proposal for SDGs would be presented to the UNGA "for consideration and appropri-ate action." This last addition sought to strengthen the role of UNGA in the process and give comfort to those who feared a loss of political clout if this body was sidelined from the ultimate outcome on the SDGs.

The next day, June 18, the SDGs group met again in the afternoon. Again, Azeredo opened the session by soberly inquiring whether we had sought solutions among ourselves and intoning that if there were out-standing issues, the Brazilian delegation would have no choice but to address them. We heard this, but most of us still expected negotiations to spill over into the next few days.

There was continued and intense discussion of the SDGs process, with some still calling for an option under UNGA while others rejected an inter-governmental process. Delegations insisted on issues they regarded as cen-tral, such as including indicative themes, but largely the textual changes proposed by the Brazilian lead were well received and recognized as neat solutions to arrive at consensus. We were picking our battles, priming for the final negotiations we expected to have over the coming days. The Brazilian facilitator proposed language to replace the explicit reference to CBDR in paragraph 249 with a phrase: "taking into account different national circumstances, capacities and priorities." This language was welcomed as a viable option by delegations from the Western group. Another important textual addition effectively acknowledged the significant unhappiness across many delegations—especially from the Western group—at the deletion of the paragraphs on priority thematic areas. New text was proposed to address this in paragraph 250, which characterized the SDGs: "We also recognize that the goals should address and be focused on priority areas for the achievement of sustainable development, being guided by this outcome document." Given that "this outcome document" included twenty-six critical thematic areas, this was as inclusive as the language could get. Throughout the discussions, a few delegations—sensing that this was the endgame—tried to make more changes, for example, regarding the number of seats in the recently named open working group. Azeredo listened attentively but remained noncommittal.

At the end of our Monday afternoon meeting, Azeredo urged us all to continue to consult among ourselves and bring solutions to the Brazilian hosts. We were informed that there would be a plenary later that evening, and we left the room wondering when the next negotiation session would take place. Negotiations on the remaining tracks had made progress under the relentless Brazilian leadership, but intractable divisions remained, and we discussed what the trade-offs could be. We still had one day to go before the formal start of the conference on Wednesday, and many expected negotiations to continue at least into the next day.

There was one development, unknown to us, that presented a massive, last-minute threat to the SDGs. As successive delegations took to the floor in the room where the SDGs group was meeting to comment on the proposed text on the evening of June 17, the EU delegate framed a question in a way that did not convey the resolute support for the SDGs that had been the case up to then. We were stunned. The EU had been one of the most faithful supporters of the SDGs, ever since the meeting in Solo, Indonesia, in July 2011. Across the room I stared at the EU delegation, trying to fathom what was going on. A few interventions later, it was the turn of John Matuszak from the US delegation. His comments clearly evidenced strong support for the establishment of an open working group. His words set off a flurry of whispered discussions in the corner of the room where the EU was sitting. More was brewing than we could have fathomed.

Last-Minute Derailment Averted

During the last negotiation sessions in New York in late May and early June, Colombia had welcomed the very positive US engagement in the discussions on the SDGs and the adoption of pragmatic positions that helped frame the conversation. The US delegation often insisted on having a maximum of ten goals and underscored the importance of ensuring that these be defined through an open, intergovernmental process with strong government ownership. A proper framework metric had to be agreed to, with measurable goals and targets to which everyone could be held accountable. Participation by the private sector was key. The US position clearly resonated with our vision, and we certainly welcomed it. The internal tensions in the US government between those who supported the new framework and those more wedded to a continuation of the MDGs—which was common in many governments—were less evident as the US stance became more proactive and engaged in the SDGs discussions under the leadership of Todd Stern.

A very different process was playing out within the UK delegation (at the time the United Kingdom was still a member of the EU, Rio+20 unfolding just four years before the Brexit vote). Throughout the process, until around May 2012, the UK delegation was led mainly by the Department of Environment, Food, and Rural Affairs (DEFRA). The UK delegation was a resolute advocate of the SDGs and with Chris Whaley, head of EU and International Coordination at DEFRA, as its lead, played a decisive role within the friends. Caroline Spelman, secretary of state for DEFRA, had publicly and staunchly defended the SDGs. However, in the run-up to the conference, the SDGs were placed under the purview of Nick Clegg, the deputy prime minister and head of the UK delegation to Rio+20. In early May, Colombian President Santos had a call with him to underscore the importance of the SDGs and of agreeing on a technical working group to develop them. Given concerns among developing countries related to financing for the SDGs, Santos underscored that "the SDGs are about implementation, and transcending rhetorical positions. Therefore, concrete SDGs will enable mobilization of resources from a wide variety of sources including the private sector." In that call, Clegg signaled continued support for the proposal.

However, the fact was that the development community in the UK, led by the Department for International Development (DFID, the government agency responsible for administering overseas aid) had participated only minimally in the SDGs process, and the negotiations had largely been left to DEFRA. As was the case across many other governments, many were convinced that the SDGs idea would ultimately not prosper. However, as the Rio+20 conference drew closer, it started to become increasingly apparent that there was growing support for the SDGs and that most likely, they would be an integral part of the outcome document. This was unwelcome.

In parallel to the Rio+20 negotiation process, there had been ongoing discussions between Secretary-General Ban Ki-moon and UK Prime Minister David Cameron to establish another high-level panel to define the new post-2015 development agenda. The report of the Global Sustainability Panel that was presented in March 2012 had fallen flat (see Chapter 7), but there was interest in setting up a new process that would apply the lessons from this failed effort to decisively influence the framing of the new post-2015 agenda. Cameron preferred that a panel in which he would have a leadership role be the one to frame a new development agenda. If its contours were already agreed to in Rio, his ability to frame and shape the new agenda would be constrained. As the option of the open working group to define the SDGs framework was clearly ascendant by then, this meant that a high-level panel format would be off the table.

Judging from the later discussions in the high-level panel on the post-2015 agenda, which was established in July 2012, in the absence of the SDGs, a panel under Cameron's leadership would likely have proposed a framework along the lines of MDG+. Cameron ultimately chaired this panel, along with the president of Liberia, Ellen Johnson Sirleaf, and the president of Indonesia, Susilo Bambang Yudhoyono. Colombia's Minister of Foreign Affairs María Ángela Holguín participated in the panel, as one of twenty-three other eminent experts. I served as her assistant, supporting her participation in that panel, and that experience enabled me to ascertain some of the nuances that had not been wholly evident to me in Rio. The story of the panel, however, would call for another book.

As the final round of negotiations in Rio drew closer, it became clear that the SDGs were going to be a core part of the final outcome; some in the UK government wanted to prevent this outcome. Providentially, in this same timeframe, the G20 meeting was being held in Los Cabos, Mexico, on June 18–19, 2012. On the sidelines of that meeting, Cameron decided that the SDGs language should be blocked. In the EU, this brought to the surface deep divisions; some delegates recalled incredibly difficult negotiations running down to the wire because there were divisions around the SDGs. In addition to the EU, the United Kingdom determined that it was essential to get the United States to support this effort. Thus, DFID led an intense démarche toward the United States, a concerted effort to get the United States to withdraw their support of the SDGs.

The United States, however, was convinced that the SDGs, properly framed and defined, offered a solid, concrete outcome for Rio+20. Strong proponents of the SDGs in the US delegation argued that within a larger negotiation domain, this was an important outcome that would simply allow a process to go forward. They considered that a constructive Rio+20 outcome could generate important capital with the G77 and China that could help in other negotiation arenas. They asserted that derailing the SDGs at this late stage was simply a very bad move that would alienate many. The United States was not swayed by DFID's appeal. Thus the United States played a decisive role in preventing the derailment of the final adoption of the SDGs.

We were not, however, aware of what was going on at that time. After the Brazilian presidency issued their consolidated outcome draft, I spent most of my time consulting within our group and reviewing language with Khan given the tightrope he had to walk between what the majority wanted for the process to define the SDGs and where progressive countries like Colombia stood. Together we had consulted on language for the SDGs process with the US delegation, and one of their most senior members had come back with a draft text that neatly defined areas of ambitious consensus. Thus, as we went into the SDGs consultation chaired by Azeredo on that Sunday, we were expecting the same issues that we had been grappling with the preceding months to surface again around the new draft text, and for these to be raised by the same suspects. We were confident that we had the support of the European Union, the United States, the friends, and several important constituencies including the Caribbean.

Thus, I was dumbfounded when the EU's intervention seemed less clearly aligned with earlier positions. Their shift in position was unexpected because these were truly the final hours of negotiation. Given how closely we had worked with the EU in support of the SDGs, it made no sense to me. Sitting across the room, I looked askance to EU colleagues trying to piece together what was happening. Finally, a delegate from an EU member country who was also a friend signaled to me to step into the hallway. There he explained that thousands of miles away, in Los Cabos, Mexico, where the G20 meeting was getting underway, David Cameron had doubled down on his opposition to the SDGs proposal. My colleague assured me that there was no consensus on this in the EU and that the ongoing discussions were incredibly difficult. It put the EU negotiators in a horrible bind. When I prodded him and asked whether this meant that the SDGs could be derailed, he shook his head and said, "I honestly don't know."

In the very last hours, the divisions in the EU and the US refusal to oppose the SDGs decided the outcome. Cameron had counted on getting the United States to lead opposition to the SDGs given that the aim was to establish a universal metric against which all countries would be accountable. Even as they realized that the SDGs were fast becoming a new reality, some in the United Kingdom thought there was sufficient latent opposition to the proposal that it was just a matter of galvanizing those forces.

But the SDGs proposal had struck a chord across governments and constituencies. Governments like the United States and other European countries stood by this new paradigm that we were collectively crafting. Even the G77 and China was now supportive of the idea even if there was still no consensus on how the post-Rio process would move forward. Later, we were told privately, at a final meeting between the UK and US delegations, the US delegation signaled that they were willing to go along with the Brazilian outcome text, and the United Kingdom realized that the game was up.

Looking back, we are convinced that in the Rio process, the SDGs were negotiated not with 193 member states but with hundreds and hundreds of delegates. In the end, enough consensus had been arrived at across such a broad array of governments and delegates that the SDGs could no longer be simply killed off. There was broad and deep and wide ownership of this new agenda.

The Final Push

By Monday, June 18, although it was the appointed day for arriving at the final outcome text according to our Brazilian hosts, many delegates expected that some negotiations would spill over, at least until June 20, when the actual conference with heads of state was due to start. Again, there were varied rumors circulating in the hallways. The tempo and dynamics were changing. Delegations had swelled with the arrival of high-level representatives and their entourages, even though many heads of state were not expected until late on June 19 or 20, especially those still at the G20 meeting in Mexico. Dignitaries and luminaries in the field of sustainable development were also arriving.

Key meetings were also taking place as the endgame was in sight. Brazil was conducting bilateral consultations around the clock to sound out the final layout of the negotiations and thus of the final outcome document, an exercise that required understanding where the last red lines were for key delegations. The overriding precept of "nothing is agreed until everything is agreed" animates all negotiations at the United Nations. Getting the final architecture right required a combination of keen insight into the negotiation process to date, which the Secretariat had ably kept track of (see Appendix 26) and of strong tactics to force consensus if needed. At this point, all the outstanding issues across the negotiations came into play, for these were the most contentious areas around which consensus had proved impossible. This is the moment that negotiators hold out for, to bargain for the most they can get as all the cards are revealed.

In these final hours, Brazil's leadership over the entire process hung in the balance. Remaining points of contention across the negotiation tracks included the future status of UNEP. In the EU, a few countries, especially France and Germany, together with Kenya, wanted to upgrade UNEP from a program to a more autonomous agency. This proposition was not wholeheartedly supported within the EU, and others, including the United States and Russia, rejected it outright.

There were also difficult discussions about the follow-up mechanism for the Commission on Sustainable Development and whether the UN Economic and Social Council should have a role in such a mechanism. On the SDGs front, a key sticking point was around a monitoring system. The EU wanted a more muscular system for reviewing and monitoring implementation of the SDGs to ensure that commitments truly bolstered more sustainable outcomes. This proposition was soundly rejected by the G77 and China, who considered that this encroached on their national policy space. Within the EU, there were difficult discussions about how much to push for priorities they had invested heavily in and to what degree to support the emerging compromise. In the hallways, it was said that in the EU there were concerns over how the Brazilian presidency would manage the negotiations. Thus, tensions were running high when the EU and Brazilian delegations met—one of the most important bilateral meetings of the many the Brazilian team was holding. Brazil played a strong hand, characterizing the EU as unreasonable and pressuring for agreement on the consensus outcome text they were crafting. Many delegates recall a highly charged, acrimonious meeting. Ultimately, after intense internal discussions, the EU member states agreed to support the hand that Brazil was playing.

At this stage, rumors were rife because there was considerable confusion as to how Brazil planned to take the process forward. On the one hand, select consultations were still happening across several key tracks, framed by Brazil's adjuration "If you are not able to come to an agreement, you leave us no option." We had been operating in a non-negotiation mode since Sunday morning as the Brazilian leadership had clearly instructed us to seek solutions among ourselves while they did likewise. In the consultations there had been intense discussions around the outstanding issues but largely not on specific text. Major issues remained unresolved, and we needed more negotiation time. On the other hand, we had been told in no uncertain terms by our hosts that the final outcome document had to be finalized that very day.

Clarity was soon forthcoming. Delegates were informed that a plenary would convene at 11 p.m. A new consolidated text was to be presented and, we all assumed, discussed. We knew that the Brazilian delegation had been holding exhaustive bilateral meetings with negotiation groups, facilitators, and individual delegations. Because these were bilateral, no one had a clear and comprehensive understanding of the final trade-offs and consensus landscape.

We all tried to get something to eat and packed into a relatively small conference room to wait for the new document. Nearby overflow rooms accommodated the huge number of delegates and constituencies that were present. The plenary time came and went. Midnight came and went. June 18, 2012, was the deadline Brazil had set to arrive at a final text, but at that late hour, there was only anticipation. As the hours passed, a subdued collegial spirit infused the room as we waited, exhausted, in a strange limbo. By that point we had spent weeks together since the formal negotiations had begun in March. We had all been in the trenches together. Every so often, some ripple of news or rumor would flicker through the room as we all waited for news of the new text. Finally, around 2 a.m., Antonio Patriota, the Brazilian foreign minister, entered the room and informed us that the final outcome document would be distributed at 7 a.m. and that the plenary would reconvene at 10:30 a.m. He told us that his intention was to make an announcement to the press that the negotiations had concluded. This was audacious. But at this late hour, no one challenged him.

This was Brazil's take-it-or-leave-it moment, and it had been masterfully played. Brazil's achievement in Rio+20 was no small feat given the overall context of multilateralism. Just six months earlier, at the UNFCCC COP in Cancún, the Mexican presidency had issued a final text—after extensive negotiations—that was essentially a take-it-or-leave document. It reflected the presidency's best effort at a package that balanced interests across delegations to achieve that hallmark of consensus—enough so everyone had a gain, enough so that everyone had a pain point. After Cancún and after the Copenhagen outcome in 2009, many delegations in the Rio+20 process, including in our group, had flatly stated that any attempt to do that again would be met with firm rejection.

Brazil had played a clean hand in two ways. First, it provided an initial consolidated text that gave delegations a good sense of what the final landing ground could look like. Second, Brazil encouraged delegations to find and come forward with solutions themselves, giving repeated advance warning that otherwise "you will leave us no choice."

Granted, no one at the time knew what they meant by "no choice," but the warning had been there. In parallel, over the course of those three days, the Brazilian delegation held many bilateral meetings. This enabled them to have frank, even if sometimes tense discussions with key delegations and negotiation groups and to scope out viable landing spaces. Because the meetings were largely bilateral or smaller in scope, the dynamics that could make discussions in the formal groups so diffi- cult were avoided. Moreover, this strategy kept delegations and groups slightly off balance because no one knew for certain what had been dis- cussed elsewhere.

Finally, Brazil had in its favor wide recognition in the G77 and China as a key delegation with a history of strong, stark positions and was seen by many as a stalwart advocate of the Global South. Brazil was also widely respected for its history of outstanding diplomacy and the legacy of Rio 1992, which it was trying to protect. At the end of the day, everyone wanted Brazil to succeed and deliver a strong outcome at Rio 2012. In short, arguably only Brazil could have pulled off what essentially became a take-it-or-leave-it move. In the end, it was an astonishingly effective process.

By the time Patriota finalized his announcement, it was around 3 a.m. Delegates headed back to their hotels for a quick shower and nap. Everyone wanted to be back at 7 a.m. to see what had been announced as the final text. Fortunately, in the early hours of the morning, the trip between the conference venue and Rio de Janeiro was under an hour. Most delegates shuffled back into the venue by 7 a.m. the morning of June 19 to receive and review the final outcome text. Then we waited. And waited. The new consolidated outcome text was only shared around 10 a.m. (see Appendix 27). There were no major surprises. The Brazilians had done a solid job of ironing out the remaining hurdles.

If there were few surprises in the overall document, on the SDGs front, there were none. The final text was the one we had worked with the previous days, with the additions and edits we had discussed.

By the time the consolidated outcome text was released, the entire Colombian delegation, with the exception of President Santos, who was flying in that evening from the G20 meeting in Cancún, had arrived in Rio de Janeiro. From our perspective, the final text was perfect. There was clearly an open (not open-ended) working group, composed of a limited number of participants (see Appendix 27). Balanced geographic representation ensured broad ownership. Critically, it called for the full participation of all stakeholders, including civil society, scientists, and UN experts. We had ensured that it would not only be the remit of governments and that it would be informed by science and technical expertise (see Chapter 9 for deeper analysis).

Moreover, given that it was based on the Green Climate Fund's Transitional Committee experience, we also welcomed the fact that an inter-agency technical support team had been established. This would help bring in the latest science and ground the deliberations in information and data that could be readily accessed by participants. What became paragraph 249 had only two significant changes (emphasized in italics for reference):

> 249. The process needs to be coordinated and coherent with the processes considering the post-2015 development agenda. The initial input to the work of the working group will be provided by the United Nations Secretary General *in consultation with national governments*. In order to provide technical support to this process and to the work of the working group, we request the UN Secretary-General to ensure all necessary input and support to this work from the UN system including through establishing an inter-agency technical support team and expert panels, as needed, drawing on all relevant expert advice. *Reports on the progress of work will be made regularly to the General Assembly.*

Delegates huddled and sat on desks, on the floor, and along hallways to review the Rio outcome document. Overall, there was a pervading sense of relief. We waited in the small plenary room for the final session of the Pre-Conference Informal Consultation. The room was packed. By then even more ministers and dignitaries had arrived. Many delegates were spread out across the desks and floor—even ministers were sitting on the floor. Finally, around noon, the Brazilian foreign minister walked into the room. He said the text was ready to be presented to and adopted by the conference ad referendum. Although a few delegations still had issues related to the International Framework for Sustainable Development and the future status of UNEP (which were not ultimately resolved until the plenary session), there was a long round of deeply felt and relieved applause. A final outcome document had been arrived at.

After Patriota gaveled the meeting to a close, he called Patti and me onto the podium to express his personal gratitude as well as that of his government for our perseverance in making the SDGs proposal a reality. He told us that Colombia had secured the success of Rio+20. Given the broad range of issues addressed at the summit and the fact that the outcome document, although quite streamlined, was still far from a clear call to action, many labeled Rio+20 a failure. However, the Brazilian government, through its able orchestration of the negotiations and the decisive final choices they had made on the SDGs paragraphs, had in fact delivered the foundations of a new development framework.

Embedded in *The Future We Want* was the linchpin of a new, radically different vision of development. The SDGs concept had been approved and, most important, a robust process agreed to that all but ensured that the path to define and develop the new framework would be as revolutionary as the concept itself.

On Thursday, June 21, 2012, during the final, historic plenary, President Santos called for action in his statement during the general debate. The focus of his intervention was entirely on the SDGs. We knew that when the dust settled, the SDGs were the cornerstone of the new development agenda. He affirmed that the SDGs were a concrete and pragmatic tool that could enable progress in delivering national, regional, and global priorities. Aware of the still latent opposition to the SDGs by many in the development arena, he noted that the SDGs built on the MDGs and were an invitation to a more ambitious and all-encompassing vision as well as to an integrated and comprehensive perspective. He expressed his gratitude for the international community's endorsement of the SDGs proposal that Colombia had incubated, which was to become the new sustainable development framework for future action. He highlighted the versatility of the SDGs: they would enable improved coordination between local authorities and national governments and facilitate engagements at regional and interregional levels, for example, on transboundary issues. In his statement, he underscored the vital role that the private sector and civil society would play in advancing the SDGs.

After he spoke and as the general debate continued, the secretary-general of the UNCSD, Sha Zukang, came down from the podium and walked over to where the Colombian delegation was sitting. After greeting and congratulating Santos, he said, "Colombia, it is not a big country. But it has big ideas that changed the history of development."

On June 22, 2012, the Rio+20 outcome document, *The Future We Want*, was formally adopted.[3] It was a fitting closure to an unbelievable eighteen-month journey. In fact, there was now an opportunity to radically redefine how we understand and tackle global development.

Notes

1. Summary of UNCSD PrepCom III (2012).

2. A notable exception was the section on energy, which the table noted would be "populated by Brazil."

3. On July 27, 2012, the UNGA endorsed the Rio+20 Outcome Document, adopting Resolution A/66/288.

9

Creating the
Open Working Group

Getting agreement on the concept of the Sustainable Development Goals (SDGs) was a decisive win in Rio+20, but the bold, disruptive framework of the SDGs was possible only thanks to the creation of an evidence-based, wholly participatory body that brought the best science and expertise into the process. The story of how the Open Working Group was established is the story of the other major battle that was waged in the Rio+20 process. This chapter describes this track of the negotiations from March to June 2012.

Creating a Forum for Transformation

From the beginning, when we came up with the SDGs idea, we had known that we would need to establish a nonpolitical forum to develop the framework because it would be impossible to do so during the already packed Rio+20 preparation process. We had determined that in Rio de Janeiro we needed to secure at least two basic outcomes: (1) agreement on the concept of the SDGs as a unique framework and (2) agreement on a process to develop them.[1] The concept paper we circulated with Guatemala as far back as August 2011 called for this. As the negotiations advanced over the first months of 2012, we gradually became confident that there would be agreement on the idea of the SDGs. However, positions on the process to develop the SDGs after Rio+20 were mired in controversy.

From our perspective, agreeing to the SDGs concept without a rigorous science-based process to develop the framework with active engagement of national and international experts—not just diplomats—was a nonstarter. I continuously asked, "What about Rio+1? What happens the day after Rio?" We knew that if the SDGs were negotiated under a business-as-usual UN format, we would end up with, at best, some kind of resolution of hard-fought political statements couched as "goals" or "targets" or another "implementation plan" that generated no traction, no change, and no movement.

Rio+10 had generated the mother of all implementation plans—the Johannesburg Plan of Implementation (JPOI). Over fifty-four pages and eleven chapters, delegates hammered out detailed recommendations across a range of issue areas, many tailored to specific regions. Yet it had no uptake after the Rio+10 conference ended. For us it was a stark reminder of what would happen if the SDGs process followed a traditional approach. We did not want the SDGs to end up in some variation of the JPOI. We wanted a metric, a tangible framework to drive action, guide implementation, and hold everyone accountable. How many declarations and resolutions had been negotiated that ultimately changed nothing?

Throughout the negotiations, two options predominated that would have hardwired precisely the kind of established processes we were convinced were absolute impediments to the transformational framework we had in mind. Colombia worked unceasingly in the final months of negotiations and in Rio de Janeiro to put on the table and garner support for a third option—one that finally became the Open Working Group (OWG).

Options on the Table

The initial Zero Draft submitted by the UNCSD co-chairs in January 2012 had nothing specific on the SDGs process after Rio. As a result of the consultations undertaken throughout February and most of March before the formal negotiation process started, many delegations and groups, including the G77 and China, put forward options. Gradually the following three main options emerged.

First was a negotiation under the UN General Assembly (UNGA). This meant a wholly political process following the rules and established negotiation format with the participation of the formal negotiation groups, such as the G77 and China and the European Union. This was the only option the majority in the G77 and China accepted. Early on the group had starkly stated that the process had to comply with three conditions:

- be intergovernmental,
- be inclusive, transparent, and open-ended, and
- be under the UNGA.

In the G77 and China version of the Zero Draft, the process entailed the establishment of an ad hoc open-ended working group under the General Assembly, which would present a report with recommendations to the UNGA at either its sixty-seventh or sixty-eighth session.[2]

Many other delegations, however, feared that under a business-as-usual UN setting with the established negotiating bodies, we would be simply setting ourselves up for exactly the kind of debacle we were living through at that moment in the Rio+20 negotiations: a politicized agenda with widely disparate views that forced minimum consensus within each group—such as the G77 and China or the EU—and then a further watering down of consensus in plenary sessions. For Colombia, the option of a process under the UNGA was our single most significant red line. Under this format, the ability of groups to shape or block negotiations was heightened, essentially guaranteeing a highly politicized process. A standard, political UN format would likely at best deliver another unwieldy cookbook of recommendations as had already happened in 2002 with the JPOI.

For this reason, the EU and others put forward a second option that called for requesting the Secretary-General "establish and coordinate a process . . . with a view to establishing a set of coherent global goals in 2015," which would then report to the UNGA. This option was favored by many delegations from the Western group, including the European Union, Switzerland, Norway, and the Republic of Korea. A Secretary-General-led process offered some delegations the apparent comfort of a more tightly led exercise. Across the UN, some heads of key agencies also preferred this option. However, this option was anathema to many who considered that a process led by the Secretary-General might not be transparent and possibly a replay of the Millennium Development Goals (MDGs) process, which was wholly top-down. Traditionally, the most common expression of this option was the creation of a panel by the Secretary-General led by one or more countries he would select.

In March 2012, the Secretary-General had launched the report of the High-Level Panel on Global Sustainability; it had been met with deafening indifference. Even though the panel had outstanding expertise and participation, the perception of a closed process contributed to sinking the report. Many delegations were opposed to agreeing to a similar exercise in Rio.

For Colombia, the option of a Secretary-General-led process was also problematic because it would be limited to a select number of countries and closed to substantive inputs from a whole range of external stakeholders and experts. The choice of leadership for the process could also limit its vision and scope as the designated chairs or presidents of the process had significant power over its framing and implementation. The SDGs process, from our perspective, had to be able to tap the best expertise around the world and translate it into a suite of concrete, measurable, actionable targets around which the whole range of stakeholders could galvanize change.

For this reason, we were immensely grateful to Mexico when Damaso Luna, their lead negotiator, put forward a third option on May 2, 2012 (see Appendix 14).[3] Mexico did not belong to a formal negotiation group and was able to exercise independence in proposing language. This option reflected discussions among the friends and most closely hewed to the format that Colombia considered essential if a robust metric was to be developed after the summit. This third option called for establishing "a process for the adoption of a single suite of SDGs" led by a group of experts to "define appropriate targets and indicators." Critically, it included that all-important word "single," signaling that there would not be a separate, parallel process to review and advance the MDGs.

At the outset of the negotiations, other options had been put forward, but they fell by the wayside during the negotiations. These included requests to the Secretary-General to variously launch a process, "provide all necessary support," or provide proposals for measuring and reporting on progress. The option for having the president of the UNGA and the president of UN Economic and Social Council "develop a meaningful framework" was also put forward. Some delegations requested that the process be undertaken in conjunction with an MDGs review.

Box 9.1   Evolution of Text on a Post-Rio Process to Develop the SDGs

---

Text on March 28, 2012:
CST 106. We agree that the SDGs should be developed through an intergovernmental process under the General Assembly that is inclusive, transparent and open to the participation of all stakeholders. This process will need to be coordinated and coherent with the processes considering the post-2015 development agenda.

continues

Box 9.1 Continued

Text on May 2, 2012:
[CST 106/ We [agree [to establish a process on—G77] [that the G77 delete] SDGS should be developed through an intergovernmental process under the General Assembly that is / propose that any SDGs would need to be internationally agreed and developed through a fully—US, RoK] inclusive, transparent and open [[to / process with—US] the participation of all stakeholders / including the UN System—G77]. This process will need to be coordinated and coherent with the [MDGs review—G77] process[es—G77 delete] considering the post-2015 development [agenda / framework—US] [in order to allow a smooth integration of SDGs into such post-2015 development agenda—Japan]. (based on suggestions before pre 105, 105, 106 and 106.alt) —Canada delete] (Canada propose consolidating OP 106 malt1 and CST 106 into CAST 106 bis; EU, Norway propose merging CEST 106 and 106 bis) (New Zealand questions link of intergovernmental process with CST 106 bis language on UN Secretary General)

"Third Option" proposed by Mexico on May 2, 2012:
CST 106 alt 2 We decide to establish a process for the adoption of a single suite of SDGs, with sustainable development and poverty eradication as the overarching focus, such a process should be country-driven whilst open to the participation of all stakeholders. We therefore decide to establish a group of experts integrated by representative [sic] of governments and relevant stakeholders and from specialized agencies with experience in environmental, social and economic aspects of sustainable development in order to define appropriate targets and indicators and to develop a mechanism for periodic follow-up and reporting on progress made towards the achievement of such goals. The UN Secretary-General should provide all the necessary support to this process.

Text on the "UNGA Option" as we headed off to Rio in June 2012:
SDG 6 alt. We agree to establish an intergovernmental process on SDGs under the UNGA that is inclusive, transparent, and open to all stakeholders. The process needs to be coordinated and coherent with the processes considering the post-2015 development agenda. —G77, Turkey

Laying the Groundwork for the OWG

During the first months of negotiations, we concentrated our efforts in getting agreement on the concept of the SDGs as a separate process from the MDGs. Gradually, enough consensus started to consolidate that we were confident that there would be agreement on some kind of SDGs framework, and I was able to shift my attention almost single-mindedly to what I called "the SDGs process." The discussions on this issue were not going well, and there was a stand-off between the groups favoring two options. The one we favored was not even on the table. Therefore, toward the end of the second round of negotiations in early May 2012, we prepared and distributed our fourth concept paper—this time endorsed by Peru and the United Arab Emirates (see Appendix 22).[4]

The paper acknowledged that while the decision in Rio was political, the subsequent process that was to be defined by member states would evolve "through targeted consultations and deliberations . . . and not [be] negotiated prima facie." Colombia had an unyielding position regarding a purely politically negotiated process for the SDGs. We argued that the SDGs process had to be evidence-based. Because that term was anathema to many, the paper restated this requirement: "The development of the SDGs must be informed by: i) existing information; ii) work already undertaken on indicators and goals, in particular the MDGs; and iii) technical inputs from national experts, regional organizations and specialized agencies."

Importantly, given serious concerns in many quarters that the SDGs would imply responsibilities that many countries did not have the wherewithal to implement, the paper stated that the process would "assess required support for implementation for each SDGs in terms of, inter alia, technology transfer and assistance, capacity building, financial support and investments, [and] institutional architecture (international and regional)." The latter element had a twofold purpose. One was to link the SDGs to the ongoing negotiations in the formal negotiation track of the International Framework for Sustainable Development. The other was to imply that as a global framework, the SDGs would require support and aggregation at international and regional levels.

We were slowly but relentlessly shaping the field for agreement on a revolutionary negotiation format and outcome within the United Nations: a technical body, supported by statisticians, that would bring in technical expertise to advise and help guide the construction of a rigorous metric that sensibly structured the daunting array of issues and themes that would need to be addressed. We wanted to have national expertise inform the process, to encourage member states to tap into their pool of experts to shape an outcome that would be scientifically and technically informed and that built deep ownership across governments and in their respective countries. National experts would also bring firsthand knowledge of what was feasible, what was needed, and how to implement whatever was agreed to. Colombia knew this was the case from the exhaustive national consultations and process that we had already undertaken (see Chapter 4). We knew that to get the kind of robust, transformational framework that was needed, deep expertise, even visionary expertise, was needed. This was not something that diplomats in New York, no matter how seasoned or bright, could deliver. We also wanted to rule out the possibility of a political outcome. We envisioned a process with a technical working group that would encourage experts from across ministries, government research institutions, and specialized agencies to be brought in, with the hope that such experts would be more indifferent to political nuances and positions and spearhead the formulation of a real metric. Given the need for political sign-off and buy-in, we proposed that this body would submit its technical, evidence-based recommendations for approval to the UNGA.

Cognizant of the fact that it is impossible to have substantive deliberations in a political setting and with the participation of all member states, known as an "open-ended" process in UN parlance, we proposed a limited membership. The Rio+20 preparatory process we were then going through—with its seemingly endless lines of bracketed text—was a firsthand experience of what an open-ended exercise could devolve into. However, limiting membership opened up a Pandora's box of concerns over lack of transparency, oblique decisions, and exclusion. We knew we had to address concerns about nontransparency—the climate change meeting in Copenhagen had imploded in part due to perception of a closed process and was still very much in many delegates' minds. Thus, we emphasized the difference between "open" and "open-ended." "Open-ended" meant that it was a process open to all member states, basically operating under the rules of procedure of the UNGA. We proposed instead that it be an "open" process, that is, fully transparent in its deliberations, meeting in full view of anyone who wanted to sit in the room, and that it be webcast. As far as we were concerned, "open" was the only real option for getting a proper metric developed and agreed on. In addition, the concept of "open" was a compromise between what the majority of G77 and China members wanted and what the Western group of countries were calling for.

However, we knew what we were up against. The third option put forward by Mexico in early May during the Third Informal Informal Consultations was an outlier that faced considerable hurdles. The proposal to develop the SDGs framework outside of well-understood processes was not just heretical; for many, it was suicidal and jeopardized any SDGs-related outcome. It essentially called for having the formal negotiation groups that were playing a leading role in the negotiations willingly give up their power and yield to an unknown and untested format. It thus meant giving up the weight and gravitas conferred by speaking on behalf of a significant group of countries. It meant agreeing to a format where individual countries—especially developing countries—might not be able to pull their own weight. Where countries with smaller delegations would not be able to rely on the muscle of a group. Where conditionalities or geopolitical dynamics might skewer the playing field. This was thus a hard, red line for most countries in the G77 and China, as well as for a few other delegations. Many others were not comfortable with the format. Delegates from the EU would tell me, "You do realize that this would mean that the EU would have no role in the negotiations?"

Aware of these concerns, we worked intensely with other delegations, especially across the friends, to frame and set out options for text. The positions put forward by friendly countries such as Mexico or Norway, crafted and defined entirely by the respective delegations, brought the kind of language we considered essential into the negotiations. Other friends in the EU were engaged in similarly intense discussions, trying to ensure progressive alignment on the many fronts of the negotiations, including a robust, technical post-Rio process. For his part, the G77 and China coordinator for the SDGs, Farrukh Khan, was fully aligned with regard to the kind of process needed. However, he had to walk a razor-thin line as any perception within the group that he was not ably and energetically positioning the language favored by the majority would have completely undermined his role.

We were desperately concerned that as the endgame approached, positions regarding the SDGs process after the summit continued to be divided and entrenched. "What about Rio+1?" became my rallying point in endless conversations and consultations. Through these conversations, we realized that a problem with the third option—an evidence-based technical process—was that few could really envision what it would entail.

We reached out to Brazil, which was now at the forefront of taking the SDGs proposal forward, to find out how they planned to push for a robust outcome on the process for developing the SDGs. As the final round of consultations in New York loomed, there was no conclusive response.

We were increasingly worried, seeing a process analogous to the journey to date of the SDGs concept. There was no time for substantive discussions and no clarity as to what a "technical" working group actually entailed, and delegates tended to move into sharply drawn positions within subgroups. The consultations we had engineered in Tarrytown and at the Ford Foundation offices had proven decisive in moving the negotiations forward in terms of broader acceptance of the SDGs concept and principles based on a better understanding of the proposal. The concept notes we had put forward with other allies had helped frame and shape the discussions. We decided that another paper was needed. I brainstormed with my team, trying to find a precedent on which we could base the paper so that it would be easier to understand for all delegations. Isabel Cavelier, who was part of our UN Framework Convention on Climate Change (UNFCCC) delegation, suggested that the Transitional Committee under the UNFCCC, which had delivered the Green Climate Fund, be used as a model. It seemed a perfect fit.

Building on our earlier concept note issued with Peru and the United Arab Emirates, we prepared a new paper where we tried to explain the format of the Transitional Committee in the simplest terms possible and, cognizant of the complexities around the issue, proposed the inclusion in the Zero Draft of a single sentence: "The SDG process will follow the model of the Transitional Committee established under the UNFCCC to develop the GCF" (see Appendix 23). In a way, this paper was analogous to the initial Colombian proposal that sought to ground the SDGs idea in Agenda 21: the aim was to show that it had already been done and establish a common precedent to give delegations more comfort in a new proposal.

I shared the proposal among a few of the friends, and several colleagues signaled that it was a constructive way forward. Khan had been an elected member of the Green Climate Fund's Transitional Committee, and he understood the model perfectly. In line with our agreement with Community of Latin American and Caribbean States (CELAC) and in deference to Brazil, we did not seek endorsements or organize side events or consultations. I framed the document mainly as a conduit for information on the Transitional Committee. Regardless, Brazil was incensed when we started to distribute copies at the beginning of the Third Informal Informal Consultations, interpreting this as a lack of recognition of the agreement in CELAC that Brazil would lead the negotiations. However, time was running out and if there was going to be guidance on this issue, it had to be now. Although we respected Brazil's role, it was essential to help delegates understand that there was an established format around which the third option could be framed. Our third option had to be rendered feasible. As was the case with our previous papers, we aimed to plant a seed and create a reference point for delegates. We felt compelled to act quickly to prevent a lost opportunity of historic dimensions if the traditional UN negotiation formats were to be avoided.

The final round of negotiations in New York (the Third Informal Informal Consultations from May 29 to June 2, 2012) before heading out to Rio confirmed the timeliness of our paper. There was a chasm between delegations on this issue. In an effort at compromise, the Secretariat had included language to the effect that a process led by the UN Secretary-General would be "a country-driven process guided by the General Assembly." The delegations of the United States, Japan, and Switzerland rejected this compromise language, calling for the SDGs to be only "agreed by the UNGA," that is, presented to the UNGA once it had been fully developed by another body. They mostly held out for a process led by the Secretary-General. The G77 and China, along with Turkey, insisted on an intergovernmental process under the UNGA and refused to countenance any other option. The third option that Mexico had introduced earlier, which Colombia and many friends strongly favored as a step in the right direction, was deleted entirely from the final draft outcome text. Such was the playing field on the future SDGs process as we left for Rio for the final round of negotiations.

At this point, Patti and I were incredibly anxious but undeterred. We decided that the paper we had shared on the Transitional Committee had been useful for putting this option on the table, but it had not penetrated the negotiation dynamic. We prepared another paper that we hoped would more clearly translate this option for the SDGs process. It was analogous to an earlier concept paper: just as we had moved from a paper grounding the SDGs idea in Agenda 21 to one more focused on the actual Rio+20 process, we were moving from a first paper that described the Transitional Committee (Appendix 23) to one that elaborated on its relevance for the third option and grounded it in the process by proposing more ambitious language for inclusion in the Zero Draft (Appendix 24). It was a formula that had worked earlier; as we arrived in Rio, we hoped it would work again.

The second paper on the Transitional Committee set out the few areas of consensus, namely, that it be intergovernmental, focused and well structured, and "informed by reviews of existing information, including work already undertaken on indicators and goals, in particular the MDGs, as well as technical inputs from national experts, regional organizations and specialized agencies." The paper spelled out salient characteristics of the Transitional Committee: that it was not just intergovernmental but also geographically balanced; it welcomed relevant inputs from all stakeholders (not only member states); and it was informed by experts. The paper highlighted key characteristics of its structure:

> [The Transitional Committee] was structured in such a way as to facilitate quality inputs and concrete outputs, e.g.:
> - Members were to have the necessary experience and skills;
> - Meetings were open to observers;
> - The [Conference of the Parties] requested that the UNFCCC Secretariat make arrangements with relevant UN agencies to provide second staff to support the work of the Transitional Committee and establish a Technical Support Unit (TSU);
> - For each meeting of the Transitional Committee a set of background papers and notes and scoping papers were prepared by the TSU to inform its work and compile relevant existing information;
> - The work of the Transitional Committee was arranged in four work-streams under a set of co-facilitators, providing clear divisions of responsibility and more detailed work on selected issues;
> - The Transitional Committee clearly documented its work; such documentation included initial elaboration of its working arrangements, as well as reports for each of its meetings detailing its progress.

Based on this analysis, the following negotiation text was proposed in our paper, keeping it as simple as possible so that it might have a better chance of making it through. We outlined a role for both the General Assembly and the Secretary-General in an effort to appease as many delegates as possible:

> SDG 6 alt. We agree that an intergovernmental process should be established to develop SDGs as a key contribution to the post 2015 framework and,
> a. Agree to establish a working group of governmental experts having the necessary experience and skills, on the basis of equitable geographical distribution, to develop recommendations on Sustainable Development Goals; the group shall submit its working arrangements to the General Assembly at its sixty-sixth session, and submitting a report on its work to the General Assembly at its sixty-seventh session;

  b. Request the Secretary-General to make arrangements to provide assistance and services that may be required to support the working group, including secondment of staff from relevant agencies and institutions.

Since the option Mexico had proposed on May 2 (see Appendix 14) had been deleted, our goal was to propose minimal language that stood a chance of remaining on the negotiation table. We shared this new paper informally among delegates, trying to broaden the playing field as we all headed into the final round of negotiations. We did not know how the stars would align in Rio.

Perseverance and Leadership in Rio de Janeiro

As recounted in Chapter 8, once in Rio de Janeiro the negotiations became even more fraught. Tensions were running high. The imminent arrival of heads of state meant we were coming down to the wire. Consultations in the G77 and China were impossibly difficult given the starkly opposing views held by members. For Khan, the group coordinator, the nature of the process to define the SDGs was potentially a time bomb. Yet the highest priority for both Khan and me was to find a way to get the third option that Mexico had proposed back on the table, following the model of the Transitional Committee, as it had yet again disappeared from the negotiation text. After the first meeting of the new SDGs group facilitated by Selwin Hart, it was clear that both the EU and the G77 and China were largely sticking to the options preferred by their respective majorities.

Building on Hart's request that we help find a pathway forward, and based on extensive consultations, Khan's experience in the GCF process, and the papers Colombia had issued, Khan and I worked to prepare a new proposal that delivered on the ambitious outcome we wanted while navigating the complex balancing act he had to deliver on. As lead negotiator for the G77 and China, he had to respect the majority's wishes to have a process under UNGA. Thus, we worked on language that respected the group's insistence on the need to establish an intergovernmental entity, while pushing the envelope by calling for the establishment of a steering committee to oversee the process—the equivalent of a technical body. I was not entirely happy with that term because I wanted to have an explicit reference to the fact that it was an "open" forum, but accepted language that Khan considered was clearer to many. A day after arriving in Rio de Janeiro, on June 14, Khan submitted this draft compromise language to the co-chairs (see Appendix 19):

SDG 6 alt. We agree to establish an intergovernmental process on SDGs under the United Nations General Assembly that is inclusive, transparent and open to all stakeholders with a view to proposing global sustainable development goals to be agreed by the UN General Assembly. An Intergovernmental Steering Committee will oversee and guide this process. It shall comprise XX members nominated by Member States through the five UN regional groups and serving in their own personal capacity with the aim of achieving fair, balanced and equitable geographic representation. At the outset, this Committee will decide on its method of work including developing modalities for the involvement of relevant stakeholders and expertise including Major Groups in its work. It will produce an interim report to the UNGA in 2013 and a final report with recommendations to the UNGA in 2014.

Based on the Transitional Committee model and Khan's experience, we proposed another paragraph:

SDG alt. bis. The process needs to be coordinated and coherent with the processes considering the post-2015 development agenda. In order to provide technical support to this process and to the work of the Intergovernmental Steering Committee, we request the United Nations Secretary-General to establish an inter-agency technical support team, drawing on all relevant expert advice.

This language created a new playing field for the negotiations. The negotiations in the coming days would allow delegations to further shape the proposal, but it clearly laid out a third option. Although nominally under UNGA—Khan had to respect the position of the majority in G77 and China—in fact it would be an intergovernmental process that would develop and propose the goals, not the UNGA itself. We knew other non-G77 delegations would reject the reference to a process being under UNGA, but Khan had remained faithful to the majority G77 and China position. Colombia and other friends were ready to ensure that the proposal explicitly stated that it would be led by experts. At this juncture, what was critical was the overarching model, which was nonpolitical (to the degree possible insofar as it was populated by people from governments) but also truly participatory. The contours of the future Open Working Group were being laid out on the negotiation table.

The play over the next seventy-two hours evidenced the degree to which negotiations are often shaped and defined by individuals. Our text succeeded in decisively changing the negotiation landscape. Ahead of the next round of negotiations the following day, Hart issued a new draft consensus text as the basis for further discussion (see Appendix 20). It was electrifying. As we had foreseen, by taking our text as a foundation and adjusting it to make it acceptable to as wide a range of delegations as possible, we had a proposal for a truly revolutionary process. Not only was it not under UNGA, it was also as distant from the genesis of the MDGs as possible. At long last, an expert-led, independent, open body was being created to define the SDGs framework. This new draft text was potentially transformational:

> We resolve to establish an inclusive and transparent intergovernmental process on SDGs that is open to all stakeholders with a view to proposing global sustainable development goals to be agreed by the United National General Assembly. A Steering Committee shall be constituted no later than the opening of the 67th session of the UNGA and shall comprise XX experts nominated by Member States through the five UN regional groups with the aim of achieving fair and balanced geographic representation. At the outset, this Committee will decide on its method of work including developing modalities to ensure the full involvement of relevant stakeholders and expertise from civil society in its work in order to provide a diversity of perspectives and experience. It will submit a report to the 68th session of the UNGA containing a proposal for sustainable development goals.

The discussion was intense in the SDGs negotiation group. Salient, recurring issues included what the roles of the scientific community and the UN would be; whether civil society representatives could participate and how; whether experts could participate, and how they would be selected and/or nominated; the number of members; how nonmembers would be informed of its deliberations or whether nonmembers could participate or observe its deliberations; the nature of recommendations or report that would be generated by the entity; and the role of UNGA in reviewing or adopting the outcome of the entity and what session of the UNGA would receive it. On the last issue, some felt it should be an expedited process, with the group constituted by the sixty-seventh UNGA session in September 2012 and delivering something by the sixty-eighth session in 2013. Others thought a lengthier timeline was needed. Overriding all these considerations was the persistent question of whether the body would be under UNGA rules or would be an independent body that would—or not, in the view of at least one delegation—report back to the UNGA. Many vocal G77 and China delegations were furious. The option they preferred, under UNGA, had disappeared. For our part, although welcoming the progress, we insisted that the group needed to be characterized as open and queried the characterization of a steering committee. We wanted to have the open descriptor front and center to emphasize the distinction with the traditional open-ended format.

For the G77 and China coordinator, the discussions called for particularly dexterous positioning. Khan was representing a group that had had divergent takes on almost every aspect of the SDGs narrative. Many could countenance allowing the SDGs to go forward only if they had the assurance of a process that they felt they had control over. This was the final, unbreachable red line. This new text was not under UNGA and was proposing an entirely new format that would, they feared, effectively sideline the G77 and China. The fact that it called for equitable geographical representation did nothing to assuage these fears. That the committee would itself define its method of work also pointed to a possible outcome that could marginalize the concerns and positions regarded as core to the development agenda by a majority of the group's members. To avoid a disastrous rupture in the G77 and China, Khan opted to hew strictly to the G77 position, insisting on a process under the UNGA, because otherwise he risked open rebellion. The EU with a few other Western countries stuck firmly to a process led by the Secretary-General with participation at the level of heads of state. Ultimately, the SDGs session concluded with no significant advances, although delegates expressed appreciation for the facilitator's effort to propose a compromise text. This late in the game, no one wanted to concede, holding out for a possible win as part of a larger negotiated package. We trusted that as the negotiations entered the final rounds, the combination of views would ultimately force a consensus position around this new option.

Khan's balancing act, as seen in the previous chapter, was unable to avoid a nasty reckoning at the next G77 coordination meeting. Yet in a way, it cleared the air. With time running out, Khan and I, together with many of the friends, agreed that we needed to get more delegations to voice support for the third option now on the table. We held hurried meetings with other delegates, spelling out the merits and benefits of this option, using the second paper on the Transitional Committee we had prepared. Several friends played a decisive role, many helping build up support in the groups they belonged to and across other delegations and constituencies. Many of these delegates were climate negotiators and were familiar with the Transitional Committee model. Many European friends had been supportive of the idea from the outset, but within the EU the idea had faced opposition because many preferred a process led by the Secretary-General. However, with the passing of the hours, it became more and more evident that those that did not want a process under the UNGA needed to hedge their positions. We worked quietly but intensely in the hallways to get key delegations that still supported the option of a Secretary-General-led process to put their support behind the new option. The uncertainty about how the negotiations were going to be run the few final days before the official start of the conference added to the tension and unease.

One key issue that remained outstanding was what to propose in terms of the actual composition of the steering committee, as in our previous submission to the SDGs facilitator we had simply written in "XX." We wanted to unpack the various battles one by one. Back in the kitchen, where we had been holding our brainstormings, we pondered various options. After some deliberation, we concluded that as a starting point, the text could call for a total of thirty representatives. The math was simple: six delegates from each of the five UN regional groups (Latin America and Caribbean Group, Western Europe and Others, Eastern Europe, Africa, and Asia). These delegates would provide for the internal, equitable representation each needed. In any case, we fully expected protracted negotiations in the coming days—no one believed the Brazilians could get agreement on a final consensus text without more rounds of negotiations—and we figured that thirty was a sensible baseline because in the ensuing negotiations, the number would likely spiral upward to sixty or more. Thirty seemed like a good starting point. Khan handed our language to the co-chairs.

There was rapid progress in narrowing down the options on the table; the backroom diplomacy was paying off. By the next day, June 15, when the SDGs splinter group facilitated by Hart met for the second time, only two options remained on the table: the option under the UNGA that the G77 and China had proposed months earlier, and the steering committee option. This was the state of play when the proceedings shifted the next day, June 16, into the mode of the Pre-Conference Informal Negotiations presided over by Brazil.

As discussed in the previous chapter, in a watershed moment for the SDGs, in the draft outcome text presented by Itamaraty, only one option was left on the table, the one creating the steering committee (see Appendix 21). Unbeknownst to us at the time, discussions on these options were also taking place at high levels in the UN. There were concerns among some delegations and in the UN that the option of a Secretary-General-led process had disappeared. Within UNDESA, which was playing a key role behind the scenes in terms of following the negotiations and crafting consensus language, Nikhil Seth argued for the importance of an intergovernmental process.

In the next round of negotiations in the SDGs negotiation group on Sunday morning, June 17, 2012, the decisive outstanding issue for all delegations was the nature of the process to define and develop the SDGs. The Brazilian text, which was entirely based on the Compilation Table of the negotiation text curated and crafted by UNDESA (see Appendix 26) and which had been issued the night before, maintained the tenor of the previous facilitator's text. Delegations were once again faced with a single, stark paragraph with only one option: an independent intergovernmental body. As a result of the preceding rounds of negotiation, the ambition of the language was notably strengthened: rather than having the intergovernmental process on SDGs "propose" global sustainable development goals, the new text affirmed that the process would "develop" these goals. There was one other paragraph numbered SDG5 on the SDGs process, which simply requested the Secretary-General to establish an interagency technical support team.

This round of the negotiations was a game changer. In issuing a negotiation draft that included only the third option, now framed as an open working group, the Brazilian presidency was signaling their full support for this pathway. At one of the most decisive points in the negotiation, Brazil played a strong hand and threw their considerable weight behind a nonpolitical forum to develop the SDGs. Given how fraught and politicized the issue was by then, this evidenced their strategic understanding of the long-term process.

That afternoon, a G77 and China coordination meeting was convened to discuss the draft outcome text from Brazil. Given the open confrontations that had occurred the preceding days, although passions were running high, efforts were made to keep the discussions on an even keel. Key delegations were adamant that if the process was not under UNGA then there could be no agreement at all. Without the G77 and China consensus there was no possibility of defining a process going forward. After tense and fruitless discussions, as the meeting was breaking up, Khan and I quickly asked key negotiators and interested parties in the room to stay on a bit longer. This was a make-or-break moment.

We ended up sitting in an awkward circle against the wood paneling of the desks, some on the floor, some on the few chairs we could find. We all knew each other from years of negotiations. At this late hour, Khan and I held onto the belief that some kind of consensus was possible. We reminded our colleagues that this was the first global agenda proposed by the Global South. We insisted that such an agenda could drive (force, if needed) the kind of major transformations needed to truly address inequality, poverty, and global public goods issues. Finally, I affirmed that while some of the concerns voiced were valid, some of the best negotiators in the world were there, together, in that room. Surely, together, we would be able to manage any threats that might arise in the future negotiations under the new format, and the gains in terms of a truly global agenda were also ours to materialize. Khan described how other groups' positions could be managed and how the new format could be capitalized to advance our core group concerns. There was a long silence and, finally, nodding. At last critical members of the G77 and China were willing to consider the establishment of a more technical working group that would not be under UNGA rules. From our perspective, this was—and history validated it—a decisive breakthrough in the negotiations. To this day Khan and I remember these negotiations as among the most difficult in our professional careers and certainly the most bitter and acrimonious.

That evening, the SDGs group was convened again, and attention centered on reviewing revised text proposed by Brazil for paragraph 251 (see Appendix 25) on the SDGs process. Many of the same issues rapidly surfaced. Other delegations echoed that there could not be a "repeat of the MDGs process," meaning a process that was not led by governments. Some were concerned that the new format would side-line governments again, even if in a very different way than had happened with the MDGs. Brazil noted that countries would appoint the experts to the committee. But the EU and a few others raised concerns regarding how the process could be led by a steering committee. The conversation evolved, as several delegates pointed to the benefits of a process that could ensure technical expertise and have political oversight in the guise of final consideration by the UNGA. New language had been proposed to ensure the involvement of all stakeholders, including "the scientific community and the UN system." There were wide-ranging discussions centered on the need for science-based inputs, how to ensure substantive inputs from a wide range of stakeholders, how experts should be nominated, and how to ensure political oversight over the process. There were also concerns that simply submitting "a proposal for sustainable development goals" to the UNGA was insufficient because it did not define an actual role for the UNGA. Several questioned the composition of the committee with thirty members. Khan and I still expected the number to be ramped up during the consultations, but our Brazilian lead, in keeping with the rigid instructions issued by our host country, did not open up the actual language for negotiation.

The OWG: A Reality Against All Odds

On Monday, June 18—which unbeknownst to us at the time turned out to be the last day of negotiations—the SDGs negotiation group met again to review the new text proposed by Brazil.[5] The main outstanding issue for all delegations remained the nature of the SDGs process after Rio+20. A few delegations voiced opposition to the proposal on the table, while others focused on specific aspects—whether there should be experts, the role of the UNGA, the name of the group that would take the world forward. There were also concerns that "initial input to the work of the working group" would be provided by the Secretary-General without input from governments. Some questioned the number of representatives, noting that thirty was too low and proposed other options. There were concerns about the designation of experts to the intergovernmental process, as several considered that this was too constraining and that it should be up to governments to determine whom they nominated.

The meeting ended as all meetings had since the Brazilian presidency took over the negotiations two days before. We were urged to undertake consultations over unresolved issues and bring solutions to the Brazilian team. Once again, there had effectively been no negotiation, just another informed discussion. Khan and I wondered, as we left the room, what would happen to the thirty slots we had defined for the SDGs process, a number we had proposed as a floor, anticipating that it would ratchet up during the next round of negotiations. By that point, we were all exhausted and confused. We were unclear about the next steps, given that our hosts had been adamant that the final outcome document had to be defined that very day.

Less than twenty hours later, with no further negotiations, the Brazilian presidency presented the final draft of the document, *The Future We Want* (see Appendix 27). There were significant changes that reflected the intense bilateral consultations the Brazilian delegation had engineered over the intervening forty-eight hours and the fierce discussions in the SDGs consultations. Paragraph 251 on the SDGs process had undergone a series of important changes (these changes are emphasized in italics below):

> 251. We resolve to establish an inclusive and transparent intergovernmental process on SDGs that is open to all stakeholders with a view to developing global sustainable development goals to be agreed by the United Nations General Assembly. *An open working group* shall be constituted no later than the opening of the 67th session of the UNGA and shall comprise of *thirty representatives,* nominated by Member States through the five UN regional groups with the aim of achieving fair, *equitable* and balanced geographic representation. At the outset,

this open working group will decide on its method of work, including developing modalities, to ensure the full involvement of relevant stakeholders and expertise from civil society, *the scientific community and the UN system* in its work in order to provide a diversity of perspectives and experience. It will submit a report to the 68th session of the UNGA containing a proposal for sustainable development goals *for consideration and appropriate action.*

Against all odds, the Open Working Group was established, a momentous decision that was formally ratified with the adoption of *The Future We Want.* The creation of the Open Working Group proved decisive, under the able leadership of co-chairs Macharia Kamau of Kenya and Csaba Kőrösi of Hungary, in enabling a science-based, expert-driven process that was ultimately able to deliver the SDGs framework. Rio+20 was thus foundational and defined the contours of a bold new global agenda, better fit for purpose to tackle the interlocked crises of the Anthropocene.

Postscript

The SDGs framework was developed through the Open Working Group, which met thirteen times from 2013 to 2014 under the leadership of Csaba Kőrösi and Macharia Kamau. Prior to starting up, it took seven months of arduous negotiations among the UN regional groups to determine which countries would participate in the thirty seats. Finally, member states agreed to use an innovative and constituency-based representation, and most of the seats ended up being shared by two or more countries. In practice, this meant that seventy countries sat on the OWG. Critically, the OWG allowed for the active participation of nongovernmental stakeholders and benefited from the expertise of civil society, the private sector, and the scientific community. Over forty UN agencies provided inputs through the UN System Technical Support Team under the umbrella of the UN System Task Team on the post-2015 development agenda.

In July 2014, the OWG adopted a report containing 17 proposed SDGs and 169 targets, to be submitted to the UNGA for consideration and action at its sixty-eighth session in 2015. In January 2015, a process of intergovernmental negotiations on the post-2015 development agenda began. UN decision A/69/L.46 stated that "the proposal of the OWG on SDGs will be the main basis for integrating the SDGs into the post-2015 development agenda, while other inputs will also be taken into consideration." The final document was arrived at after eight negotiation sessions that culminated in August 2015. On September 25, 2015, at the UN Sustainable Development Summit, the UNGA formally adopted document A/70/L.1, "Transforming Our World: The 2030 Agenda for Sustainable Development." The SDGs are at its core. Box 9.2 sets out the seventeen agreed SDGs.

Box 9.2   The Sustainable Development Goals

Goal 1. End poverty in all its forms everywhere.

Goal 2. End hunger, achieve food security and improved nutrition, and promote sustainable agriculture.

Goal 3. Ensure healthy lives and promote well-being for all at all ages.

Goal 4. Ensure inclusive and equitable quality education and promote lifelong learning opportunities for all.

Goal 5. Achieve gender equality and empower all women and girls.

Goal 6. Ensure availability and sustainable management of water and sanitation for all.

Goal 7. Ensure access to affordable, reliable, sustainable, and modern energy for all.

Goal 8. Promote sustained, inclusive, and sustainable economic growth, full and productive employment, and decent work for all.

Goal 9. Build resilient infrastructure, promote inclusive and sustainable industrialization, and foster innovation.

Goal 10. Reduce inequality within and among countries.

Goal 11. Make cities and human settlements inclusive, safe, resilient, and sustainable.

Goal 12. Ensure sustainable consumption and production patterns.

Goal 13. Take urgent action to combat climate change and its impacts.*

Goal 14. Conserve and sustainably use the oceans, seas, and marine resources for sustainable development.

Goal 15. Protect, restore, and promote sustainable use of terrestrial ecosystems, sustainably manage forests, combat desertification, halt and reverse land degradation, and halt biodiversity loss.

Goal 16. Promote peaceful and inclusive societies for sustainable development, provide access to justice for all, and build effective, accountable, and inclusive institutions at all levels.

Goal 17. Strengthen the Means of Implementation and revitalize the Global Partnership for Sustainable Development.

Note: *Acknowledging that the United Nations Framework Convention on Climate Change is the primary international, intergovernmental forum for negotiating the global response to climate change.

Notes

1. Because we were not confident that we would be able to set up the kind of process we envisioned, we fought for a third outcome to create future guardrails for the SDGs: agreement on a preliminary, indicative set of goals. As we have seen, this negotiation track ultimately failed.

2. The UNGA sessions are counted starting with the first one in 1946–1947. The sixty-seventh session refers to the 2011–2012 session. Resolutions, reports, and so on are defined according to this nomenclature.

3. Appendix 14 contains the Mexican proposal in paragraph CST106 alt 2, which is also found in Box 9.1.

4. See Chapter 6 for an in-depth discussion of this fourth concept paper.

5. The text on the SDGs process was essentially unchanged, except for a few key additions: (1) it was to have thirty representatives; (2) "the scientific community and the UN system" would participate in addition to civil society; and (3) a report to the sixty-eighth session of the UNGA would be submitted with a proposal for SDGs for "consideration and appropriate action."

10

Transformative Implementation

Transformative implementation is hard. It requires creating movements to amplify the political space and will for transformative policies, investments, and strategies. The pull of the status quo, of what we came to understand as an MDG+ mentality, needs to be overcome. The Sustainable Development Goals (SDGs) journey yields instructive insights and lessons that may be germane to some of the challenges we face in the coming decades in tackling the crises of the Anthropocene.

The SDGs as we know them today—a largely actionable and measurable metric that was negotiated with the participation of all UN member states and a stunning number of constituencies—are proof that the boundaries of what is possible are fluid. The forces arrayed against an idea that so many considered radical and impractical were daunting, and there were many turns and moments where the process could have gone awry. Yet, ultimately, the idea not only survived but thrived. Credit goes to the two co-chairs of the Open Working Group, who understood and maximized the transformative potential of this format. It is interesting to recall that almost as soon as the Rio+20 conference finished, many pundits rushed to label the conference a dismal failure. Few realized that in the final political declaration was the seed of a revamped international development agenda.

The Relevance of the SDGs

For us, a most critical and long-lasting contribution of the SDGs is the fact that they have become a common language that all manner of constituencies, initiatives, and strategies around the planet are using to earmark their actions and convey that these are part of a bigger whole, alluding to shared responsibilities and intentions and visions. The SDGs offer coherence and structure for systemic changes, and for the vast range of targeted and interlinked actions needed to deliver such changes. In doing so, they enable practitioners, politicians, entrepreneurs, local authorities, scientists, and diplomats to talk about the complexity of development in a clearer and more concise way that is broadly understood. Just in this they have already been transformative. The SDGs offer both a lens through which to understand the magnitude and scope of the interrelated crises we are facing as well as pathways for crafting innovative, durable solutions that can drive disruption—to increase our resilience, decrease our emissions, and establish building blocks for a more equitable world. The SDGs have become both a grammar for the development agenda and a shorthand for systemic action.

Although it is beyond the purview of this book to provide a comprehensive analysis of SDGs implementation since 2015, in the years since their adoption whole ecosystems have organically grown around them. Innumerable organizations, universities, think tanks, and research institutes have spawned tools and analyses to help countries, businesses, and constituencies implement the SDGs in the integrated, systemic way that we envisioned for them and track results. Equally important, across the private and financial sectors, the SDGs have become a referent, initially helping shape corporate social responsibility standards but also, increasingly and more decisively, incentivizing changes in the actual business models of companies around the world. Vibrant coalitions have come together around specific targets, capitalizing on the convening power and visibility that the SDGs afford to a range of priority thematic areas. Critically, many governments have structured their national development plans around the SDGs and created governance spaces to advance more coherent development action across sectors. On the formal front within the UN, as established in the Rio Declaration, the High-Level Political Forum, which meets yearly in July, has progressively involved more and more countries voluntarily reporting their progress on SDGs implementation.[1]

This must be understood as only a beginning. We are far from making the SDGs a reality across our societies and economies and mindsets. Trends in poverty, inequality, and planetary boundaries attest that we have not begun to really take up SDGs implementation as envisioned. Starting with our collective mindset, we must change how we frame and understand the problems to be tackled. We must catch ourselves in the act of simply adjusting the status quo and willing ourselves to believe that that will somehow deliver change. It is sobering that a key rallying cry to action in the midst of the Covid-19 pandemic as we write this book is to "build back better." Or a variation, "to build back greener." With earnest intent, humans keep trying to get the outcomes that science demands without commensurate transformative efforts, as if somehow doing the same but "better" will ultimately deliver different outcomes or pathways. It is exactly the same mindset and approach that insisted, back in 2012, that all we needed was to tweak the Millennium Development Goals (MDGs) and continue with development as usual. In the absence of Colombia's proposal and efforts with a dedicated cohort of colleagues, in 2015 the world would in all likelihood have simply adopted an MDG+ framework—and this narrow, divisive, and inadequate framework would have been our collective touchstone for tackling the multitude of development challenges the world faces over the coming decades.

The relentless climate and biodiversity crises, as well as the growing and increasingly entrenched inequality that the pandemic has both highlighted and aggravated, demand a collective commitment to building back differently. Radically differently. And yet the collective drive for transformation is, ultimately, absent. The reality of the massive fiscal spending by governments triggered by the Covid-19 pandemic shows that once again we are merely massaging the status quo rather than driving any kind of deep-rooted change. Of the US$14.6 trillion in announced spending across the world's largest fifty countries in 2020, only US$1.9 trillion (13.0 percent) was directed to long-term recovery-type measures, and of that, US$341 billion (18.0 percent) to green recovery initiatives. Considering total spending, only US$368 billion (2.5 percent) was announced for green initiatives.[2] At the same time, our current emissions trajectory is heading to at least 2.4C degrees of warming[3] and global power generation from coal is surging to an all-time high.[4]

A Single Agenda

The system-wide pathways and responses that the SDGs seek to drive are those needed to tackle the climate change, biodiversity, and pollution crises. To overcome recalcitrant poverty and inequality. We are encouraged that there is growing understanding and acceptance that integrated implementation is key—whether across jurisdictions or supply chains or energy systems. And yet, as a global society we maintain divides across the agendas and platforms that have been set up to deal with problems that are ultimately one and the same.

The fact that the SDGs and climate change are seen as separate and distinct is merely another symptom of incumbent mindsets and narrow, siloed thinking. The only reason climate change is not more explicitly detailed in the SDGs is because in 2011 and 2012, the highly charged climate negotiations under the UN Framework Convention on Climate Change were running parallel to the post-2015 process. There were fears that including more explicit language on climate in the SDGs could derail or set back the Framework Convention negotiations, which were struggling to advance a more ambitious outcome, with challenging contexts and developments in prior conferences of the parties. Yet even if the two agendas grew out of completely separate intergovernmental processes, they must be implemented as one—just as the SDGs arose from the forced merger of the Rio track and the MDGs track. Colombia ultimately forced this consolidation to happen in 2012 to yield the SDGs; who will step up and do the same?

Progress on the climate and the SDGs translates equally into the imperative of tackling the biodiversity extinction crisis. Somehow, as a species, we are mostly still under the delusion that what happens to biodiversity is an unfortunate externality, a regrettable effect of our production and consumption choices but ultimately not relevant to humans. As we wantonly breach planetary boundaries, the arrogance and grievousness of this mindset is becoming increasingly palpable; the Covid-19 pandemic brought to the fore unexpected pathways of devastating impacts. There is in fact nothing wholly environmental. There is a full circle between the progressive degradation of ecosystems, the relentless dimming of biodiversity, deepening food and water insecurity, and the increasing waves of climate refugees we are already witnessing. On the ground and in terms of planetary systems, the climate and biodiversity crises are interconnected—and compounding, as is the convergent crisis of pollution and waste. Recent research indicates that in 2021, 55 percent of global GDP was moderately or highly dependent on biodiversity and ecosystem services.[5] The SDGs evidence that ultimately all environmental matters will transcend into the economic and social realms.

For example, the UNFCCC Conference of the Parties (COP26) in 2021 in Glasgow, Scotland, was a watershed in that natural climate solutions and the role of Indigenous peoples and local communities took on a new and urgent primacy, with far-reaching commitments to halt deforestation. This time we hope that improved monitoring and traceability systems, as well as more active and decided engagement by the private sector, will actually deliver on the intentions. Several coalitions to tackle various fronts of the climate crisis were launched. The question now is how the many commitments and coalitions from Glasgow will be furthered in the next global gathering at the CBD COP15 in Kunming, China. What will it take to have a single agenda that creates implacable momentum by progressively capitalizing on and leveraging the still widely insufficient funding and political will needed to turn our economies and societies around? How do we create *a single arc of ambition* linking all these agendas together so that the efforts of businesses, the finance sector, communities, governments, and science can progressively add up?

These agendas also underpin the growing equity crisis—within countries, among countries, between generations—that will be the defining sociopolitical factor of the coming decades. This book was written as the 2021 IPCC report was published.[6] The growing reach of climate-related impacts in countries at all levels of development includes wildfires, droughts, floods, and major storms and hurricanes. No degree of exceptionalism can be claimed in the face of this phenomenon. Millions more will be progressively left behind as climate change narrows the safe operating space for life as we know it,[7] and it will become progressively more difficult to lift—and keep—them out of poverty. Achieving and sustaining equity for humankind is indelibly rooted in addressing the relentless progression of emissions and species loss that are ultimately irreversible. Only through integrated approaches will humanity be able to imagine, engineer, and deliver comprehensive solutions that effectively address the web of drivers and values that make the world so profoundly unequal and unsustainable. It is imperative that we break out of the ethos and mindset that led us into the current quandary. The SDGs can help us remove sectoral blinders and mobilize the collective political will and financial muscle to transmute the systems that gird our lives and are determining the destiny of ecosystems and other species. The SDGs are no silver bullet, but they are a blueprint for tackling the imperatives of sustainable development in ways that are multisectoral, forward-looking, inclusive, and—necessarily—disruptive.

Lessons from an Improbable Journey

The SDGs journey was in many ways both improbable and unexpected. Certainly at the outset we had no inkling of the challenges and opposition we would encounter. As the process unfolded, a small movement germinated around the SDGs that grew and flourished over the next few years. This movement was ultimately responsible for the scope and ambition of the new framework and for its broad uptake across countries, constituencies, and companies. Throughout that journey, we learned many lessons and, as we wrote this book, we reflected on a few that may be relevant to others who also seek to spur disruption and transformation.

Our first lesson is an imperative: learn to recognize when an existing mindset and framework is offered up as if it were new or transformative. This is what would have happened had the MDGs simply been rolled over in 2015, merely revamped and updated. Had that been the case, without a transformational approach, it would have been impossible to even deliver on MDGs+. As we complete our work on this book in 2021, the siren call of "build back better" or "build back greener" threatens to lead us into the same trap.

Our second lesson is that resistance is often proportional to the magnitude of the shift you are trying to make happen. If everyone is against you, you are likely onto something. This means that you must have dogged confidence in the endgame you believe to be transformational (or necessary for transformation), and never give up. If you have a vision or idea, persist. Patti used to say I was a Rottweiler, refusing to let go no matter how desperate or desolate the situation seemed. Tenacity is needed to build a movement and achieve breakthroughs.

Our third lesson is that a truly global agenda cannot be based on national interests. Colombia stood to gain nothing by advancing this idea. Moreover, we tackled and thought through valid concerns around potential conditionalities and possible repercussions on development priorities. Implementation was always going to be as challenging for Colombia as for others. I remember an intense discussion on the need to have a goal on energy with delegates from West Africa, a region where many countries are highly reliant on fossil fuel exports. I was told that I did not understand what such a goal could entail and that I did not care because it was not relevant for Colombia. They were shocked to learn that Colombia is actually a major exporter of fossil fuels. Shock turned to bewilderment—why in the world would Colombia push for a goal on energy? (In addition to the fact that we were proposing a new global agenda as objectively as possible, another factor that made Colombia such an effective conduit for this idea is the fact that we were perceived as a marginal country and thus an improbable champion for such an agenda.)

Our fourth lesson concerns the need to bring others along. Facilitating a shift is not just an act of faith but also one of translation. To build and maintain momentum for systemic change, a fertile ecosystem across diverse constituencies and (often opposing) interests has to be created and nurtured. At its simplest, it speaks to the need to make it relevant. *Relevance* speaks to the capacity to help a range of interests, constituencies, and leaders understand a proposal in terms they can relate to and understand. Although it might seem counterintuitive, it is equally important to help people understand why they should support an idea and why they oppose it. This is what we aimed for—especially as the process was getting underway—with the consultations in Bogotá and Tarrytown and the endless side events and informal meetings we hosted or participated in together with the friends. Certainly, we wanted to build a better understanding of the value and virtue of the SDGs idea, but we were equally keen to help those who disagreed with it understand the premises on which they founded their position. This had two pay-offs: it enabled people to crystallize their ideas and thus made it more feasible to have informed discussions; most important, it demonstrated that there was not a hidden agenda and that we meant it when we affirmed that we wanted to co-create the proposal, that it was a journey we were all on together. In this process of collectively unpacking the idea, many gradually came to see why it was relevant and useful for advancing their own interests. As they became translators, they embarked on the pathway to becoming champions.

Our fifth lesson—the flip side of the coin for broad engagement—concerns the need to ensure that what is proposed is actionable with a transformational intent. In other words, there has to be the understanding and the will to ensure that action will decisively break out of entrenched or incumbent domains and result in deep changes across systems. The story of the struggle to create the Open Working Group speaks precisely to this. What was the point of agreeing to a concept for a new metric if the process for getting there did not exist? Our years of experience in multilateral negotiations indicated that under a business-as-usual scenario, the idea would devolve into either an extensive shopping list around areas where there was already consensus or some kind of political declaration. It is telling that the hardest struggles in the Rio+20 process were precisely around this post-Rio process, as we recount in Chapter 9. As humans we may ultimately make peace with radical ideas and ambitious announcements but too often balk at the actions that will create real shifts that actually deliver. The penchant for summits, high-level panels, and other vainglorious events where grand announcements and commitments can be made with no accountability ultimately reinforces the status quo. The question always needs to be, what will it take to make it happen?

Our sixth lesson builds on the fifth: deep change is often only possible by working around formal processes or established pathways that have locked in existing mindsets and understandings of what is possible or desirable. In the case of the SDGs, the breakthrough trail was one of informal diplomacy. By forging a small but determined coalition, we were able to ultimately subvert two established processes and bridge the enduring chasm between them: the global environmental negotiations that have yielded international treaties and summits like Rio+20 in one track and the global development arena and its MDGs in the other. We were also able to change the agenda for Rio+20, which had already been defined with a UN resolution. Applying this lesson now challenges us to imagine how the needed political will, policy space, and financial realignment can be metabolized to activate and force the dramatic shifts needed in the face of such interlinked, mutually reinforcing crises.

This leads us to our seventh, most vital lesson: everyone counts. As we explained in Chapter 1, it takes a village. The SDGs idea gained traction and momentum because it was built from the bottom up, through a widely divergent and inclusive process that, while recognizing the need to align an intergovernmental dynamic, saw civil society as equals at the table. With the exception of the March 2012 consultation at the Ford Foundation, which was an extension of negotiations, all the international consultations we convened included civil society representatives, and we ensured they had a prominent seat and an active voice at the table. In terms of governments, we sought to engage actively across all regional groups as well as with negotiation groups that have helped bring attention to common realities in different arenas, including the least developed countries, the small island developing states, and the landlocked developing countries.

"It Always Seems Impossible Until It's Done."
—Nelson Mandela

The story of the SDGs is a story of how the reinforcing ripples of individual initiative, collective action, and multilateralism can deliver unexpected change. It speaks to the fact that vision, perseverance, and translation can change what is deemed possible and desirable, and bring about profound changes in mindsets, values, and actions. This book is an invitation to each of us, in our daily lives, to shift lifestyles, reduce our impact, demand from our leaders, and disrupt. I have often said that the "mother of all SDGs" is SDG12 on Sustainable Consumption and Production patterns because delivering on this goal will require far-reaching, systemic changes in ways that include most of the other SDGs' targets. Critically, it will demand action at all levels, from individual consumers and voters to governments and corporations. We must all do something. We must hold governments and the financial and productive sectors accountable to the commitments implicit in the SDGs and in the climate change and biodiversity agendas. The genesis of the SDGs proves that it is possible to massively disrupt the status quo, and once a new vision takes hold, many are inspired to action. Bold synergies are now needed to simultaneously achieve net-zero emissions by 2050, stem the destruction of and protect our biodiversity, and boost equity for people around the globe. Help make it happen.

Notes

1. The High-Level Political Forum on Sustainable Development is the main UN platform in which governments report about the progress and implementation of the SDGs. The follow-up and review are conducted in a transparent and open manner.

2. O'Callaghan and Murdock (2020).

3. Climate Action Tracker (2021), 6.

4. Coal (2021), 32.

5. Kelly (2020).

6. IPCC (2021).

7. Rockström et al. (2009).

Acronyms

ALBA	Bolivarian Alliance for the Peoples of Our America
CARICOM	Caribbean Community
CBD	Convention on Biological Diversity
CBDR	common but differentiated responsibilities
CELAC	Community of Latin American and Caribbean States
COP	Conference of the Parties
CSD	Commission on Sustainable Development
CST	co-chairs' suggested text
DEFRA	UK Department of Environment, Food, and Rural Affairs
DESA	UN Department of Economic and Social Affairs
DFID	UK Department for International Development
ECLAC	Economic Commission for Latin America and the Caribbean
ECOSOC	UN Economic and Social Council
GCF	Green Climate Fund
IGO	intergovernmental organization
IFSD	International Framework for Sustainable Development
JPOI	Johannesburg Plan of Implementation
LDC	least developed country
MDGs	Millennium Development Goals
MEA	multilateral environmental agreement
MoI	Means of Implementation
NCST	new co-chairs' suggested text

ODA	official development assistance
OECD	Organisation for Economic Co-operation and Development
OWG	Open Working Group
SDGs	Sustainable Development Goals
SIDS	small island developing states
TSU	Technical Support Unit
UAE	United Arab Emirates
UNCCD	UN Convention to Combat Desertification
UNCSD	UN Conference on Sustainable Development
UNCTAD	United Nations Conference on Trade and Development
UNDP	UN Development Programme
UNEP	UN Environment Programme
UNFCCC	UN Framework Convention on Climate Change
UNGA	UN General Assembly
UNSG	UN Secretary-General
WRI	World Resources Institute

Timeline of the
SDGs Process

2010

May 17–19   First session of the Preparatory Committee for UNCSD
                   (PrepCom I), New York

2011

January   *Initial SDGs idea proposed**
January 10–11   First Intersessional Meeting of the UN Conference
                   on Sustainable Development (UNCSD)
February   *First Concept Paper linking SDGs to Agenda 21 issued*
March 7–8   Second session of the Preparatory Committee for
                   UNCSD (PrepCom II), New York
February–May   *Informal positioning in New York*
May 27   *First intergovernmental SDGs Meeting, Colombian
                   Permanent Mission to the UN*
July 19–21   High-Level Dialogue on the International Framework
                   for Sustainable Development, Solo, Indonesia
August 21–22   First Brazilian Consultation on Rio+20, Rio de Janeiro
August 22   *Second Concept Paper on SDGs issued with Guatemala*
September 3–5   Department of Public Information/Non-Governmental
                   Organization (DPI/NGO) Conference, "Sustainable
                   Societies, Responsive Citizens," Bonn, Germany
September 7–9   ECLAC Regional Preparatory Meeting for Latin
                   America and the Caribbean on UNCSD,
                   Santiago de Chile, Chile
September 13–18   United Nations General Assembly General Debate
November 1   Deadline for submissions on Zero Draft
November 4–5   *First International Consultation on SDGs, Bogotá*
December 14–15   Second Intersessional Meeting of UNCSD, New York

---

*Events and developments in italics are those led by Colombia.

December 15   *Third Concept Paper on SDGs issued with Guatemala and Peru*

2012

January 10   Zero Draft issued by the co-chairs

January 23–24   *International Consultation on SDGs, Retreat on SDGs "Rio+20, and the Post-2015 Development Agenda," Tarrytown Estate, NY*

January 25–27   Launch of Zero Draft and consultations in New York

January 31–
February 2   Latin American and Caribbean Environment Ministers
    Forum, Quito, Ecuador

February   Internal consultations on Zero Draft by negotiation groups

February 13   *Presentation by Colombia of the SDGs concept to the G77 and China Group's Second Committee members*

February 20–22   UNEP Administrative Council, Nairobi, Kenya

February 28–29   United Nations System Experts' meeting on Rio+20, New York

March 5   G77 and China issues own version of Zero Draft

March 13–17   *Demarche to Delhi, India, to meet with officials and discuss the SDGs proposal*

March 19–27   First Informal Informal Consultation and Third Intersessional Meeting, New York

March 24   *International Consultation on SDGs, Ford Foundation, New York*

April 23–May 4   Second Informal Informal Consultation, New York

May 3   *Fourth Concept Paper on SDGs issued with Peru and UAE*

April 23–25   Stockholm+40, Stockholm, Sweden

May 29–June 2   Third Informal Informal Consultation, New York

May 30   *Concept Paper on Transitional Committee as Format for Post-Rio Process*

June 13–15   Third Informal Informal Consultation continues, Rio de Janeiro
    Second Concept Paper on Transitional Committee as Format for Post-Rio Process

June 15   (short-lived) Third session of the Preparatory Committee for UNCSD (PrepCom III)

June 16–18   Pre-Conference Informal Negotiations led by Brazil, Rio de Janeiro

June 20–22   Rio+20 (UN Conference on Sustainable Development)

June 22   Adoption of the outcome document, *The Future We Want*

2013–2014   Thirteen sessions of the Open Working Group

July 2014   OWG adopts a report containing 17 proposed SDGs and 169 targets

2015

September 25   UN Sustainable Development Summit formally adopts Document A/70/L.1 "Transforming Our World: The 2030 Agenda for Sustainable Development." The SDGs are at its core.

Appendix 1:
The Millenium Development Goals
(MDGs)—A Brief Explanation

On September 18, 2000, the United Nations adopted the Millennium Declaration (General Assembly Resolution A/RES/55/2), a far-reaching document that tackled an array of issues, from peace and security to development and poverty eradication and protection of the environment. It reaffirmed existing commitments on human rights, democracy, and good governance. It included no goals. A year later, the Secretary-General issued a report, *Road Map Towards the Implementation of the United Nations Development Declaration* (A/56/326, September 6, 2001) that included in an annex a list of eight Millennium Development Goals with targets and indicators and a completion date of 2015. This report explained that "as part of the preparation of the present report, consultations were held among members of the United Nations Secretariat and representatives of IMF, OECD and the World Bank in order to harmonize reporting on the development goals of the Millennium Declaration and the international development goals." The group discussed the targets and some relevant indicators with a view to developing a comprehensive set of indicators for the MDGs. The main reference document was section III of the UN Declaration "Development and poverty eradication." It is noteworthy that in drafting these goals and operationalizing them with targets, no consultations were held with UN member states.

The report noted that "the Millennium Development Goals focuses [*sic*] on sustainable development, . . . reduc[ing] poverty, including finding solutions to hunger, malnutrition and disease. . . . To achieve progress, the developing countries will need the political and financial commitment of their richer country partners" (Section III, Development and poverty eradication, A/56/326, 3, 18–26, 32–36). The report explicitly locked in differentiated responsibilities across the Global North and Global South.

Incrementally, the MDGs became part of the international development agenda based on the Secretary-General's *Road Map*, as set out in General Assembly

Resolution A/RES/56/95 of January 30, 2002. This document is an example of the careful language used to refer to the MDGs given that they did not originate from an intergovernmental process. Operative paragraph 2 of this resolution "recommends that the 'road map' be considered as a useful guide in the implementation of the Millennium Declaration by the United Nations system, and invites Member States, as well as Bretton Woods institutions, the World Trade Organization and other interested parties to consider the 'road map' when formulating plans for implementing goals related to the Declaration."

Building on General Assembly efforts, in March 2002 the International Conference on Financing for Development, held in Monterrey, Mexico, agreed to the Monterrey Consensus,[1] which stated that "to fulfil internationally agreed development goals, including those contained in the Millennium Declaration, to eliminate poverty, improve social conditions and raise living standards, and protect our environment" required "mobilizing and increasing the effective use of financial resources" (para. 3). Calling for a "new partnership between developed and developing countries" (para. 4), the consensus recognized "the link between financing of development and attaining internationally agreed development goals and objectives, including those contained in the Millennium Declaration, in measuring development progress and helping to guide development priorities" (para. 71).

Gradually the MDGs became the reference framework used to align international development cooperation with national and international strategies. Over time, governments and cooperation and aid agencies structured development plans and strategies around the MDGs and constituencies evolved around the world focused on these goals' implementation, supported by philanthropies, foundations, nongovernmental organizations, and other stakeholder groups.

Millennium Development Goals

- Eradicate extreme poverty and hunger
- Achieve universal primary education
- Promote gender equality and empower women
- Reduce child mortality
- Improve maternal health
- Combat HIV/AIDS, malaria, and other diseases
- Ensure environmental sustainability
- Global partnership for development[2]

Notes

1. Monterrey Consensus of the International Conference on Financing for Development, March 18–22, 2002, http://www.un.org/en/events/pastevents/pdfs/MonterreyConsensus.pdf.
2. From https://www.un.org/millenniumgoals/.

Appendix 2:
Negotiation at
the United Nations

To an outsider, United Nations processes and resolutions may seem confusing. However, there is a clear internal logic that simply needs to be understood. Negotiating is an interactive process, and multilateral negotiations involving hundreds of interests and positions face a range of difficulties and challenges. Yet this is precisely the strength and the magic of multilateralism. Despite the profound differences in beliefs, opinions, and worldviews, 193 countries mostly manage to work together and approve common resolutions that ultimately aim to make the world a better place. UN resolutions are sometimes difficult to read and understand because consensus is hard work, requiring progressive balancing of positions as language is crafted to reflect member states' interests in text that all can live with. Once a resolution is adopted, member states are freely and willingly called on to implement it, which is a major achievement on its own.

Negotiation Formats
There are different types of negotiation. Many issues are efficiently negotiated in open-ended formats, which means that all 193 countries sit in a large room and deliberate on an issue. Interpretation to the six official languages (Arabic, Chinese, English, French, Russian, Spanish) is normally available, but English tends to be the prevailing language in negotiations. Delegates go over each paragraph in a text with one or two representatives from selected countries facilitating. It is a time-consuming process, but once the text is closed and consensus is reached, the issue becomes a negotiated reality that can be acted on.

In the open-ended format, the major formal groups play a decisive role. The largest negotiating groups of the Global South are the Group of 77 and China (134 member states from Africa, Asia, Latin America, and the Caribbean), which deals mainly with humanitarian, economic, and environmental issues and the Non-Aligned Movement (120 member states from Africa, Asia, Latin America, and the Caribbean), which deals mainly with disarmament and several social and political issues. The European Union, which represents twenty-seven countries from the Global North, is an important counterpart. Countries that do not belong to a formal negotiation group can play a pivotal role in the negotiations because they have the independence to state their own positions without first arriving at consensus in a group. This includes countries such as Australia, Canada, Japan, Mexico, New Zealand, Norway, Russia, Republic of Korea, Switzerland, and the United States. These same countries, with the exception of Russia, also participate in JUSCANZ (a name derived from the combination of its founding members: Japan, the United States, Canada, Australia and New Zealand), an informal coalition of countries largely from one of the five UN regional groups, the Western European and Others Group (WEOG). During the Rio+20 process, JUSCANZ did not play a distinct role.

Given the range of countries and disparate national contexts, forging consensus in each group can be quite difficult. This is especially the case for the G77 and China, which covers a vast range of geographic, economic, social, and cultural realities. Its remarkably diverse membership often makes it challenging to find and agree to common positions. One hundred thirty-four countries, ranging from major economies like India and Brazil to small island states and landlocked countries like Tonga and Tajikistan, have vastly different national realities and priorities. In addition, over the years some more political positions have evolved within the group, not all of which members subscribe to. One of the most salient is the principle of common but differentiated responsibilities (CBDR) in its broadest application.

In principle, for every negotiation, there are daily G77 and China coordination meetings as a first order of business in the morning and on specific negotiation tracks to strategize on the various negotiation items. The plenary meetings take stock across the negotiation tracks to gauge progress, identify priority concerns and issues, define strategies, and deal with operational issues. At these meetings, diverging positions across the members surface constantly and call for dexterous diplomatic efforts on the part of the group's presidency to either find consensus language and positions or to define pathways for advancing toward a collective endgame. Coordinators are assigned to the lead on the different negotiation tracks in a given process.

For formal negotiations, each group designates coordinators who are tasked with negotiating on their behalf in plenary sessions and formal negotiation formats, and they set up thematic coordination meetings that usually meet in the evening after the multilateral negotiation suspends for the day. A challenge with this approach, as clearly evidenced in the Rio+20 negotiations, is that often consensus in a group is arrived at only after lengthy internal negotiations that result in agreement around a lowest common denominator. Group representatives thus come to the plenary and other formal negotiation sessions with hard-won internal consensus positions that are difficult to readily change in response to the evolving negotiations. This means that as the negotiations advance, space for accommodating and responding to the areas of debate is often quite constrained. The coordinator often has to go back to the relevant political group to discuss and find a new consensus before continuing the formal discussions. In particularly difficult negotiations, such as those under the UN Framework Convention on Climate Change (UNFCCC), it has not been uncommon for the day's agenda to come to a standstill while some kind of consensus is thrashed out, for example, within the G77 and China; once a compromise within G77 and China has been found, the negotiations continue between that group and the other delegations. Where a majority of countries in a group support a particular position, the coordinator tries to base the group's negotiation tactics around it.

Given the complexities and often highly politicized dynamics of an open-ended process, a very different and innovative format was proposed for the process to develop the Sustainable Development Goals (SDGs) framework. Colombia proposed instead an "open" format, which ultimately became the Open Working Group. This format proposed that only a limited number of government representatives would participate, which crucially meant that the formal negotiation groups (like the G77 and China or the EU) would not. The aim was to enable a less politicized and more technical discussion. A fully transparent working modality was proposed that allowed everyone to observe and be represented in the discussions. Such an "open" format is uncommon in the United Nations.

Under all negotiation formats, the chairs or co-chairs of open-ended negotiations may create specific work streams—as was the case in Rio+20 around specific thematic areas or issues—or will invite member states to work under a facilitator in a smaller group to reach consensus and report back to the larger group. All interested countries can participate. These more informal negotiation formats—whether to tackle specific issues that are particularly contentious or need more substantive discussions or for ironing out different positions—are vital to enable negotiations to advance and complement the formal plenary settings.

These more informal negotiation formats promote enhanced communication and allow the necessary compromises across delegations' positions to find common ground and consensus. The informal format also allows for opinions and views to be shared more openly. Consensus language can be brought back for consideration in a formal plenary setting. The downside to these more informal formats is that there is no official translation, and meetings are conducted in English, which limits many delegations' ability to actively participate. As a rule of thumb, the more informal a setting, the more intense and decisive the negotiations can be. Thus, in addition to "informal consultations," there are also "informal informal consultations." It is telling of the complexity of the Rio+20 negotiations that the process was structured around a series of "Informal Informal Consultations." Other variants of these informal formats include meetings of friends of the chair and groups appointed by a chair or co-chair to help iron out intractable issues.

The "huddle" merits special mention because many critical decisions in negotiations, especially in the climate change arena, have been arrived at through this mechanism. A huddle is a somewhat impromptu moment when a group of negotiators start to congregate somewhere in the plenary room during an active session, usually after hours or even days of fraught negotiations, and an intense, no-holds-barred discussion takes place. The trigger for a huddle is when a few of the lead negotiators start to converge somewhere on the plenary floor and other delegates rush over to keep abreast of any developments. In this setting, the final trade-offs across the negotiation tracks or decisions on the key pending issues are quickly defined. The decisionmaking process is transparent in that it unfolds in plain view of all participants, but in fact, few participate. The final configuration of climate pledges as "nationally determined contributions" under the UNFCCC is just one of many examples of a critical decision decided through a huddle. This particular huddle took place at COP19 in Warsaw and went on to shape the structure of the 2015 Paris Agreement.

There is a significant degree of flexibility across these formats depending on the negotiation. The aim is always to promote the degree and type of dialogue needed to address national positions, tackle red lines, and gradually arrive at the "perfect paragraph" that everyone can live with. The formal and informal modalities coexist and often advance in parallel. Discussions in hallways and over coffee, such as in the well-known Vienna Café at the UN headquarters, are also essential for consensus building.

The Rio+20 Outcome Document, including the SDGs, was negotiated following these various formats. The SDGs are a result of a rich multilateral negotiation process. Consensus building takes time, but it is worth it.

Draft Text, Amendments, and Brackets

Under a standard UN process, draft text is negotiated through amendments. This means that any delegation can propose changes to any paragraph, and these will be reflected with an annotation of the starting document. Text that has been proposed but not accepted by all member states is put in square brackets. UN procedures state that

> When draft texts are being actively negotiated (e.g., draft conventions and programs of action being negotiated at a conference), alternative versions of a paragraph may be proposed. All versions of the paragraph should be placed in square brackets. . . . The initial version is normally numbered with an Arabic numeral and is followed by the alternative versions proposed, which are identified sequentially as follows: bis, ter, quater, quinquies or quinquiens, sexies or sexiens. . . . These terms and the square brackets are removed once agreement has been reached on the text. The agreed paragraphs are then numbered consecutively in the normal way.[1]

In several of the appendixes that reflect the actual negotiation texts, the reader will find examples of bracketed text. We briefly take one passage to demystify how to read through the brackets and illustrate the evolution a paragraph may go through.

> SDG2. We recognize that the development of goals could also be useful for pursuing focused and coherent action on sustainable development. In this regard, and [building on /**complementing –Japan**] [**the experience of –EU, Iceland, Switzerland, Nor-**

UN Editorial Manual Online, "Paragraphs and Subparagraphs," UN Department for General Assembly and Conference Management, https://www.un.org/dgacm/en/content/editorial-manual /para-subpara.

way] the Millennium Development Goals, we agree to develop [a set of –EU delete] global sustainable development goals (SDGs) that address and incorporate **[in a balanced way –EU, Australia, Switzerland]** all three dimensions of sustainable development and their interlinkages. These goals should be [incorporated in/**developed in conjunction with, and contribute to –EU, Iceland, Switzerland, Japan, ROK retain]** the United Nations Development Agenda beyond 2015, thus [contributing to the achievement of sustainable development and –EU, Iceland delete] serving as a driver for implementation and mainstreaming of sustainable development **[at the global, regional, national levels and –EU]** in the United Nations system as a whole.

SDG2 alt. We recognize the importance and utility of a set of sustainable development goals, which are based on Agenda 21 and JPOI, fully respect Rio Principles, in particular common but differentiated responsibilities, build upon commitments already made, respect international law and contribute to the full implementation of the outcomes of major Summits in economic, social and environmental fields, taking into account that these goals should be incorporated in the United Nations Development Agenda beyond 2015, thus contributing to the achievement of sustainable development and serving as a driver for implementation and mainstreaming of sustainable development in the United Nations system as a whole. –G77, Turkey

Text negotiation is a fluid and complex process. The key for anyone wanting to follow the process is to differentiate between text that has been approved by consensus or text that has not and understand the source of newly proposed text. Text that is proposed by one or more parties is registered in brackets; these are only removed when/if the text is approved. With particularly complex negotiations like this one, some text is put in bold letters to make it easier to read. The country or group that proposed the text is annotated at the end of each insert.

At this stage of the negotiations, participants had been given proposed text for SDG2. Through sequential rounds of interventions, some countries suggested changes to the text. Reading through the first two sets of brackets in order in the first paragraph, you can tell that

- Japan asked to include a reference to "complementing the MDGs"; and
- The EU, Iceland, Switzerland, and Norway proposed the reference be to "building on the experience of the MDGs."

You can also see that while the proposed text referred to developing "a set of global SDGs," the EU had asked that "a set of" be deleted, so that the text refers instead to developing "global SDGs."

You can see that the second paragraph in the excerpt is numbered SDG2 alt. This indicates that there has been a proposal to include a paragraph put forward by the G77 and China and Turkey. Because the proposal is not yet agreed, it appears in brackets.

Once the whole draft text is negotiated and approved, then and only then are the paragraphs numbered sequentially again. This is a practical method to see and keep track of the evolution of the draft text, but it means that the same paragraph may be labeled several different ways through the negotiation process, and then go on to be known by another number altogether when the final outcome has been edited and is published.

Agreed Text: Reference (Ad Referendum or Ad Ref)

When paragraphs are negotiated, amended, and cleaned up and everyone agrees on the text, the square brackets around the paragraph are removed and the text is characterized as *ad ref* or *ad referendum*. This means that there is consensus on the wording and that in principle it is agreed; however, the touchstone of all UN negotiations is that "nothing is agreed until everything is agreed." Thus, final agreement will be pending until the entire "negotiation package" is finalized and agreed to. Marking text as *ad ref* enables delegates to see how the negotiations are advancing and focus their attention on paragraphs still containing brackets. As was the case in Rio+20, negotiations can last several months, and sometimes new delegates come in or start to participate in negotiation tracks for the first time. The *ad ref* marker is an important signal that at least in principle, a specific paragraph has been agreed to.

Appendix 3:
First Concept Paper on the SDGs—
Colombia, February 8, 2011

I. Introduction

The definition of the scope and outcome of Rio+20, in particular with regards to "Green Economy", has become increasingly complex and thorny as the debate advances, and threatens to become a progressively rhetorical exercise through which diverse positions become more entrenched and polarized. The Government of Colombia considers that Rio + 20 constitutes a critical opportunity for the international community to agree on a concrete approach that transcends intellectual debates and delivers means for measuring—in accordance with the contexts and priorities of each country—both advances as well as bottlenecks in efforts to balance sustained socio-economic growth with the sustainable use of natural resources and the conservation of ecosystem services. There are experiences, such as the MDGs, that indicate that when there are objectives to guide the international community's efforts towards a collective goal, it becomes easier for governments and institutions to work together to reach them. **A key outcome of Rio+20 is that of "securing political commitment to Sustainable Development." However, concrete ways of grounding that commitment are needed.** Therefore, Colombia is proposing that a key outcome of the Rio + 20 process be the definition and agreement of a suite of *Sustainable Development Goals (SDGs),* equivalent to the MDGs. These SDGs would translate the Green Economy/Sustainable Development debate into tangible goals, which would focus the broad debate at a practical level, and enable the preparatory process to productively address key issues for which measurable progress would be welcome.

Moreover, the SDGs approach would generate a series of additional benefits: Objectives agreed to internationally could be underpinned by targets—as is the case with the MDGs—and could also subsequently be translated into a suite of indicators that reflect the realities and priorities at national levels. They would thus be fully aligned with national contexts and could therefore be a useful tool for guiding public policies. The SDGs would play an important role in the identification of gaps and needs in countries, for example in terms of means of implementation, institutional strengthening, and capacity building to increase absorptive capacity for new technologies. Defined internationally, like the MDGs, these would serve both for comparing results as well as furthering opportunities for cooperation, including South-South cooperation. The definition of the SDGs would contribute to focusing the preparatory process towards Rio+20, thus achieving more substantive and concrete results. A process framed along these lines would build upon the Johannesburg WSSD Plan of Implementation as well as Agenda 21. The SDGs would contribute to positioning the three pillars as cross-cutting building blocks for development throughout the UN system.

II. The Proposal

The process of defining the SDGs should be rich and challenging, an exercise through which the international community can sort through a wide range of issues and concerns in order to prioritize those which are considered to be most indicative of current needs to balance socio-economic growth with responsible environmental stewardship. The process should result in the definition of a small number of key Objectives that could be further elaborated through a suite of targets, much like the MDGs.

The SDGs would be based on Agenda 21 given that it already maps our requirements for sustainable development. This would also avoid reopening debates as Agenda 21 does not need to be renegotiated. The SDGs could provide a logical sequence and structure to the process launched almost 20 years ago: in 1992 the guiding principles were agreed to as well as a road map for sustainable development; in 2002 a Plan of Implementation was defined; and now in 2012 we could consider identifying goals in order to better identify gaps and needs and provide for more structured implementation of the principles and goals defined 20 years ago. Where relevant, given that Agenda 21 addresses socio-economic issues, MDGs could be updated and adopted as SDGs. The two sets of objectives should be fully complementary. It is worth noting that while the MDGs applied only to developing countries, the SDGs would have universal application. In principle, a suite of no more than 10—possibly less—Objectives would be agreed to. However, it would be necessary to cluster some of the Agenda 21 chapters given that: It was adopted 20 years ago and key issues, such as climate change, were not priorities then; and, the SDGs should focus on a small suite of key issues, not on all 21 thematic chapters. Proposed initial refocusing, clustering and additions to the Agenda 21 chapters would be as follows:

Chapter 9 on Atmosphere, to focus on Climate Change Mitigation, including energy issues. New chapter on Climate Change Adaptation, including Disaster Risk Management, which would include improved climate resilience of infrastructure. **Chapter 12** to focus more comprehensively on Land Degradation. **Chapter 13** on Mountain Ecosystems to be eliminated as issues related vulnerability would be covered under the new Adaptation chapter. **Chapter 14** on Sustainable Agriculture, to explicitly include food security. **Chapter 16** on Biotechnology, could be eliminated as this is a complex issue being addressed in other, more appropriate, for a. **Chapters 19–22** which deal with various types of waste could be clustered into a single objective which could have specific targets for each type of waste.

To help jump start the discussion and focus the debate, a suite of potential SDGs is described below as simple examples. The process of actually defining and agreeing on these Objectives would demand a robust negotiating process. **Chapter 2 - Commodity Markets and Policies:** Commodity policies at national and international levels enhance the contribution of the commodity sector to sustainable development, taking into account environmental considerations. **Chapter 3 - Combating Poverty:** Community-based mechanisms improve access to resources needed to enhance livelihood options, *MDG 1 - Halve, between 2012 and 20___, the proportion of people whose income is less than $1 a day.* **Chapter 4 - Changing Consumption Patterns:** Public policies that discourage unsustainable patterns of production and consumption are under implementation by 20___. **Chapter 5 - Demographic Dynamics & Sustainability:** Appropriate policies and programs are in place to address migrations resulting from environmental disruptions, with special attention to women and vulnerable groups. **Chapter 6 - Protecting & Promoting Human Health:** The burden of environmentally triggered diseases on GDP is reduced by ___% by 20___, national strategies to strengthen environmental health in order to reduce health burdens resulting from negative environmental conditions are under implementation by 20___, *MDG 5—Achieve universal access to reproductive health, MDG 5—Reduce by three fourths the maternal mortality ratio.* **Chapter 7 - Promoting Sustainable Human Settlement Development:** Living conditions in urban and peri-urban areas include adequate incomes, diets, housing and services by 20___, environmentally sound urban development and expansion, and land utilization, promoted through public policies. **Chapter 8 - Integrating Environment & Development in Decision-Making:** Metrics for measuring GDP include impacts due to loss of ecosystem services and progressive environmental degradation by 20___, Progressive identification and elimination of all subsidies that promote the unsustainable use of natural resources or which contribute to negative environmental impacts by 20___, Environmental education policies that promote understanding of the value of ecosystem services, the scope of environmental impacts, and the need for risk strategies are place for at least primary and secondary schooling by 20___. **Chapter 9 - [Protection of the Atmosphere] Climate Change Mitigation:** ___% of national energy needs are met from renewable sources by 20___, Energy efficiency standards are in place and under implementation at national level, National low carbon development strategies are designed and under implementation by 20___

NEW Chapter - **Climate Change Adaptation** - 100% of new large infrastructure investments have undergone a climate resilience analysis by 20___, National adaptation to climate change plans are designed and under implementation by 20___, Appropriate land-use planning and management strategies for both arable and non-arable land in mountain-fed watershed areas developed to prevent soil erosion, and maintain ecosystem service functions throughout watersheds. **Chapter 10 - Integrated Approach to the Planning & Management of Land Resources:** Integrated watershed management is a basis for land use planning by 20___. **Chapter 11 - Combating Deforestation:** Negative changes in forest cover are not registered and forest conditions are stable by 20___. **Chapter 12 - [Managing Fragile Ecosystems:]**

Combating Desertification & Drought: Measures are in place to maximize the sustainable use of existing land suitable for agriculture and address land degradation trends, as well as to halt deforestation caused by the expansion of the agricultural frontier. **[Chapter 13** - Managing Fragile Ecosystems: Sustainable Mountain Development - *Deleted and vulnerable ecosystems addressed under new chapter on adaptation*]

 Chapter 14 - Promoting Sustainable Agriculture & [Rural Development] Food Security: Food security is enhanced through sustainable exploitation of natural resources and sound agricultural practices, ___% of the population, in particular rural communities, children and inhabitants of urban slums, has access to sufficient and healthy food by 20__. **Chapter 15 - Conservation of Biological Diversity:** 17% of each terrestrial biome and 10% of each marine biome in the respective EEZ, in each country, is effectively protected *(in accordance with the CBD Strategic Plan for Biodiversity 2011-2021)* **[Chapter 16 - Environmentally Sound Management of Biotechnology] Chapter 17 -Protection of the Oceans, all Kinds of Seas, Including Enclosed & Semi-enclosed Seas, & Coastal Areas & the Protection, Rational Use & Development of their Living Resources:** Populations of marine species are maintained at levels that can produce the maximum sustainable yield as qualified by relevant environmental and economic factors, taking into consideration relationships among species and reducing impacts on non-target species.

 Chapter 18 - Protection of the Quality & Supply of Freshwater Resources: Application of Integrated Approaches to the Development, Management & Use of Water Resources: Sectoral water use efficiency plans are in place by 20__. **Chapter 14 - Promoting Sustainable Agriculture & [Rural Development] Food Security:** Food security is enhanced through sustainable exploitation of natural resources and sound agricultural practices ___% of the population, in particular rural communities, children and inhabitants of urban slums, has access to sufficient and healthy food by 20__. **Chapter 15 - Conservation of Biological Diversity:** 17% of each terrestrial biome and 10% of each marine biome in the respective EEZ, in each country, is effectively protected *(in accordance with the CBD Strategic Plan for Biodiversity 2011-2021)*

 [Chapter 16 - Environmentally Sound Management of Biotechnology] Chapter 17 - Protection of the Oceans, all Kinds of Seas, Including Enclosed & Semi-enclosed Seas, & Coastal Areas & the Protection, Rational Use & Development of their Living Resources: Populations of marine species are maintained at levels that can produce the maximum sustainable yield as qualified by relevant environmental and economic factors, taking into consideration relationships among species and reducing impacts on non-target species. **Chapter 18 - Protection of the Quality & Supply of Freshwater Resources: Application of Integrated Approaches to the Development, Management & Use of Water Resources:** Sectoral water use efficiency plans are in place by 20__.

Appendix 4:
Notes from the First Consultation on the SDGs, May 27, 2011

Rio + 20
SDGs   27 May - NY

Tscang - Btsw
J.nero-Arct   China - concern over new int'l standards
Nutero - UK   1) - poverty eradication = MDGs
Dong - Cun /Gua   2)   - need rempli x end to balance out
Jemen - Sing   3) fewer SDGs - brief
Paolo - Bz   5th health + poverty - avoid duplication
Mohamed - Egypt   4) common but dif responsibilities
Chile -   MDG 'partnership clause'
Jeanine - Switz   · dev - ∆ Consumpt +
Edundo - Sp   · M + I
Claire - Fr   Singapore - common but dif respon
                       - 2 sets x each ch?
Jnge - Mx   - M+I?
Lynn - USA

                   Botswana - already had this discussion in G77
                        + v. MDG model
                   Guatemala - A21 - back to beginnings
                      - gives benchmarks
                      - redefine how engagement / cooperation will happen
                   Egypt - + ment b/
                        dif b/w structure + outcome (response to Tscang)
                        - need combine both
                      → could be major outcome x Rio
                      - integrate agendas of MDGs + SD
                        " 3 pillars
                      - end MDGs - think beyond 2015
                      - quantifiable targets x MDG
                         y.t for SD - mostly genetic -

Appendix 5:
Second Concept Paper on the SDGs—
Colombia and Guatemala,
August 23, 2011

I. Introduction

The Governments of Colombia and Guatemala consider that Rio + 20 constitutes a critical opportunity for the international community to agree on a concrete approach that delivers means for measuring—in accordance with the contexts and priorities of each country—both advances as well as bottlenecks in efforts to balance sustained socio-economic growth with the sustainable use of natural resources and the conservation of ecosystem services. There are experiences, such as the MDGs, that indicate that when there are objectives to guide the international community's efforts towards a collective goal, it becomes easier for governments and institutions to work together to reach them. **A key outcome of Rio+20 is that of "securing political commitment to Sustainable Development." However, concrete ways of grounding that commitment are needed.**

Therefore, Colombia and Guatemala are proposing that a key outcome of the Rio + 20 process be the definition and agreement of a suite of *Sustainable Development Goals (SDGs)*, similar and supportive of the MDGs. These SDGs would focus the broad debate at a practical level, and enable the preparatory process to productively address key issues for which measurable progress would be welcome. Moreover, the SDGs approach would generate a series of additional benefits:

Objectives agreed to internationally could eventually be underpinned by targets—as is the case with the MDGs—that reflect the realities and priorities at national levels. They would thus be fully aligned with national contexts and could therefore be a useful tool for guiding public policies. The SDGs would play an important role in the identification of gaps and needs in countries, for example in terms of means of implementation, institutional strengthening, and capacity building to increase absorptive capacity for new technologies. Defined internationally, like the MDGs, these would serve both for comparing results as well as furthering opportunities for cooperation, including South-South cooperation.

The definition of the SDGs would contribute to focusing the preparatory process towards Rio+20, thus achieving more substantive and concrete results. A process framed along these lines would build upon the Johannesburg WSSD Plan of Implementation as well as Agenda 21. The SDGs would contribute to positioning the three pillars as cross-cutting building blocks for development throughout the UN system.

II. The Proposal

The process of defining the SDGs should be rich and useful, an exercise through which the international community can prioritize those issues which are the most indicative of current needs to balance socio-economic growth with responsible environmental stewardship. The process should result in the definition of a small number of key Objectives that could be later elaborated through a suite of targets, much like the MDGs. The SDGs would be based on Agenda 21 given that it already maps our requirements for sustainable development. This would also avoid reopening debates as Agenda 21 does not need to be renegotiated.

The SDGs could provide a logical sequence and structure to the process launched almost 20 years ago: in 1992 the guiding principles were agreed to as well as a road map for sustainable development; in 2002 a Plan of Implementation was defined; and now in 2012 we could consider identifying goals in order to better identify gaps and needs and provide for more structured implementation of the principles and goals defined 20 years ago. The SDGs and the MDGs should be fully complementary. It is worth noting that while the MDGs applied only to developing countries, the SDGs would have universal application.

III. The Way Forward

The Rio+20 process is complex, and there are many activities, consultations and decisions that need to be undertaken at national, regional and global levels *in the remaining months to June 2012*. Therefore, it is necessary to gauge a practical level of ambition for the development of the SDGs by *June 2012*. It is proposed that a reasonable deliverable by June 2012 at Rio would be **agreement on suite of Objectives at a broad level**. This would mean prioritizing those themes and issues that are considered critical factors in moving forward the sustainable development agenda, inspired on Agenda 21. *These could broadly include issues such as*: Combating Poverty; Changing Consumption Patterns; Promoting Sustainable Human Settlement Development; Biodiversity and Forests; Oceans; Water Resources; Advancing Food Security; Energy, including from renewable sources.

The expected results at the Rio Summit would be two pronged: 1) a definition of the thematic Objectives and, 2) an agreement on a mandate to subsequently define (post-Rio): i) How these Objectives would be further developed—this would include decisions, for example, on: definition of goals (as with the MDGs) and/or indicators for the Objectives whether these goals would be at global, regional and/or national levels how these goals might reflect the integration of the 3 pillars in each Objective interlinkages between the Objectives themselves. ii) A process that could converge with the revision of the MDGs given that it will soon be necessary to undertake this exercise as the MDGs have a deadline of 2015. Tackling both processes in a coordinated or converging manner could be a win-win situation as the international community would ultimately benefit from a more solid, coherent and comprehensive suite of Objectives.

Thus, this would be a reasonable level of ambition: By June 2012, to define the suite of Sustainable Development Objectives. During the Conference, a mandate would be agreed to for further developing the Objectives and defining possible options such as those detailed above. There would not be a need to prejudge the outcome in the remaining months leading up to Rio.

Appendix 6:
Executive Coordination Team
Compilation of Zero Draft Submissions,
November 1, 2011

Table A6.1   Top Ten Issues in Submissions

Number	Member States	Political Groups	Regional Preparatory Meetings	Major Groups	UN and IGOs
1	Participation	Participation	Participation	Participation	Adaptation
2	Consumption and Production	Adaptation	Adaptation	Adaptation	Participation
3	SDGs	Capacity Building	SDGs	Accountability	Capacity Building
4	Adaptation	Accountability	Principle 10 / Access to Information	Transparency	SDGs
5	Capacity Building	Transparency	Consumption and Production	Mitigation	Mitigation
6	Transparency	Mitigation	Productivity	SDGs	Productivity
7	Desertification	Consumption and Production	Desertification Building	Capacity Growth	Green
8	Green Growth	Desertification	Urbanization	Principle 10 / Access to Information	Consumption and Production
9	Means of Implementation (MOI)	Urbanization	Environmental Governance	Productivity	Accountability
10	Mitigation	Common but Differentiated Responsibility	Common but Differentiated Responsibility	Consumption and Production	Urbanization

Note: This table, adapted from a compilation by the Executive Coordination Team, ranks the ten top issues as reflected in Zero Draft submissions.

Table A6.2 Summary of Submissions

Number	Initiative/ Concepts	All Submissions	Member States	Political Groups	Regional Preperatory Meetings	Major Groups	UN and IGOs	Level of Interest
1	Participation	334	53	4	5	241	31	Excellent
2	Adaptation	227	36	4	4	151	32	Excellent
3	Accountability	170	24	3	0	127	16	Excellent
4	SDGs	170	37	1	4	102	26	Excellent
5	Transparency	166	31	3	1	118	13	Excellent
6	Mitigation	160	27	3	2	103	25	Excellent
7	Capacity Building	159	35	4	2	90	28	Excellent
8	Consumption and Production	135	38	3	3	74	17	Excellent
9	Productivity	135	27	1	3	82	22	Excellent
10	Principle 10/Access to Information	124	17	0	4	90	13	Excellent
11	Desertification	113	30	2	3	63	15	Excellent
12	Urbanization	113	21	2	3	71	16	Excellent
13	Green Growth	98	28	1	1	47	21	High
14	Environmental governance	91	26	1	3	51	10	High
15	Poverty Alleviation	78	9	1	0	59	9	Strong
16	Common but differentiated responsibility	76	24	2	3	35	12	Strong
17	Means of implementation (MoI)	72	28	2	3	36	3	Strong
18	Green Economy Roadmap	66	10	1	0	50	5	Strong
19	Sustainable Development Council	61	24	1	2	28	6	Strong
20	Precautionary Principle	57	3	1	2	50	1	Good
21	Planetary Boundaries/Environmental Limits	53	12	1	0	36	4	Good
22	Rio Principles	44	17	1	3	16	6	Good
23	Disaster Preparedness	41	11	0	1	22	7	Good
24	Carrying Capacity	39	5	1	1	30	2	Medium
25	Social Inclusion	39	7	1	1	18	12	Medium

continues

Table A6.2 Continued

Number	Initiative/ Concepts	All Submissions	Member States	Political Groups	Regional Preperatory Meetings	Major Groups	UN and IGOs	Level of Interest
26	Decoupling	37	7	0	1	21	8	Medium
27	Polluter Pays	33	5	0	0	26	2	Medium
28	Market Mechanisms	31	6	1	0	21	3	Medium
29	Beyond GDP	31	2	0	0	25	4	Medium
30	Just Transition	30	3	1	1	19	6	Medium
31	Blue Economy	25	4	2	2	13	4	Medium
32	Sustainable Tourism	25	6	1	1	13	4	Medium
33	Water-Food-Energy Nexus	23	3	1	1	14	4	Medium
34	National sustainable development strategies (NSDS)	22	10	1	0	8	3	Medium
35	Intergenerational equity/justice	22	2	0	0	19	1	Medium
36	Sustainable Agriculture & Food	21	2	0	0	11	8	Medium
37	Ombudsperson for Future Generations	20	0	0	1	18	1	Some
38	Rights-based approach	20	3	0	1	12	4	Some
39	Tipping point	18	0	0	0	17	1	Some
40	Corporate Sustainability	17	1	0	0	14	2	Some
41	Multi-Stakeholder dialogue/process	16	2	0	0	13	1	Some
42	ISO 26000	16	2	1	0	9	4	Some
43	Fiscal Reform	15	2	0	0	9	4	Some
44	Ecosystem Approach	15	2	0	0	9	4	Some
45	Strengthening/Reforming UNEP	14	8	0	1	4	1	Some
46	UN Environment Organization (UNEO)	11	4	0	0	6	1	Some
47	World Environment Organization (WEO)	11	4	0	0	6	1	Some
48	Low Carbon Economy	9	1	0	0	6	2	Some
49	Green & Fair Economy	8	1	0	0	7	0	Some
50	Green Stimulus	8	2	0	0	4	2	Some

continues

Table A6.2 Continued

Number	Initiative/ Concepts	All Submissions	Member States	Political Groups	Regional Preparatory Meetings	Major Groups	UN and IGOs	Level of Interest
51	Life Cycle Approach	8	2	0	0	5	1	Some
52	International Court for the Environment	8	0	0	0	8	0	Some
53	BASD 2012	7	0	0	0	6	1	Some
54	Financial Stability	7	2	0	0	5	0	Some
55	Intergovernmental Panel on Sustainable Development	7	2	0	1	4	0	Some
56	Climate Investment Fund	6	2	0	0	2	2	Some
57	Full Cost Accounting	6	0	0	0	6	0	Some
58	Ecocide	4	0	0	0	4	0	Some
59	Internalization of externalities	4	0	0	0	3	1	Some
60	Investing in People	4	0	0	0	3	1	Some
61	Economic Democracy	3	0	0	0	3	0	Some
62	Environmental tribunal	2	0	0	0	2	0	Some

Note: This table, adapted from a compilation by the Executive Coordination Team, ranks the initiatives/concepts raised in the Zero Draft submissions by level of interest (far right column). The scale used is 100+ = excellent; 81 to 100 = high; 61 to 80 = strong; 41 to 60 = good; 21 to 40 = medium; 1 to 20 = some.

Appendix 7:
Chair's Summary—Bogotá
Consultations on the SDGs Proposal,
November 4–5, 2011

Informal Consultations on the proposal of SDG were held in Bogotá on 4 to 5 November 2011, chaired by Vice Minister for Multilateral Affairs, Patti Londoño. The informal setting encouraged an open and creative exchange of views among a representative group of member states as well as of UN Agencies and NGOs. In keeping with the format of the consultations, no formal report will be issued. However, the interactions were so substantive that, in order to continue developing the proposal collectively, it was felt that it would be useful to share the thrust of the discussions and some of the main issues and aspects considered.

1. Scope of the SDGs
Overall, it was considered that the proposal offers a means for ensuring that there are concrete results coming out of Rio+20. There is growing understanding that the SDGs may be tools for addressing concrete global challenges with national dimensions. From the discussions it emerged that the SDGs could:

- Assist the international community in prioritizing key challenges and in identifying means and requirements for effectively integrating the three pillars of sustainable development
- Catalyze action towards implementation at national and local levels
- Support countries so that they can define new development pathways for themselves
- Orient requirements for governance arrangements at international levels
- Ensure greater coherence and coordination at international and regional levels, as well as at national levels

- Foster targeted innovation and science-based solutions
- Promote specific partnerships to address specific issues or needs
- Enable the international community to work on concrete issues that underpin sustained poverty reduction and decoupling of environmental impacts from economic growth

In a world that will face increasing natural resource and land scarcities, how can human wellbeing be supported? What kind of trade-offs may need to be considered? These scenarios are a cause for concern, but also for opportunities to secure improved resource productivity and efficiency, more employment options, and greater social inclusion. This is what the SDGs are about. The SDGs focus on planetary issues that require support and coherence at international levels, and resolution and implementation at national and local levels.

2. Guiding Principles
The need for guiding principles for the SDGs was underlined, and some considerations were reiterated throughout the Consultations. The SDGs should be:

- Universal and comprehensive, and therefore relevant for all countries
- Based on Agenda 21 and the Johannesburg Plan of Implementation
- Forward looking and build upon already existing agreements and principles
- An innovative and bold response for the integration of the three dimensions (social, economic and environment) in an effective and practical manner
- Focused on global challenges and issues that are widely acknowledged as concerns for the international community (i.e. non-threatening issues)
- Tailored to the circumstances and priorities of each country; there is no "one-size-fits-all"
- Reliant on the full participation of key stakeholders, including private sector, for implementation
- . . . an inspiration to the next generation

3. Identification of Priority Areas and Related Issues
SDGs are meant to focus on key global challenges that are critical for ensuring the wellbeing of people everywhere, including through sound stewardship of the natural resource base and services on which so many—and so many economies—depend. Key concerns of the international community, which were iterated by many participants, indicated themes which could be prioritized as SDGs:

- Food security
- Energy access, including with renewable sources
- Water, integrated management and sanitation issues

- Oceans, including fisheries
- Sustainable human settlements (cities)
- Biodiversity and forestry
- Employment
- Women and youth

One participant proposed a SDG on "Physical development planning" which would encompass urban planning and land use.

A Pilot Exercise: Discovering the Merits of a SDG
In order to better appreciate the logic of the SDGs for addressing complex issues, a dynamic discussion took place on "Food Security." As anticipated, once the focus was on a concrete issue, a range of specific considerations was brought to the fore, as well as options and requirements for effective implementation. *There was no rhetoric, little politics, and the discussion was substantive, constructive and targeted on implementation issues.* This is what the SDGs are about. Most importantly, the three dimensions of sustainable development were integrated in tangible manners. Discussions covered areas such as land tenure and access; nutrition; price volatility; distribution and supply; changing consumption patterns; resource footprint (water, pesticides, etc.); land degradation; sustainable intensification; rural development; and subsidies. Economic and environmental drivers that underpin social requirements were naturally articulated.

---

4. Linkage Between MDGs and SDGs
The relationship between the MDGs and the SDGs was the subject of intense discussions. There was no consensus on an approach but it was agreed that there is a need for further consultations on this issue. Some considerations that were iterated were:

- The MDGs are widely acknowledged as a highly successful and key approach for enabling international cooperation at all levels.
- There is full consensus that the MDGs must not be in any way undermined by any other process and that they should be amply supported. The MDGs must continue their planned trajectory to 2015.
- There were suggestions that the SDGs could provide a useful input to the MDG review process and to the definition of the post-2015 framework. Some noted that the MDGs do not sufficiently address underlying economic and environmental issues and drivers.
- There was broad agreement that there must be coherence between the existing MDGs and the proposed SDGs.
- Many considered that the SDGs, which could focus on major global challenges such as food security, would therefore complement the scope of the MDGs.

5. The Way Forward to June 2012 and Beyond

It was widely agreed that although lengthy negotiations on the SDGs are unwelcome, there is a need for further consultations and discussion on the content of the SDGs and their relation to the MDGs.

As called for in the Colombia-Guatemala proposal, many agreed that it would be important to launch the SDG process in Rio in June 2012, and that it should be possible to agree on a suite of thematic Objectives by June 2012.

As part of the mandate coming out of Rio, iterated calls were made for a "gap analysis" to be undertaken of the core issues of the sustainable development agenda— a stocktaking across the three pillars—in order to provide governments and stakeholders with a better understanding of key areas or mechanisms that require prioritization.

Some of the options discussed for further developing the SDGs included:

- Definition of a suite of SDGs by June 2012 that could then start to be worked on, through a gap analysis and/or other mechanisms, to "learn by doing" in terms of identification of international governance requirements, national implementation requirements, areas for action across the three pillars, etc. Additional SDGs could be defined over the following year through targeted consultations.
- Definition of a suite of SDGs, no more than 8 or 10 and ideally fewer. These could have aspirational global targets. Interested countries could develop concrete targets to guide their own internal development agendas. This would be a combination of a top-down (internationally) and bottom-up (nationally) approach which would be developed over the following year(s).

Overall, there was broad agreement that a mandate would need to be agreed at the Conference for taking the SDGs forward.

As one participant succinctly noted, "The SDGs should be universal and comprehensive but they should also be concrete and deliver results." The challenge is to define a mandate that achieves this at both levels.

In addition to the relation between the SDGs and the MDGs, other concerns were voiced regarding issues that will need to be addressed in further elaborating the proposal. Among the most salient:

- How to reconcile the universal dimension of the SDGs with the fact that these will need to be tailored to specific national circumstances, i.e. one-size-does-not-fit all.
- How to approach issues of implementation, recognizing that implementation includes not just financial resources but also institutional and governance capacities at national level, as well as issues such as absorptive capacity for new technologies, dissemination of best practices, and inclusion of key stakeholders ranging from youth to private sector for effective implementation.
- Linking up with private sector and IFIs.

Finally, many noted that the SDGs could contribute to a new way of measuring development that does not focus primarily on economic growth. The need to measure sustainability, in terms for example of resource footprints and social equity, were noted.

Appendix 8:
Third Concept Paper on the SDGs—
Colombia, Guatemala, and Peru,
December 13, 2011

I. The Proposal

A key outcome of Rio+20 is that of "securing renewed political commitment to Sustainable Development." Concrete ways for grounding this commitment are needed. The Governments of Colombia, Guatemala and Peru affirm that Rio+20 constitutes an historic opportunity for agreeing on a concrete and substantive approach that enables continued and robust political commitment to the three pillars of sustainable development. Agreement on a set of Goals would serve to guide and focus the international community's efforts on the work needed to address these issues. It needs the participation of all key stakeholders. The SDGs would also support the MDGs which remain a cornerstone of the UN development agenda.

The proposal for agreement on a suite of *Sustainable Development Goals (SDGs)* in June 2012 seeks to set in place a process to effectively address issues that underpin human welfare. Some of the benefits of the SDGs are that they:

- Build upon Agenda 21 and the Johannesburg WSSD Plan of Implementation;
- Catalyze implementation at national and local levels, in response to national realities and priorities;
- Assist the international community in focusing on key challenges that demand coherence and coordination at all levels;
- Catalyze means of implementation at the international level and assist in identifying gaps and needs in developing countries;
- Contribute to positioning the three pillars as cross-cutting building blocks for development throughout the UN system;

214

- Compliment the MDGs and enable stakeholders at all levels to work on concrete issues that focus on poverty eradication and on reducing environmental impacts from increased economic growth; and,
- Have universal application

> *The SDGs provide a logical sequence and structure to the process launched almost 20 years ago: in 1992 the guiding principles were agreed to as well as a road map for sustainable development; in 2002 a Plan of Implementation was defined; and in 2012 we would work on the SDGs in order to better identify gaps and needs, and provide for more structured implementation of critical sustainable development priorities.*

II. The Way Forward

Given the importance of the UNCSD and the high-level participation that the UNCSD will convene, part of the outcome of UNCSD should be at two levels:

1) Agreement on the Themes of the SDGs

The outcome of the UNCSD would include agreement on the overarching themes of the Sustainable Development Goals based on (a) social and economic dimensions; and (b) conservation and management of resources for development. (i.e., Sections I and II of Agenda 21). These themes should focus issues that have gained increased political attention, such as:

- Food security
- Energy access, including with renewable sources
- Oceans, including fisheries
- Sustainable human settlements (cities)
- Water, integrated management

2) Agreement on the Process to Finalize the SDGs Framework

Scope for work would include:

- Further elaboration of the Goal for each theme, including the targets for each goal and how each goal would be supported; and,
- Timeline of 12–18 months post Rio + 20.
- The SDGs would be adopted by the UN General Assembly in 2013. The SDGs could also be integrated into the MDG post 2015 framework.

Appendix 9:
Chair's Summary of the Tarrytown Retreat on the SDGs—Tarrytown, NY, January 23–24, 2012

Informal consultations on the proposal for Sustainable Development Goals (SDGs) in the context of Rio+20 and the post-2015 development agenda were held in Tarrytown, NY from 23 to 24 January 2012, with the participation of 44 countries, representatives of NGOs, and representatives of the UN and UN agencies. The informal setting encouraged an open and substantive exchange of views on a range of issues related to the process for developing the SDGs in the preparatory process to Rio and beyond, a discussion that is related to the definition of the post 2015 framework. The Retreat was chaired by Colombia, whose delegate underscored that the discussions were intended to provide an opportunity for a representative group of stakeholders to explore various aspects of the SDG proposal and contribute to its further development. The following is a summary of the main points that emerged from the deliberations.

There was broad agreement on **four core aspects**:

- Rio+20 is a milestone event and the international community should strive for a high level of ambition, with clear and robust outcomes in the form of a renewed and focused sustainable development agenda.
- Sustainable Development Goals are understood in the context of the post-2015 development framework. SDGs have a definitive added value and will be further elaborated and completed within the post-2015 process.
- There should be a single unified process leading to the definition of the post-2015 framework, building upon government consultations as well as inputs from stakeholders, and expert and scientific advice.
- There should be a single set of international development goals with sustainable development and poverty eradication the overarching focus.

SDGs in the Rio+20 Preparatory Process:
Elements & Deliverables

The discussions pointed towards a multi-step process to decide on the SDG framework: from (1) agreement on guiding characteristics of SDGs; to (2) an eventual agreement on architecture and themes; to (3) subsequent agreement on the goals together with targets and indicators.

There was strong support for including **SDG guiding characteristics** in the Zero Draft, including:

- Poverty eradication as an overarching goal;
- Universal relevance of the SDGs, but allowing for varied country and regional circumstances and priorities and capacity for implementation of specific voluntary targets;
- Action-oriented;
- Strongly linked to Agenda 21 and JPoI;
- Effectively address and integrate the economic, social and environmental dimensions of sustainable development;
- Enable articulation of the nexus between the different issue areas covered by the SDGs;
- Voluntary application, in keeping with national realities, priorities, and capacities;
- Time bound and measurable, with targets and indicators; and,
- Few in number and easy to communicate and understand.

In addition, the following **considerations** were reiterated throughout the discussions:

- There was a clear understanding that the formulation of SDGs should not divert or in any way undermine the focus of the international community on achieving the MDGs by 2015.
- SDG should build upon and complement the MDGs, and reflect lessons from MDG implementation.
- In line with keeping the SDGs simple, succinct and few, many underscored the need for the SDGs to set clear and focused priorities, which was a key strength of the MDGs.
- A possible approach for setting priorities and defining the SDGs is to focus on the major development challenges that the international community needs to address.
- In addition to the definition of themes or issue areas for the SDGs, it is equally important to define cross-cutting issues. These issues are no less important than those to be captured in an SDG, and indeed are critical given their prevalence and relevance. Cross-cutting issues could include aspects such as technology transfer, capacity building, means of implementation, climate change, equity and gender.

• In the development of the SDGs, consideration must be given to the institutional and governance arrangements required for their implementation, taking into consideration the current mandate and work of existing agencies, as well as gaps and future requirements. It will equally be important to work with an understanding of relevant existing agreements and programs.
• The capacity of developing countries for managing information and data, and for reporting, will need to be strengthened.
• Implementation will require the support and commitment of all stakeholders, including civil society and the private sector, so their participation in the process is fundamental.

With regards to **possible deliverables by June 2012**, there were a wide range of views that reflect differing levels of ambition for Rio as well as different understandings of the required process for defining the SDGs. It was recalled that the MDGs were not negotiated but rather derived from the Millennium Declaration and then defined through an expert process.

• Some delegations considered that a more measured process is required, with inputs by expert panels, including academia, private sector and NGOs to define the SDGs, given the transcendent role they are expected to play in the development agenda in the future.
• However other delegations insisted that it is critical to launch them in an event of the magnitude and visibility of Rio+20, and given existing mandates and work on core issues, it is possible to already identify the themes of the SDGs by June. The further development of the SDGs can then be tasked to the post-2015 process.
• Given the divergence of views a third option was proposed that called for the identification of 1-3 preliminary pilot SDGs that could be further developed in the aftermath of Rio within the post-2015 process through expert group advice. This will provide a valuable opportunity for learning-by-doing in terms of better understanding the nature, scope and complexity of the SDGs.

Based on the advances and agreements arrived at by June 2012, a **mandate** will need to be defined for further defining and/or developing the SDGs after the Conference. The mandate could include: purpose and long-term vision for SDGs; key characteristics to guide development of SDGs; priority themes and architecture; and guidance on an inclusive process for the post 2015 development agenda;

Overall Process: Possible Architecture
For the process leading up to Rio+20, two levels of interaction where discussed:

• the need to create opportunities within the negotiations to enable the continuation of substantive discussions such as those at the Retreat; and,

• entry points and opportunities to interact and participate in the preparations for the post-2015 process from the onset.

There was broad agreement that it would be helpful to **continue substantive discussions** which enable everyone to collectively arrive at a better understanding of the SDGs and the post-2015 framework, given the uncertainties, complexities and array of possible options. There was good consensus that it would be far more productive to collectively come to a more concise understanding of the process and the proposal, in terms of identifying both areas of convergence as well as those of divergence, before embarking on detailed drafting and negotiation exercises. It was also underlined that despite the usefulness of these informal consultations, it was fundamentally important to ensure that future consultations were fully open-ended and included all Member States. Therefore, it was agreed that it would be necessary to consult with the co-Chairs and Bureau on appropriate mechanisms for enabling more in-depth discussions on these issues.

With respect to the **post-2015 process**, representatives of UNDESA and UNDP informed retreat participants of the UN Task Team on the post-2015 process that has been established by the Secretary-General, which will develop the road map for the post-2015 agenda process. Following Rio+20, the Secretary-General has announced his intention to convene a high level/expert panel to guide work on the post-2015 agenda and that will report to the 2013 UNGA. In response to several delegations that noted that the post-2015 framework needs to be defined through an intergovernmental process, UNDP affirmed that it was envisioned that the work of the Task Team be very transparent and inclusive, and in the service of the Member States. There would be opportunities for participation and regular information. It is noted, however, that several other delegations did not support work on the SDGs beyond Rio through an intergovernmental process.

Several participants noted that it would be important to find an **effective mechanism** that would provide for an inclusive and participatory process, but one informed by relevant expertise to deliver judicious and balanced outcomes in the aftermath of Rio+20. There was discussion of options, including the possibility of establishing an expert group with participation of government experts presented by UN regional groups, key agencies such as UNDP and UNEP, specialized agencies depending on the focus of work, representatives of civil society and think tanks from South and North. A Rio+20 outcome on SDGs could provide guidance to the Secretary-General on what form such a mechanism could take.

Appendix 10:
Co-Chairs' Draft—*The Future*
We Want, January 10, 2012

B. Accelerating and Measuring Progress

105. We recognize that goals, targets and milestones are essential for measuring and accelerating progress towards sustainable development and agree to launch an inclusive process to devise by 2015:

   a) a set of global Sustainable Development Goals that reflect an integrated and balanced treatment of the three dimensions of sustainable development, are consistent with the principles of Agenda 21, and are universal and applicable to all countries but allowing for differentiated approaches among countries;
   b) a mechanism for periodic follow-up and reporting on progress made toward their achievement.

106. We invite all stakeholders to join this process and request the UN Secretary-General to coordinate this process.

107. We propose that the Sustainable Development Goals could include sustainable consumption and production patterns as well as priority areas such as oceans; food security and sustainable agriculture; sustainable energy for all; water access and efficiency; sustainable cities; green jobs, decent work and social inclusion; and disaster risk reduction and resilience.

108. We consider that the Sustainable Development Goals should complement and strengthen the MDGs in the development agenda for the post-2015 period, with a view to establishing a set of goals in 2015 which are part of the post-2015 UN Development Agenda.

109. We also propose that progress towards these Goals should be measured by appropriate indicators and evaluated by specific targets to be achieved possibly by 2030, and request the Secretary-General for proposals in this regard.

110. We resolve to strengthen the capacity of all countries to collect and analyze data and information needed to support the monitoring of progress towards the Sustainable Development Goals. We request the Secretary-General, with the support of interested donors, the UN system, international organizations and other entities, to promote a global partnership in this regard.

111. We also recognize the limitations of GDP as a measure of well-being. We agree to further develop and strengthen indicators complementing GDP that integrate economic, social and environmental dimensions in a balanced manner. We request the Secretary-General to establish a process in consultation with the UN system and other relevant organizations.

Appendix 11:
G77 and China Zero Draft Text,
March 5, 2012

~~B. Accelerating and measuring progress~~ Sustainable Development Goals

~~105. We recognize that goals, targets and milestones are essential for measuring and accelerating progress towards sustainable development and agree to launch an inclusive process to devise by 2015;~~

~~a) a set of global Sustainable Development Goals that reflect an integrated and balanced treatment of the three dimensions of sustainable development, are consistent with the principles of Agenda 21, and are universal and applicable to all countries but allowing for differentiated approaches among countries;~~

~~b) a mechanism for periodic follow-up and on progress made toward their achievement.~~

~~106. We invite all stakeholders to join this process and request the UN Secretary-General to coordinate this process.~~

~~107. We propose that the Sustainable Development Goals could include sustainable consumption and production patterns as well as priority areas such as oceans; food security and sustainable agriculture; sustainable energy for all; water access and efficiency; sustainable cities; green jobs; decent work and social inclusion; and disaster risk reduction and resilience.~~

~~108. We consider that the Sustainable Development Goals should complement and strengthen the MDGs in the development agenda for the post-2015 period, with a view to establishing a set of goals in 2015 which are part of the post-2015 UN Development Agenda.~~

~~109. We also propose that progress towards those Goals should be measured by appropriate indicators and evaluated by specific targets to be achieved possibly by 2030, and request the Secretary-General for proposals in this regard.~~

~~110. We resolve to strengthen the capacity of all countries to collect and analyze data and information needed to support the monitoring of progress towards the Sustainable Development Goals. We request the Secretary-General, with the support of interested donors, the UN system, international organizations and other entities, to promote a global partnership in this regard.~~

In accordance with A/RES/65/1 we call for the General Assembly to continue to review, on an annual basis, the progress made towards the achievement of the Millennium Development Goals, including in the implementation of the outcome document and request the President of the General Assembly at its sixty-eighth session to organize a special event in 2013 to follow up efforts made towards achieving the Millennium Development Goals (agreed ad ref)

We recognize that some progress has been made towards attainment of MDGs. However, we are deeply concerned that most LDCs, SIDS and African countries remain off-track in achieving most of the MDGs by 2015 and beyond (agreed ad ref)

We also recognize that all the Millennium Development Goals are interconnected and mutually reinforcing and can therefore be best achieved when pursued in a holistic and comprehensive manner. Whereas there could be need to formulate sustainable development goals, we emphasize that they must neither be used as a pretext for avoiding international commitments towards meeting MDGs targets nor pose new conditionalities for accessing to development assistance (agreed ad ref)

We underscore the continued relevance of the outcomes of all major United Nations conferences and summits in the economic, social and related fields and the commitments contained therein, including the Millennium Development Goals, which have raised awareness and continue to generate real and important development gains. Together these outcomes and commitments have played a vital role in shaping a broad development vision and constitute the overarching framework for the development activities of the United Nations. We strongly reiterate our determination to ensure the timely and full implementation of these outcomes and commitments. We recognize the importance of the MDGs in ensuring coherence in the delivery of the development objective by the UN System as a whole both at national and international levels (agreed ad ref)

We recognize that goals can be useful for pursuing sustainable development, taking into account the need for an integrated approach incorporating economic, social and environmental dimensions and recognizing their interlinkages and avoiding dealing with them in separate or parallel tracks. In this regard Sustainable Development Goals, built upon the MDGs, could be a driver for implementation and mainstreaming of sustainable development as well as of integration of its three dimensions (agreed ad ref)

We therefore agree to undertake the establishment of a ~~single~~ *set of SDGs consistent with Agenda 21 and JPOI in full compliance with the Rio Principles in particular CBDR (Colombia)*

We consider that the SDGs should complement and strengthen the MDGs in the development agenda for the post-2015 period (Colombia)

We recognize the importance and utility of a set of Sustainable Development Goals which are based on Agenda 21 and JPOI, fully respect Rio Principles in particular CBDR, build upon commitments already made, respect international law and contribute to the full implementation of the outcomes of all major summits in the economic, social and environmental field taking into account that these goals should ensure a holistic coherence with the goals set in Agenda 21 and JPOI (agreed ad ref)

SDGs should be guided by the following principles and characteristics: (agreed ad ref)

- achieve poverty eradication (agreed ad ref)
- integrate in a balanced manner the three dimensions of sustainable development, (agreed ad ref)
- respect the sovereignty of States over their natural resources in accordance with the UN Charter and principles of international law, without causing damage to the environment of other States or of areas beyond the limits of national jurisdiction (agreed ad ref)
- be consistent with the Rio principles particularly the Principle of Common But Differentiated Responsibilities (agreed ad ref)
- ensure the implementation of Agenda 21 and JPOI, and the outcomes of all UN major summits in economic, social and environmental field (agreed ad ref)
- build upon and complement the MDGs and renew and strengthen commitment towards their achievement (agreed ad ref)
- take into account different national realities, capacities and development priorities (agreed ad ref)
- rely on government driven implementation with involvement of all relevant stakeholders (agreed ad ref)
- contribute to the monitoring of fulfillment of developed countries' international commitments especially those related to financial resources, technology transfer and capacity building (agreed ad ref)
- shall include means of implementation for developing countries, including under each goal (agreed ad ref)
- give special attention to the countries in special situation and to disadvantaged and vulnerable people (agreed ad ref)
- not place additional restriction or burdens on developing countries or dilute responsibilities of developed countries (agreed ad ref)
- contribute to fulfill the right to development and achieving equity at all levels (agreed ad ref)
- should respect policy space and national development priorities of each country, in particular avoiding the establishment of mechanism for monitoring national policies (agreed ad ref)
- applicable to all countries consistent with the principle of common but differentiated responsibilities (agreed ad ref)

We agree to establish under the General Assembly, an inclusive, transparent, member states driven Ad-Hoc Open-ended Working Group to develop and design the Sustainable Development Goals. The Ad-Hoc Open-ended Working Group shall conclude its work by the 67 General Assembly and present a report with recommendations based on discussion and taking into account the inputs and contributions presented by member states. [We emphasize the importance of support the engagement of developing countries' expertise in this process] (pending)

Alt. We agree to establish, under the General Assembly, an inclusive, transparent, member state driven and owned intergovernmental process to develop and design the SDGs. That process shall conclude its work by the sixty-eighth session of the UNGA and present a report with recommendations based on its discussions and taking into account the inputs and contributions presented by member states.

Appendix 12:
March 27, 2012,
Section B at 6 p.m.—
Negotiation Text

B. Accelerating and measuring progress

B. [Accelerating and measuring progress/ Sustainable Development Goals-G77] [US, Canada, New Zealand reserve this entire section] [Propose that this section be structured in 4 paragraphs: 1 para on characteristics, 1 para on process (merge 106 into 108), 1 para on potential issues, areas and themes (107), 1 para on measurement of progress (109) –Switzerland, ROK, New Zealand] [Propose alternative structure: 1. Vision on Sustainable Development Goals. 2. Principles that should guide Sustainable Development Goals. 3. Process: 3.1. Has to be intergovernmental. 3.2. Has to be inclusive, transparent and open-ended. 3.3. Has to be under the UN General Assembly –G77]

[Pre 105. We encourage countries to develop the capacity to monitor and integrate environmental, social, and economic data, in order to value natural and social capital, and integrate that data in national accounts and development plans. –US, Canada; Switzerland, ROK move and merge with 110; G77 delete]

[Pre 105 alt. We emphasize that Sustainable Development Goals (SDGs) as well as an inclusive Green Economy in the context of Sustainable Development and Poverty Eradication and an enhanced Institutional Framework for Sustainable Development are important elements for progress –EU; G77 delete]

[Pre 105 alt bis. We [agree/consider-G77] to advance global and coherent Sustainable Development Goals that complement and strengthen the development agenda for the post-2015 period which fully encompass the three dimensions of sustainable development in a balanced and synergistic way and which are consistent with the principles of the 1992 Rio Declaration, Agenda

225

21 and the JPOI, are universal and applicable to all countries –EU; Switzerland move to section I]

105. We recognize that goals, targets and milestones are essential for measuring and accelerating progress towards sustainable development and agree to launch an inclusive process to devise by 2015:

a) a set of global Sustainable Development Goals that reflect an integrated and balanced treatment of the three dimensions of sustainable development, are consistent with the principles of Agenda 21, and are universal and applicable to all countries but allowing for differentiated approaches among countries;

b) a mechanism for periodic follow-up and reporting on progress made toward their achievement.

[105. We recognize that goals, targets and milestones **[based on a core set of principles –Liechtenstein, Canada] [are essential for [focused and coherent action, and –EU]/together with enhanced data and information can contribute to –US, Canada]** measuring and accelerating progress towards sustainable development and **[to this end –Norway]** [agree to launch [an inclusive –Mexico delete] **process /a fully participatory, inclusive and transparent process involving all stakeholders and coordinated by the UN Secretary-General –Liechtenstein, Canada]** [to devise [by 2015 –Japan delete]/**develop a set of sustainable development goals. These goals should –Norway/support a focused effort to inform post-2015 development planning by: –US, Canada /that progress should be measured against appropriate targets and indicators. –EU, move para 105 after para pre37, which is proposed to be in section V]**

[[105 bis. a)/**We agree to advance –EU]** [a set of –EU delete] global **[and coherent –EU]** Sustainable Development Goals **/considering sustainable development goals –US, Canada]** that –Norway delete] **[could be incorporated into any post-2015 framework and –US, Canada]** [reflect [an integrated and /a –Switzerland] balanced treatment of **/complement and strengthen the development agenda for the post-2015 period, full encompass- EU]** [and-Switzerland] **/integrate –New Zealand]** the three dimensions of sustainable development, **[in a balanced and synergistic way-EU] [are developed with consideration of cross-cutting themes –Australia, Canada] [are gender responsive, –Iceland] [reaffirming the Rio principles –Liechtenstein] [are/ and -Japan / and be –Norway]** [consisting with the **[Rio –Norway]** principles of **[the 1992 Rio Declaration –EU]** Agenda 21 –Japan delete], **[and the Johannesburg Plan of Implementation, –EU] [are based on and ensure the full equal enjoyment of human rights/protection and promotion of human rights, democracy, the rule of law and good governance, gender equality and women's empowerment –Liechtenstein]** and **[are b) be –Norway]** [universal and –New Zealand delete] applicable to all countries **/nationally-defined and relevant and universally applicable or accepted –US, Canada] [but while –Norway** allow[ing for differentiated approaches among countries –US delete/ **different paths to achievement –New Zealand, ROK] [enabling, all countries to translate it into national commitment to policy coherence for sustainability through appropriate legislative mechanisms –Liechtenstein; Switzerland reserves]**

b) [a/**exploring –US**] [**fully accountable –Liechtenstein**] mechanism for/**be sub-ject to –Norway**] periodic follow-up and reporting on progress made toward their achievement. (*Move as the last point –Norway, Canada*) [**in the context of any post-2015 development plans –US**] [**that is carried out openly and transpar-ently with the full and effective participation of all stakeholders, including civil society, and particularly people living in poverty –Liechtenstein; Switzerland reserves; EU move to 106bis**]

[**b) bis appropriate linkages to the institutional framework for sustainable development to support implementation and reporting. –Australia; Switzer-land reserve**]

[**b) ter build on the successful aspects of the MDGs and be concise, action-ori-ented [measurable –Switzerland] and limited in number; –Norway, Switzer-land, New Zealand**]

[**b) quat be designed to galvanize support and coordinated action for sustain-able development and poverty eradication –Norway; Switzerland delete**] –G77 delete entire paragraph]

(*Move after proposed Mexico's 105 ter*)

[**105.alt.1 In accordance with A/RES/65/1 we call for the General Assembly to continue to review, on an annual basis, the progress made towards the achieve-ment of the Millennium Development Goals, including in the implementation of the outcome document and request the President of the General Assembly at its sixty-eighth session to organize a special event in 2013 to follow up efforts made towards achieving the Millennium Development Goals –G77; Switzer-land delete; Canada prefer to work on 105; ROK move to Section I**]

[**105. alt 1 bis. We recognize that some progress has been made towards attain-ment of MDGs. However, we are deeply concerned that most LDCs, SIDS and African countries remain off-track in achieving most of the MDGs by 2015 and beyond. –G77; Switzerland delete; ROK move to section I**]

[**105. alt 1 ter. We also recognize that all the Millennium Development Goals are interconnected and mutually reinforcing and can therefore be best achieved when pursued in a holistic and comprehensive manner. Whereas there could be a need to formulate sustainable development goals, we emphasize that they must neither be used as a pretext for avoiding international commitments towards meeting MDGs targets nor pose new conditionalities for accessing development assistance. –G77; Switzerland delete; ROK move to section I**]

[**105. alt 1 quat. We underscore the continued relevance of the outcomes of all major United Nations conferences and summits in the economic, social and related fields and the commitments contained therein, including the Millen-nium Development Goals, which have raised awareness and continue to gener-ate real and important development gains. Together these outcomes and com-mitments have played a vital role in shaping a broad development vision and constitute the overarching framework for the development activities of the United Nations. We strongly reiterate our determination to ensure the timely** and full implementation of these outcomes and commitments. We recognize the importance of the MDGs in ensuring coherence in the delivery of the development objective by the UN System as a whole both at national and international levels. -G77; Switzerland delete; ROK move to Section I]

[105.alt 1 quint. We recognize that goals can be useful for pursuing sustainable development, taking into account the need for an integrated approach incorporating economic, social and environmental dimensions and recognizing their interlinkages and avoiding dealing with them in separate or parallel tracks. In this regard Sustainable Development Goals, built upon the MDGs, could be a driver for implementation and mainstreaming of sustainable development as well as integration of its three dimensions. –G77; Switzerland delete; ROK merge with 105]

[105. alt 1 sext. We recognize the importance and utility of a set of Sustainable Development Goals which are based on Agenda 21 and JPOI, fully respect Rio Principles [in particular CBDR-EU bracket], build upon commitment already made, respect international law and contribute to the full implementation of the outcomes of all major summits in the economic, social and environmental field taking into account that these goals should ensure a holistic coherence with the goals set in Agenda 21 and JPOI –G77; Switzerland, ROK delete]

[105. alt 1 sept. SDGs should be guided by the following principles and characteristics:

a) [Achieve poverty eradication –Switzerland delete / "poverty eradication" borrow from JPOI para 1.2 –EU];

b) Integrate in a balanced manner the three dimensions of sustainable development;

c) Respect the sovereignty of States over their natural resources in accordance with the UN Charter and principles of international law, without causing damage to the environment of other States or of areas beyond the limits of national jurisdiction;

d) Be consistent with the Rio principles particularly the Principle of Common But Differentiated Responsibilities;

e) Ensure the implementation of Agenda 21 and JPOI, and the outcomes of all UN major summits in economic, social and environmental field;

f) Build upon and complement the MDGs and renew and strengthen commitment towards their achievement;

g) Take into account different national realities, capacities and development priorities;

h) Rely on government driven implementation with involvement of all relevant stakeholders;

i) Contribute to the monitoring of fulfillment of developed countries' international commitments especially those related to financial resources, technology transfer and capacity building; –EU reserve]

j) Shall include means of implementation for developing countries, including under each goal; –EU reserve]

k) Give special attention to the countries in special situation and to disadvantaged and vulnerable people;

l) Not place additional restrictions or burdens on developing countries or dilute responsibilities of developed countries- EU reserve]

m) Contribute to fulfill the right to development and achieving equity at all levels;

n) Should respect policy space and national development priorities of each country, in particular avoiding the establishment of mechanism for monitoring national policies;

o) Applicable to all countries consistent with the principle of common but differentiated responsibilities. –G77; Switzerland delete; ROK bracket entire para]

p) Sustainable Development Goals shall be voluntary in nature –G77]

[105. alt 2. We recognize that goals, targets and milestones are essential for measuring and accelerating progress towards sustainable development, in this regard we decide to launch a process for the adoption of a single suite of Sustainable Development Goals –Mexico; Switzerland, G77 delete]

[105. alt 2 bis. We affirm that there should be a single set of goals with sustainable development and poverty eradication as the overarching focus –Mexico; Switzerland, G77 delete]

106. We invite all stakeholders to join this process and request the UN Secretary-General to coordinate this process.

[Move 106 to 108 –Switzerland]

[106. We [invite all stakeholders to join this process and –EU delete] [request/**look forward to the efforts of** –US, Canada] the UN Secretary-General to [**launch and** –EU] coordinate /**in relation to**- US] [this/an inclusive –EU delete] [process / **effort** –US] [process **to elaborate Sustainable Development Goals by 2015, with the participation of all relevant stakeholders. This process should be coordinated and coherent with the MDG review, without deviating efforts from the achievement of the MDGs. It will be important to have an overarching framework for post-2015 that addresses key challenges in a holistic and coherent way** –EU] action by developing a strategy for sustainable development, including in it the component of an energy-ecological balance –Kazakhstan, Belarus]. -G77 delete paragraph]

[106. alt We decide that the process to set the SDGs should be country-driven while open to the participation of all stakeholders and request the UN Secretary-General to provide all the necessary support to this process. –Mexico; G77 delete]

[106. alt 1 We request the UN Secretary-General to launch and coordinate an inclusive process to elaborate Sustainable Development Goals by 2015, with the participation of all relevant stakeholders. This process should be coordinated and coherent with the MDG review, without deviating efforts from the achievement of the MDGs. It will be important to have an overarching framework for post-2015 that addresses key challenges in a holistic and coherent way. –EU, ROK; G77 delete]

[106. alt 1 bis We also agree that progress towards these goals should be measured by appropriate indicators and evaluated by possible specific targets to be achieved possibly by 2030, and request proposals from the Secretary-General in this regard, as well as proposals for periodic follow up and reporting on progress made towards their achievement. –EU; G77 delete]

[106. bis We invite all stakeholders to join this process and request the President of the General Assembly and the President of the ECOSOC to develop a meaningful framework for civil society engagement to ensure participation by those directly concerned by extreme poverty and sustainable development. – Mexico; Switzerland move to 108; G77 reserve]

107. We propose that the Sustainable Development Goals could include sustainable consumption and production patterns as well as priority areas such as oceans; food security and sustainable agriculture; sustainable energy for all; water access and efficiency; sustainable cities; green jobs; decent work and social inclusion; and disaster risk reduction and resilience.

[107. We [propose/agree- Australia, ROK] that the Sustainable Development Goals could/ should –Australia] include [ecosystem preservation, –Kazakhstan, Belarus] [sustainable consumption and production patters as well as priority areas [such as oceans; [forests, biodiversity, education [and universal literacy – Switzerland] –Liechtenstein] food security and sustainable agriculture; [sustainable land management; –Iceland] sustainable energy for all –Kazakhstan retain]; [water access and efficiency/ access and efficient use of water –ROK] [[gender equality and the empowerment of women- Iceland]; health –Liechtenstein] sustainable cities; [resource-efficient and responsible industrial production,- Serbia][green jobs, Liechtenstein delete] decent work, [,green [and decent-ROK] jobs- Liechtenstein] [climate change –Switzerland, ROK] [sustainable chemicals and waste management, sustainable water management, violence and vulnerability, equitable economic rules, poverty reduction, transparent and accountable global institutions and partnerships –Switzerland] and social inclusion; [gender equality and the empowerment of women –Iceland, ROK / [political and civil rights –Switzerland] access to information and participation, social protection –Liechtenstein]; [the empowerment of women and education for sustainable development –Israel] and disaster risk reduction and resilience –Australia bracketed; Japan, ROK delete] –Mexico delete] –G77, Japan delete paragraph]

[107. alt 1 We propose that any goals for sustainable development be targeted, measurable, high-level, transparent, and, to help ensure sustained commitment, focused on a small number of priority items. –US, Canada, New Zealand, Australia; G77 delete]

[107. alt 2 We propose that priority areas to be covered by the Sustainable Development Goals should include sustainable energy for all, food security and sustainable water management, as well as areas such as sustainable consumption and production patterns, oceans; sustainable human settlements; decent green jobs; disaster risk reduction and resilience. All the goals should contribute to reducing poverty, inequity and gender inequality and promote sustainable management of ecosystems and natural resources. An expert mechanism should be established by the Secretary-General to elaborate and refine the goals before their adoption by member states. –Norway; Mexico, G77 delete]

[107. alt 3 We propose that the Sustainable Development Goals should be limited in number and easily communicable. They should include key thematic areas, their interlinkages and cross-cutting issues, giving particular consideration to areas covered in Chapter V, Section A. –EU, New Zealand; Japan reserve; G77 delete]

108. We consider that the Sustainable Development Goals should complement and strengthen the MDGs in the development agenda for the post-2015 period, with a view to establishing a set of goals in 2015 which are part of the post-2015 UN Development Agenda.

[108. [We agree that Sustainable Development Goals should be developed through a transparent UN system wide process led by the UN Secretary-General, drawing on expert advice and involving member states, as well as stakeholders. –Switzerland] We consider that [this process for establishing –Switzerland] the Sustainable Development Goals should /sustainable development goals could –US, Canada] complement and strengthen the MDGs [[in the development agenda for/and any goals developed for –US, Canada] the post-2015 period- Norway delete], with a view to [establishing / elaborating- US, Canada] a [single –Australia, Norway] [set of [global-Norway] goals/more coherent international development agenda – US, Canada] in 2015 [which are part of/while being closely coordinated with the MDG review process and with the overall aim of informing and strengthening – Canada/as a key component of –Norway] the post-[2015 UN Development Agenda. [These goals should be developed through an inclusive process involving all stakeholders, and we request the UN Secretary-General to coordinate this process. –Norway] and be integrated into a set of post-2015 development goals – Japan] –US; EU delete and merge with 106; G77, Mexico delete paragraph]

[108. alt 1 We consider that the Sustainable Development Goals should be informed by a full and meaningful review of existing development goals, including the MDGs, and be fully integrated into a global over-arching post-2015 UN Development Framework with sustainable development and poverty eradication at its core. –Liechtenstein; G77 delete]

[108. alt 2 We agree that the adoption of Sustainable Development Goals in 2015 should be part of the post-2015 UN Development Agenda, in this respect we recognize that Sustainable Development Goals should complement and strengthen the MDGs in the development agenda for the post-2015 period. Mexico; G77 delete]

(Move as 105 bis –Mexico)

[108 bis. We decide to set off a process for a single post 2015 framework in order to further develop the SDGs; define appropriate targets and indicators and to develop a mechanism for periodic follow-up and reporting on progress made towards the achievement of such goals. To this end, we recommend to the General Assembly to establish a Group of Experts integrated by representatives of governments and relevant stakeholders and from specialized agencies with expertise in the environmental, social and economic aspects of sustainable development. –Mexico; Canada reserve; G77 delete]

109. We also propose that progress towards these Goals should be measured by appropriate indicators and evaluated by specific targets to be achieved possibly by 2030, and request the Secretary-General for proposals in this regard.

[109. We also [propose / **agree –EU**] that progress towards these [Goals /**goals-US**] should be measured [by/**in an –Japan**] appropriate [manner-Japan] [range of – Canada] indicators and evaluated by [**possible –EU**] specific targets [to be achieved possibly by [**2030/2032- Switzerland**], [**with strong benchmarks of progress at regular intervals- Liechtenstein**] and request the Secretary-General for proposals in this regard /**defined at the national level –US**] [**, as well as for periodic follow-up and reporting on progress made toward achievement –EU**]. –G77, Mexico, EU delete paragraph, move to 106 bis]

110. We resolve to strengthen the capacity of all countries to collect and analyze data and information needed to support the monitoring of progress towards the Sustainable Development Goals. We request the Secretary-General, with the support of interested donors, the UN system, international organizations and other entities, to promote a global partnership in this regard.

[110. We resolve to strengthen the capacity of all countries to collect and analyze data and information needed to support the monitoring of progress towards [**the sustainable development including –New Zealand**] the Sustainable Development Goals. [**Such information should also support policymaking processes. The shared environmental information system (SEIS) in the pan-European region illustrates a successful approach to supporting countries' efforts –Serbia; Switzerland reserve**] [**and in this connection we support the relevant work of the UN Statistical Commission on economic and environmental accounting and further request the Commission to advance in a process of identifying appropriate consensual statistical indicators with the aim of measuring progress in the achievement of these goals –Mexico; Switzerland reserve**]] [We /and further-Mexico] [request the Secretary-General [, with the support of interested [donors/**countries –Japan, ROK**], the UN system, international organizations and other [entities/**stakeholders –Liechtenstein**], to promote a global partnership in this regard/**to ensure that the work on strengthening this capacity is integrated into the schemes and measures on capacity building included in chapters III and V of this document, and further coordinated with existing relevant capacity development schemes in the UN system –EU** /**encourage the international community and the relevant bodies of the United Nations system to assist the efforts of developing countries in this regard by providing capacity-building and technical support. –New Zealand**] –EU to revert] – G77 delete paragraph; **US bracketed; EU reserve; Canada merge with pre105**]

111. We also recognize the limitations of GDP as a measure of well-being. We agree to further develop and strengthen indicators complementing GDP that integrate economic, social and environmental dimensions in a balanced manner. We request the Secretary-General to establish a process in consultation with the UN system and other relevant organizations.

[111. We also recognize the limitations of GDP as a measure of [well-being/**sustainable growth –EU, Canada**] We [agree/**intend –US, Canada**] to further develop [[**methods of accounting for natural capital and social well-being, and to use these measurements in our national systems to assess progress, encourage transparency and accountability, and inform policy decisions –Canada**]. We agree to further develop and [strengthen/**improve –EU**] indicators [**and wealth accounts –Canada**; Switzerland, ROK delete] [complementing/**to complement –EU, Canada**] GDP [**and measures progress towards sustainable development –EU, Canada**] [that integrate/**integrating –EU**] economic, social and environmental dimensions in a balanced manner [**taking into account the contributions of and impacts on men and women –US, Canada; Switzerland delete/based on appropriate statistical and geospatial information. In this regard, we** [support/**take into account –ROK**] **the work of the OECD in creating and developing green growth indicators. –ROK**; Canada delete] We request the Secretary-General to [establish/**explore –US, Canada, New Zealand**] a process [in consultation with the UN system [, **a broad range of stakeholders including civil society, research community –Liechtenstein, New Zealand**] and other relevant organizations/**to collate such information and track progress at a national level –EU**] [in this regard –US, Canada] –G77 delete paragraph; **EU to come back on placement; Liechtenstein, New Zealand move to end of Section V.A as a separate section therein including comments and addition already made**]

[**111. bis We decide to establish an integrated and scientifically credible global sustainable development assessment to support decision-making processes at appropriate levels, to assist member states in identifying policy options to speed up the achievement of the sustainable development goals and to inform, including through an agreed Summary for Policy Makers, the discussions of ECOSOC and request the Secretary-General, through the Department of Economic and Social Affairs, UNDP and UNEP to lead a system-wide effort in this regard. – Mexico; G77 delete**]

Appendix 13:
Co-Chairs Conslidated
Suggested Negotiation Text,
March 28, 2012

CST B. Sustainable Development Goals

CST 105. We acknowledge that the MDGs have generated real and important development gains, and have played a vital role as part of a broad development vision and framework for the development activities of the United Nations. We recognize the importance of the MDGs in ensuring coherence in the delivery of the development objective by the UN System as a whole both at national and international levels.

CST 105 bis. We recognize that goals can be useful for pursuing sustainable development, taking into account the need for an integrated approach incorporating economic, social and environmental dimensions and recognizing their interlinkages and avoiding dealing with them in separate or parallel tracks. In this regard Sustainable Development Goals (SDGs), built upon the MDGs to whose timely achievement we remain firmly committed, could be a driver for implementation and mainstreaming of sustainable development, as well as of integration of its three dimensions.

CST 105 ter. We recognize the importance and utility of a set of SDGs which are based on Agenda 21 and JPOI, fully respect all Rio Principles, build upon commitment already made, respect international law and contribute to the full implementation of the outcomes of all major summits in the economic, social and environmental fields.

CST 105 quat. SDGs should contribute to achieving the three overarching objectives and essential requirements for sustainable development as defined in the JPOI: poverty eradication, changing unsustainable patterns of production and consumption and protecting and managing the natural resource base of economic and social development. They should build upon and complement the MDGs and renew and strengthen commitment towards their achievement.

CST 105 quint. SDGs should be action-oriented; concise and readily communicable; limited in number and focused on priority areas; universally applicable while taking into account different national realities, capacities and development priorities; and voluntary in nature.

CST 105 sext. SDGs should also give due consideration to cross-cutting issues including social equity and gender equality as well as the means of implementation.

CST 106. We agree that the SDGs should be developed through an intergovernmental process under the General Assembly that is inclusive, transparent and open to the participation of all stakeholders. This process will need to be coordinated and coherent with the processes considering the post-2015 development agenda.

CST 106 bis. We request the UN Secretary General to launch and coordinate a process to elaborate SDGs by 2015, which will include reporting to the UN General Assembly, drawing on expert advice and be based on the participation of all relevant stakeholders.

CST 107. We propose that the SDGs address key priority areas, their interlinkages and cross-cutting issues, giving particular consideration to areas covered in Chapter V, Section A.

CST 109. Progress towards the SDGs should be measured in an appropriate manner by a set of appropriate indicators and evaluated by specific targets. We request the Secretary-General for proposals in this regard as well as for periodic reporting on progress made towards the achievement of the SDGs to the General Assembly.

Appendix 14:
Negotiation Text,
May 2, 2012, 10 p.m.

B. [Accelerating and measuring progress / **Sustainable Development Goals-G77**] **US, Canada, New Zealand reserve this entire section**]

CST B. [Sustainable Development Goals/**Integrating Sustainable Development in a post-2015 development framework –US, RoK delete**]

Note: EU propose retain original title or move para 111 to end of Section V.A

[Propose that this section be structured in 4 paragraphs: 1 para on characteristics, 1 para on process (merge 106 into 108, 1 para on potential issues, areas and themes (107), 1 para on measurement of progress (109) –Switzerland, RoK, New Zealand] (Merged with G77's proposed organizational structure to form overarching structure of section)

[Propose alternative structure: 1. Vision on Sustainable Development Goals. 2. Principles that should guide Sustainable Development Goals. 3. Process (Merged with Switzerland's proposed organizational structure to form overarching structure of section) 3.1. Has to be intergovernmental. 3.2. Has to be inclusive, transparent and open-ended. 3.3. Has to be under the UN General Assembly (Merged into CST106) –G77]

CST 105. [**We emphasize that Sustainable Development Goals (SDGs) as well as an inclusive Green Economy in the context of Sustainable Development and Poverty Eradication and an enhanced Institutional Framework for Sustainable Development are important elements for progress. –EU, RoK; New Zealand questions placement**] We [acknowledge/**underscore –EU**] that [**as a tool –G77**] the MDGs have [[generated/**sharpened the focus on –US**] real and important development gains, and have **–G77 delete**] played a vital role as part of a broad development vision and framework for the development activities of the United Nations [**for international cooperation, national priority setting and mobilization of stakeholders and resources towards a common goal, –Switzerland**] [**, as well as at national and**

236

regional level –EU, Switzerland], [and national governments –US]. [We recognize the importance of the MDGs in [ensuring/**fostering-US**] coherence in the delivery of the development objective by the UN System as a whole both at national and international levels. **–G77, New Zealand delete**] [**We remain firmly committed to the timely achievement of the MDGs. –New Zealand**] (105.alt 1 quat)

CST 105 bis. We recognize that goals [[can be/**could be** –US/**are** Switzerland] [useful/**are essential** –EU, Norway, RoK] for pursuing [focused and coherent action on –EU, RoK] sustainable development, taking into account the need for an integrated approach incorporating economic, social and environmental dimensions and recognizing their interlinkages and avoiding dealing with them in separate or parallel tracks. In this regard [**aspirational** –US] Sustainable Development Goals (SDGs), [built/**building-Canada**] upon /**complementing** –Japan] [**the experience with** – EU, Switzerland] the MDGs [to whose timely achievement we remain firmly committed, –New Zealand delete] –US delete] could be a driver for implementation and mainstreaming of sustainable development, as well as of integration of its three dimensions. (105. alt 1 quint)

[CST 105 ter. We recognize the importance and utility of [a set of –EU, Switzerland delete] SDGs which are based on [**a core set of principles, including respect for international law, in particular human rights law, democracy, good governance, gender equality and women's empowerment, and the rule of law, and which contribute to the full implementation of** –Liechtenstein] Agenda 21 and JPOI [, **the Rio Principles** –Liechtenstein] [**the Rio outcome and the MDGs assessment** – Switzerland, Liechtenstein], [**and the** –Liechtenstein] [fully respect all Rio Principles, build upon commitment already made, respect international law and contribute to the full implementation of the –**Liechtenstein delete**] outcomes of all major summits in the economic, social and environmental fields [, **while taking into account recent changes and development. –Japan**] (105. alt 1 sext) –**G77, US delete para**]

CST 105 ter alt. We remain firmly committed to the timely achievement of the existing MDGs. The development of any SDGs should reinforce that commitment and not detract from our efforts in that regard –US

CST 105 ter alt2. We therefore agree to develop a set of global SDGs which address all three dimensions of sustainable development and their interlinkages, and are consistent with Agenda 21, the Rio Principles, and the JPoI. –Norway

[CST 105 quat. [**We propose that any** –US] SDGs should contribute to achieving the three overarching objectives and essential requirements for sustainable development as defined in the JPOI: poverty eradication, changing unsustainable patterns of production and consumption and protecting and managing the natural resources base of economic and social development. [They should [build upon [the strength of the MDGs –EU] [and/strengthen and –Japan] complement –Switzerland delete] the [m-commitment towards [their/the –Switzerland] achievement [**and play a critical factor in the formation of a post-2015 development agenda- Japan**] [of their objectives and furthermore define a universal sustainable development agenda – Switzerland] / **SDGs should be built upon the foundation of the Millennium Declaration and should be integrated into the development of a post-2015** development framework. –US] [, contributing to an overarching framework for post-2015 that encompasses the three dimensions of sustainable development which goals that address key challenges in a holistic and coherent way –EU, Switzerland, New Zealand] (105.alt 1 sept) –G77 delete para; US reserves on para]

[CST 105 quint. [SDGs should / **We propose any SDGs would need to –US, New Zealand delete**] be action-oriented; concise and readily communicable; limited in number and focused on priority areas; universally applicable while taking into account different national realities, capacities and development priorities [; and [voluntary/**aspirational –Norway**] in nature –New Zealand delete]. (From 105, pre 105 alt bis, 105 alt 1 sept, 105 alt2, 105 b ter, 105 bis, 105 bis b ter, 105.alt 1 quint) –G77 delete para]

[CST 105 sext. [**All the –Norway**] SDGs should [also give due consideration to /address –Norway] cross-cutting issues including [**good governance –EU, Switzerland, Liechtenstein, New Zealand**] [**poverty eradication –Norway**] social [**inclusion, –EU, Switzerland, Liechtenstein; US delete**] equity [and/, –EU] gender equality [**and women's empowerment –EU, Switzerland, Liechtenstein, New Zealand, Norway**] [**sustainable resource management –Norway**] [as well as [**to –EU, Liechtenstein**] the means of implementation –US delete] [, especially for the most vulnerable groups and the poorest countries –EU, Liechtenstein]. (105.bis.a, 105.alt 1 sept) –G77 delete para; US reserves on para]

[**105.alt 1 bis We recognize that some progress has been made towards attainment of MDGs. However, we are deeply concerned that most LDCs, SIDs and African countries remain off-track due to the absence of resources in achieving most of the MDGs by 2015 and beyond. –G77; Switzerland delete; RoK move to section I] G77 retain**

[**105.alt 1 sept SDGs should be guided by the following principles and characteristics:**

a) [Achieve poverty eradication/ "Poverty eradication . . ." borrow from JPOI para 1.2 –EU];

b) Integrate in a balanced manner the three dimensions of sustainable development;

c) Respect the sovereignty of States over their natural resources in accordance with the UN Charter and principles of international law, without causing damage to the environment of other States or of areas beyond the limits of national jurisdiction;

d) Be consistent with the Rio principles particularly the Principle of Common But Differentiated Responsibilities;

e) Ensure the implementation of Agenda 21 and JPOI, and the outcomes of all UN major summits in economic, social and environmental field;

f) Build upon and complement the MDGs and renew and strengthen commitment towards their achievement;

g) Take into account different national realities, capacities and development priorities;

h) Rely on government driven implementation with involvement of all relevant stakeholders;

i) Contribute to the monitoring of fulfillment of developed countries' international commitments especially those related to financial resources, technology transfer and capacity building; –EU reserve]

j) Shall include means of implementation for developing countries, including under each goal; –EU reserve]

k) Give special attention to the countries in special situation and to disadvantaged and vulnerable people;

l) Not place additional restrictions or burdens on developing countries or dilute responsibilities of developed countries; –EU reserve]

m) Contribute to fulfill the right to development and achieving equity at all levels;

n) Should respect policy space and national development priorities of each country, in particular avoiding the establishment of mechanism for monitoring national policies;

o) Applicable to all countries consistent with the principle of common but differentiated responsibilities. –G77; Switzerland –delete; –RoK bracket entire para]

[p) Sustainable Development Goals shall be voluntary in nature –G77] [RoK bracket entire para; Switzerland reflect all dimensions of sustainable development in the entire para] G77, Mexico retain para. (Merged and streamlined into CST 105 and CST 107)

[CST 106f. We [agree [to establish a process on –G77] [that the –G77 delete] SDGs should be developed through an intergovernmental process under the General Assembly that is / propose that any SDGs would need to be internationally agreed and developed through a fully –US, RoK] inclusive, transparent and open [[to/process with –US] the participation of all stakeholders/including the UN System –G77]. This process will need to be coordinated and coherent with the [MDGs review –G77] process[es –G77 delete] considering the post-2015 development [agenda/framework –US] [in order to allow a smooth integration of SDGs into such post-2015 development agenda –Japan]. (based on suggestions before pre 105, 105, 106 and 106.alt) –Canada delete] (Canada propose consolidating Op 106 alt 1 and CST106 into CST106 bis; EU, Norway propose merging CST106 and CST106 bis) (New Zealand questions link of intergovernmental process with CST 106 bis language on UN Secretary General)

CST106 bis We request the UN Secretary General to launch and coordinate [an intergovernmental process –New Zealand] [a/an inclusive –Canada] process to [elaborate [a limited number of –Canada] SDGs [complementary to the MDG framework –Canada] by 2015, [which will include reporting to the UN General Assembly, /ensure that SDGs are reflected in any post-2015 development framework –US, Japan] drawing on expert advice and [be –US delete] based on –Canada delete] [with- Canada] the participation of all relevant stakeholders [building upon past work and efforts –Australia]. [This process will need to be coordinated and coherent with the processes considering the post-2015 development agenda,

without deviating efforts from the achievement of the MDGs. It will be important to have an overarching framework for post-2015 that addresses key challenges in a holistic and coherent way. –Canada, Australia proposes merging with CST106 alt] (From 105, 106, 106 alt, 106 alt 1 and 106bis, and guidelines on process from G77's proposed organizational structure) (Canada underscores the importance of the concepts presented in CST106 and CST106 bis being contained within a single, uninterrupted paragraph)

CST106 alt. We request the UN Secretary General to launch and coordinate a process to elaborate SDGs, which will include reporting to the UN General Assembly, drawing on expert advice and evidence [before their adoption by Member States –Norway]. This process should be inclusive, transparent, and open to the participation of all relevant stakeholders, as well as fully coordinated and coherent with the process considering the post-2015 framework. – EU, Switzerland, Norway, RoK]

CST106 alt2. We decide to establish a process for the adoption of a single suite of SDGs, with sustainable development and poverty eradication as the overarching focus, such process should be country-driven whilst open to the participation of all stakeholders. We therefore decide to establish a group of experts integrated by representative of governments and relevant stakeholders and from specialized agencies with experience in environment, social and economic aspects of sustainable development in order to define appropriate targets and indicators and to develop a mechanism for periodic follow-up and reporting on progress made towards the achievement of such goals. UN Secretary-General should provide all necessary support to this process. –Mexico]

[CST107. We propose that the SDGs address [**the following indicative –Switzerland, New Zealand, Australia**] [**areas related to the following indicative list –Mexico**] key priority areas [their interlinkages and cross-cutting issues, giving particular consideration to areas [covered in Chapter V, section A/such as Sustainable Energy for All, food security, sustainable water management and sustainable consumption and production –Norway]. –Switzerland delete] (From 105 alt 2 bis, 107, 107 alt 2 and 107 alt 3) –**G77, US delete para**] (EU propose move to after CST105 sext and merge)

[CST109. Progress towards the SDGs should be measured in an appropriate manner by a set of appropriate indicators and [evaluated by /**assessed on the basis of -US, New Zealand**] specific targets [**that could be set at multiple levels –US**]. [We request the Secretary-General [for proposals int his regard as well/**to –EU, Norway**] report[ing –EU delete] on progress [made towards the achievement of the SDGs to [**the Sustainable Development Council and –Switzerland, RoK**] [**ECOSOC and –Mexico**] the General Assembly –US delete] –Japan delete]. (From 109, 106 alt 1 bis) –**G77 delete para**]

CST109 alt. We decide to establish the sustainable development outlook as an integrated and scientifically-credible global sustainable development assessment to support the decision-making process at appropriate levels to assist member states in identifying policy options to speed up the achievement of the SDGs –Mexico]

Appendix 15:
Section B—Negotiation Text,
May 4, 2012, 4 p.m.

B. [Accelerating and measuring progress / **Sustainable Development Goals –G77**] **US, Canada, New Zealand reserve this entire section**]

CST B. Sustainable Development Goals/**Integrating Sustainable Development in a Post-2015 development framework –US; ROK delete**]

[**NCST. Sustainable Development Goals/Integrating Sustainable Development [Goals] in a post-2015 development framework –US**]

Note: EU propose retain original title or move para 111 to end of Section V.A.

NCST 105. We underscore that the MDGs are a useful tool in focusing achievement of specific development gains as part of a broad development vision and framework for the development activities of the United Nations, for national priority setting and for mobilization of stakeholders and resources towards common goals. We therefore remain firmly committed to their full and timely achievement [agreed ad ref] [EU supports para but suggest move after NCST 105bis; ROK questions placement; G77 retain placement from CST.105]

NCST 105bis. We [also –EU delete] recognize that the development goals could [**also-G77, EU**] be useful for pursuing focused and coherent action on sustainable development, taking into account the need for and integrated approach incorporating its three dimensions. In this regard, [, **and building on/complementing –Japan**] the **Millennium Development Goals –G77**] we agree to [develop a set of [**global-Norway, Australia, Kazakhstan**] sustainable development goals (SDGs) that address [**and incorporate-Switzerland**] all three dimensions of sustainable development and their interlinkages –ROK, EU / **incorporating the three dimensions of sustainable development and their interlinkages in the post-2015 UN development agenda –US; EU delete**] [**and contribute to an overarching post-2015 framework –EU**].

241

[These SDGs should be a driver for implementation and mainstreaming of [the-G77] sustainable development-EU [agenda [including-Canada] in the United Nation's system as a whole –G77, Kazakhstan] / This agenda should contribute to the achievement of sustainable development –US] EU move to beginning of section (from CST 105bis, CST ter alt 2, CST 105 quat, CST 105 sext)

NCST 105. We propose that [the SDGs / any goals-US] should also contribute to meeting the essential [requirements/components-US] for sustainable development [as defined in the JPOI, namely, poverty eradication, changing unsustainable patterns of consumption and production, and protecting and managing natural resource base of economic and social development –US delete]. They should address [cross-cutting EU reserve] issues including, inter alia [social-EU delete] equity and [social-EU] inclusion, [rule of law and good governance –Liechtenstein, EU, Switzerland] gender equality and women's empowerment [US delete entire paragraph] [New Zealand, Australia questions paragraph in view of duplication in para 105 quint] [G77, Russian Federation delete para and prefer work on 105 quint] [Norway, EU, Switzerland retain para] (from CST 105 quint, quint and sext)

CST 105 quint. [SDGs should /We propose any SDGs would need to –US; New Zealand delete] be action-oriented; concise and readily communicable; limited in number and focused on priority areas; universally applicable while taking into account different national realities, capacities and development priorities [; and voluntary / aspirational –Norway] in nature –New Zealand delete]. (From 105, pre 105 alt bis, 105 alt 1 sept, 105 alt 2, 105b ter, 105 bis, 105 bis b ter, 105 alt 1 quint) –G77 delete para] Merged into NCST 105 quint.

[105 alt 1 bis. We recognize that some progress has been made towards attainment of MDGs. However, we are deeply concerned that most LDCs, SIDS and African countries remain off-track due to the absence of resources in achieving most of the MDGs by 2015 and beyond. –G77; Switzerland delete; ROK move to Section I] G77 retain]

[NCST 105 quint. We affirm that [SDGs –ROK, New Zealand, EU retain/any goals- US, HolySee, EU] should be guided by the following [principles and characteristics –US, HolySee delete]:

a) Build upon the foundation of the Millennium Declaration [EU combine with (f); Norway combine b)]
b) [Complement –Japan/Build upon –Switzerland; Japan delete] the MDGs and renew and strengthen commitment towards [their/the-Switzerland] achievement [of their objectives-Switzerland]; [New Zealand duplicative with NCST 105]
c) Achieve [extreme-US] poverty eradication; [EU, Switzerland, Norway combine with (d); Holy See retain original]
   pre (d) Promote democracy and strengthen rule of law, as well as respect for human rights and fundamental freedom –Liechtenstein, EU]
d) Contribute to advancing the other two overarching objectives of sustainable development as agreed in JPOI, namely [poverty eradication-Switzerland] changing consumption and production patterns and protecting and managing

the natural resource base for economic and social development; [**US delete d**]; **HolySee reserve**]

e) Integrate in a balanced manner the three dimensions of sustainable development; [**US delete subpara; Norway, EU retain**]

f) Be consistent with the Rio principles [, **while taking into account of recent changes in development –Japan**]; [**US delete subpara; HolySee, New Zealand retain original; Norway combine with g)**)]

g) Advance the implementation of Agenda 21 and JPOI, and the [outcomes of all UN major summits in economic, social and environmental field **–US delete**] [**US delete subpara; HolySee reserve**]

h) Respect the sovereignty of States over their natural resources in accordance wit the UN Charter and principles of international law, without causing damage to the environment of other States or of areas beyond the limits of national jurisdiction; [**US reserve; Canada, Switzerland, New Zealand, Norway, EU delete**]

i) Be applicable to all countries [consistent with the principle of common but differentiated responsibilities **–Canada, Switzerland, Norway delete; EU calls for correct quotation of Rio Principle 7 if specific references to CBDR is necessary here**]; [**US delete, New Zealand subpara; Norway combine with j)**)]

j) [Take / **Be universally applicable while taking –Switzerland, New Zealand, EU/ while taking Norway**] into account different national realities, capacities and development priorities; [**US delete subpara**]

k) Rely on government driven implementation with involvement of all relevant stakeholders [**US, Switzerland, Norway, EU delete subpara**]

l) Contribute to the monitoring of fulfillment of [**developed –Switzerland, New Zealand delete**] countries' international commitments [**including those relating to financial resources –Switzerland, HolySee**] especially those related to financial resources, technology transfer and capacity building; [**US, Canada, EU delete subpara; ROK reserve**]

m) Shall include means of implementation for developing countries [, including under each goal **–Switzerland, New Zealand delete**]; [**US, Canada, EU delete subpara; ROK reserve**]

n) Give special attention to countries in special situations and to disadvantaged and vulnerable people; [**US, ROK, EU reserve**]

o) Not place additional restrictions or burdens on developing countries or dilute responsibilities of developed countries; [**–EU reserve**] [**US, Canada, Switzerland, New Zealand, Norway delete subpara; ROK reserve; HolySee retain original**]

p) Contribute to [fulfilling the right to **–Switzerland delete**] [**sustainable – Switzerland**] development and achieving equity at all levels; [**US, New Zealand, EU delete subpara; HolySee retain original**]

q) Be [**action-oriented and –Switzerland, New Zealand**] aspirational in nature; [**Norway, EU retain**]

r) Be concise and readily communicable; [**Norway, EU retain**]

s) Limited in number and focused on priority areas. [**Norway, EU retain**]

[EU, US, Japan, Canada, Switzerland prefers CST 105 quint; Liechtenstein, Australia flexible] [G77 retain NCST original para entirely] (from CST105 ter alt, CST105 quat, CST105 quint, 105 alt 1 sept, CST106 alt2)

NCST 106. [We agree/**request-US**] [to establish a country-driven [intergovernmental-**Norway delete**] process [**to further develop the –Norway**] [**on-Norway delete**] SDGs under the General Assembly / **that the SDGs should be developed through a process guided by the General Assembly-Switzerland, Norway/ the Secretary-General to launch and coordinate a process on the post-2015 UN development agenda which, integrates the three dimensions of sustainable development, and US**] [**that-US delete**] is inclusive, transparent and open to participation of all relevant stakeholders, including the UN System, and [that draws on / **it should be driven by –Switzerland**] relevant expert advice and [**science based –Kazakhstan**] evidence. [The UN Secretary-General should provide all the necessary support to his process. This process will need to be [fully -**ROK delete**] with the MDG review process considering the post-2015 development [agenda/**framework –Switzerland**] in order to allow a smooth integration of SDGs into this [agenda/**framework – Switzerland**] –**US delete**] /**with a view to establish a single set of goals in 2015 –Norway**] [We also propose that any SDGs be internationally agreed by [Member States/**the General Assembly –HolySee**] –**US reserves; ROK delete**] [**EU retains CST106 alt; Canada, Japan reserve entire para, prefer language that makes it clear that we will not launch 2 separate processes**] (from CST106,CST106 bis, CST106 alt and CST106 alt2)

[**CST106.alt.1. We request the UN Secretary-General to launch and coordinate a process to elaborate SDGs, which will include reporting to the UN General Assembly, drawing on expert advice and evidence before their adoption by Member States. This process should be inclusive, transparent, and open to the participation of all relevant stakeholders, as well as fully coordinated and coherent with the process considering the post-2015 framework –EU**]

[**CST106.alt.2. We agree to establish an intergovernmental process on SDGs under the UN General Assembly that is inclusive, transparent, and open to participation of all stakeholders. This process needs to be coordinated and coherent with the processes considering the post-2015 UN development agenda- G77 retain**]

[CST 107. We propose that the SDGs address [**the following indicative –Switzerland, New Zealand, Australia**] [**areas related to the following indicative list-Mexico**] key priority areas [, their interlinkages and cross-cutting issues, giving particular consideration to areas [covered in Chapter V, section A/such as Sustainable Energy for All, food security, sustainable water management and sustainable consumption and production –Norway] [Switzerland delete] **G77, US delete para**] (from 105 alt2bis, 107, 107alt 2, and 107 alt 3) (EU propose move to after CST105 sext and merge)

Stopped here at 4pm, May 4.

[CST 109. Progress towards the SDGs should be measured in an appropriate manner by a set of appropriate indicators and [evaluated by/**assessed on the basis of –**

US, New Zealand] specific targets **[that could be set at multiple levels-US]**. [We request the Secretary-General for [proposals in this regard as well / **to –EU, Norway]** [as for -EU delete] periodic **[ally –EU, Norway]** repor[ing –EU delete] on progress [made towards the achievement of the SDGs to **[the Sustainable Development Council and –Switzerland, ROK] [ECOSOC and –Mexico]** the General Assembly **–US delete]** –Japan delete] (From 109, 106 alt 1 bis) **–G77 delete para]**

NCST 109. We underline that progress towards the SDGs should be measured in an appropriate manner by an agreed set of indicators and assessed on the basis of specific targets that could be differentiated depending on countries' levels of development and national specificities. (from CST109)

[CST 109 alt. We decide to establish a sustainable development outlook as an integrated and scientifically-credible global sustainable development assessment to support the decision-making process as appropriate levels to assist member states in identifying policy options to speed up the achievement of the SDGs –Mexico]

NCST 109 alt. We recognize the need for an integrated, scientifically-credible global sustainable development assessment to support national decision-making processes in the identification of policy options for the national implementation of the SDGs. In this regard, we call on the Secretary-General of the United Nations to make proposals on this assessment to the UNGA for the subsequent consideration by Member States.

[CST 111. We also recognize the limitations of GDP as a measure of well-being and sustainable growth. As a complement to [measuring –EU delete] GDP, we [intend/**resolve –EU, Switzerland]** to further develop methods of accounting for natural capital and social well-being **[and to elaborate and adopt a set of harmonized, science-based [generally applicable –Switzerland] and easy to use indicators for –EU, Switzerland]** [, and to use these measurements in our –EU delete] national [systems to assess progress, / **and global assessments of sustainable development –EU, Switzerland]** encourage transparency and accountability, and inform policy decisions. **[We request the Secretary-General to coordinate the preparation of such indicators in consultation with the UN System and all other relevant organizations, having regard to the UN system of economic and environmental accounts –EU, Switzerland]** [US, G77 delete para] (From pre 105 and 111) (EU, Switzerland, Norway, Australia propose move para to end of section V.A); New Zealand questions placement]

[CST 111 alt. Recognizing that appropriate indicators for measuring progress on all dimensions of sustainable development may be lacking, we underline the importance of developing methods for better measuring sustainability and social well-being that would provide a framework for assessing progress, encouraging transparency and accountability, and informing policy decisions. –US]

[CST 111 alt 2. We decide to give a mandate to the UN Statistical Commission to identify appropriate consensual statistical indicators with the aim of measuring progress in the achievement of SDGs on the basis of the current economic and environmental accounting –Mexico; Norway reserves position

Appendix 16:
Negotiation Text,
May 22, 2012

B. Sustainable Development Goals [and Measuring progress beyond GDP]

SDG1. We underscore that the MDGs are a useful tool in focusing achievement of specific development gains as part of a broad development vision and framework for the development activities of the United Nations, for national priority setting and for mobilization of stakeholders and resources towards common goals. We therefore remain firmly committed to their full and timely achievement (agreed ad ref)

SDG2. We recognize that the development of goals could also be useful for pursuing focused and coherent action on sustainable development. In this regard, and building on the Millennium Development Goals, we agree to develop a set of global sustainable development goals (SDGs) that address and incorporate all three dimensions of sustainable development and their interlinkages. These goals should be incorporated in the United Nations Development Agenda beyond 2015 thus contributing to the achievement of sustainable development and serving as a driver for implementation and mainstreaming of sustainable development in the United Nations system as a whole.

SDG3. We propose that the goals should build upon the Millennium Declaration, respect the UN Charter and principles of international law, be consistent with the Rio principles and contribute to advance the implementation of Agenda 21 and JPOI, including poverty eradication, changing unsustainable patterns of consumption and production, and protecting and managing the natural resource base of economic and social development.

SDG4. We also propose that any SDGs should be action-oriented, concise and readily communicable, limited in number, aspirational, and universally applicable to all countries while taking into account different national realities, capacities and development priorities. Implementation should be government-driven with involvement of all relevant stakeholders.

SDG5. We also recognize that the goals should address and be focused on priority areas for the achievement of sustainable development including inter alia, energy, water, food security, oceans and sustainable consumption and production as well as cross-cutting issues like equity and social inclusion, rule of law and good governance, gender equality and women's empowerment.

SDG6. We reiterate our request to the Secretary-General to make recommendations in his annual reports for further steps to realize the United Nations Development Agenda beyond 2015. We further request the Secretary-General to integrate the three dimensions of sustainable development in the United Nations Development Agenda beyond 2015 and establish a coordinated process with a view to establishing a set of coherent global goals in 2015. This process should be a country-driven process guided by the General Assembly and be inclusive, transparent, open to participation of all relevant stakeholders, including the UN System, and draw on relevant expert advice and science-based evidence. We also propose that any SDGs be agreed by the UN General Assembly.

SDG7. We underline that progress towards the SDGs should be measured by an agreed and appropriate set of indicators and assessed on the basis of specific targets that could be differentiated depending on countries' levels of development and national specificities.

SDG8. We recognize that there is a need for an integrated and scientifically-credible global sustainable development report, to support the decision-making process at appropriate levels and assist countries in identifying policy options and achieving the agreed SDGs. Such an outlook could draw upon and synthesize the elements of existing outlooks produced by various UN and other international institutions, depending on theme, and should foster closer collaboration among them. In this regard, we call on the Secretary-General of the United Nations to make proposals for such a report to the UNGA for the subsequent consideration by member states.

Appendix 17:
Negotiation Text,
May 30, 2012, 6 p.m.

B. Sustainable Development Goals [and Measuring Progress beyond GDP – G77, Australia delete/ in a Post-2015 Development Framework –US]

SDG1. We underscore that the MDGs are a useful tool in focusing achievement of specific development gains as part of a broad development vision and framework for the development activities of the United Nations, for national priority setting and for mobilization of stakeholders and resources towards common goals. We therefore remain firmly committed to their full and timely achievement. [agreed ad ref]

SDG2. We recognize that the development of goals could also be useful for pursuing focused and coherent action on sustainable development. In this regard, and [building on /**complementing –Japan**] [**the experience of –EU, Iceland, Switzerland, Norway**] the Millennium Development Goals, we agree to develop [a set of –EU delete] global sustainable development goals (SDGs) that address and incorporate [**in a balanced way –EU, Australia, Switzerland**] all three dimensions of sustainable development and their interlinkages. These goals should be [incorporated in/**developed in conjunction with, and contribute to –EU, Iceland, Switzerland, Japan, ROK retain**] the United Nations Development Agenda beyond 2015, thus [contributing to the achievement of sustainable development and –EU, Iceland delete] serving as a driver for implementation and mainstreaming of sustainable development [**at the global, regional, national levels and –EU**] in the United Nations system as a whole.

[**SDG2 alt. We recognize the importance and utility of a set of sustainable development goals, which are based on Agenda 21 and JPOI, fully respect Rio Principles, in particular common but differentiated responsibilities, build upon commitments already made, respect international law and contribute to the full implementation of the outcomes of major Summits in economic, social and envi-**

ronmental fields, taking into account that these goals should be incorporated in the United Nations Development Agenda beyond 2015, thus contributing to the achievement of sustainable development and serving as a driver for implementation and mainstreaming of sustainable development in the United Nations system as a whole. –G77, Turkey]

SDG3. We [propose/**stress- EU, Switzerland**] that the [goals/**SDGs-EU, Switzerland**] should build upon [**and complement existing commitments and goals, including as set out in –EU, Australia, Iceland, Switzerland, Norway**] the Millennium Development Declaration [**and this Declaration -EU**] [, respect the [purposes and principles of the –Liechtenstein] UN Charter and [principles of/**be consistent with our obligations under –Liechtenstein**] international law [,**in particular human rights law –Liechtenstein**], [be consistent with –Liechtenstein delete] the Rio principles [, **while taking into account recent changes in development –Japan**] and –US delete] contribute to advance the implementation of Agenda 21 and JPOI [, including poverty eradication, changing unsustainable patterns of consumption and production, and protecting and managing natural resource base of economic and social development –US, G77 delete].

[SDG4. We also propose that any SDGs should be action-oriented, concise and [readily communicable / **easy to communicate –US, Norway**], limited number, aspirational [**and global in nature –US**], [and universally applicable to all countries while taking into account/**with voluntary national action towards the goals in line with –US**] different national realities, capacities and development priorities. Implementation should [be government-driven / **driven by all levels of government-EU**] with [**the full –EU**] involvement of /**involve governments and –US**] [all / **other – Switzerland**] relevant stakeholders. –G77 delete para; Norway retain original text]

[SDG5. We also recognize that the [goals / **SDGs-EU**] should address and be focused on priority areas for the achievement of sustainable development [including/**which could include –Canada/such as-EU, Japan, Australia, Switzerland, Norway**] [inter alia –EU, Japan delete], energy, water, food security [,/**and -US**] oceans [and sustainable consumption and production –US delete] as well as crosscutting issues like [equity and –US delete] social inclusion [**decent work –EU, ROK**] rule of law and good governance, gender equality and women's empowerment –US reserves; G77 delete para; Norway retain]

[**SDG4+5alt. We also recognize that the goals should address and be focused on priority areas for the achievement of sustainable development. We also underscore that the SDGs should be action-oriented, concise and** ~~readily communicable~~ **(easy to communicate), limited in number, aspirational, and universally applicable to all countries while taking into account different national realities, capacities and development priorities and** ~~not limit~~ **(respecting) the national policy space. Implementation should be government-driven with involvement of all relevant stakeholders, as appropriate –G77, Turkey] (Mexico)**

[SDG6. We reiterate our request to the Secretary-General to make recommendations in his annual reports for further steps to realize the United Nations Development Agenda beyond 2015. We further request the Secretary-General [**to make**

recommendations to –EU, ROK] integrate the three dimensions of sustainable development in the United Nations Development Agenda beyond 2015 [and establish a coordinated process/, and **to establish and coordinate a process –EU; Switzerland retain]** with a view to establishing a set of coherent global goals in 2015. This process should be [a country-driven process guided by the General Assembly and be –EU, US, Switzerland delete] inclusive, transparent, open to participation of all relevant stakeholders, including the UN System, and draw on relevant expert advice and science-based evidence. [We also propose that any SDGs be agreed by the UN General Assembly. –EU, Japan, Switzerland delete; US reserves] –G77, Turkey delete para]

[SDG6 alt. We agree to establish an intergovernmental process on SDGs under the United Nations General Assembly that is inclusive, transparent and open to all stakeholders. The process needs to be coordinated and coherent with the processes considering the post-2015 development agenda –G77, Turkey]

[SDG7. We underline that progress towards the SDGs should be measured by [an agreed and appropriate set of / **a menu of global –US, Norway]** indicators and [assessed on the basis of specific –US delete] targets [that could be differentiated **[by countries –EU]** depending on [countries' /**their –EU]** levels of development and national specificities –US delete]. **[We call on the Secretary-General on the United Nations to make recommendations also in this regard –EU, ROK]** –G77 delete para; Turkey, Switzerland retain original text]

[SDG8. We recognize that there is a need for an integrated and [scientifically-credible/**science and evidence-based -EU]** global sustainable development report, to support the decision-making process at appropriate levels and assist countries in identifying policy options and achieving the agreed SDGs. Such an outlook could draw upon and synthesize the elements of existing outlooks produced by various UN and other international institutions, depending on theme, and should foster closer collaboration among them. [In this regard, we call on the Secretary-General on the United Nations to make proposals for such a report to the UNGA for the subsequent consideration by Member States –US reserves] –G77 delete para; Turkey, Norway retain original text]

[SDG8 alt. We recognize that there is a need for global, integrated and scientifically-based information on sustainable development. In this regard, we request the relevant bodies of the United Nations System, within their respective mandates, to support regional economic commissions to collect and compile national inputs in order to inform this global effort. We further commit to mobilizing financial resources and capacity building, particularly for the developing countries to achieve this endeavor. –G77]

Appendix 18:
Negotiation Text,
June 2, 2012, 5 p.m.

**B. Sustainable Development Goals [and Measuring Progress beyond GDP –
G77, Australia delete / in a Post-2015 Development Framework –US]**

SDG 1. We underscore that the MDGs are a useful tool in focusing achievement of
specific development gains as part of a broad development vision and framework for
the development activities of the United Nations, for national priority setting and for
mobilisation of stakeholders and resources towards common goals. We therefore
remain firmly committed to their full and timely achievement. **[agreed ad ref]**

SDG 2. We recognize that the development of goals could also be useful for pursuing focused and coherent action on sustainable development. We further recognize the importance and utility of a set of sustainable development goals, which
are based on Agenda 21 and JPOI, fully respect the Rio Principles, in particular
common but differentiated responsibilities, build upon commitments already
made, respect international law and contribute to the full implementation of the
outcomes of all major Summits in economic, social and environmental fields, taking into account that these goals should ensure a holistic coherence with the goals
set out in Agenda 21. These goals should address and incorporate in a balanced
way all three dimensions of sustainable development and their inter-linkages
These goals should be incorporated and integrated in the United Nations Development Agenda beyond 2015, thus contributing to the achievement of sustainable
development and serving as a driver for implementation and mainstreaming of
sustainable development in the United Nations system as a whole. The development of these goals should not divert focus or effort from the achievement of the
Millennium Development Goals.

SDG 5. We also recognize that the goals should address and be focused on priority areas for the achievement of sustainable development. We also underscore that SDGs should be action-oriented, concise and easy to communicate, limited in number, aspirational, global in nature and universally applicable to all countries while taking into account different national realities, capacities and development priorities and respecting national policies and priorities. Implementation should be driven by governments with the involvement of all relevant stakeholders, as appropriate.

[SDG 5 bis. We also recognize that the [goals / **SDGs –EU**] should address and be focused on priority areas for the achievement of sustainable development [including / **which could include –Canada / such as –EU, Japan, Australia, Switzerland, Norway**][, inter alia –EU, Japan delete], energy, water, food security [, / **and –US**] oceans [and sustainable consumption and production –US delete] as well as cross-cutting issues like [equity and –US delete] social inclusion, **[decent work, –EU, ROK]** rule of law and good governance, gender equality and women's empowerment. –US reserves; G77 delete para; Norway retain]

[SDG 6. We reiterate our request to the Secretary-General to make recommendations in his annual reports for further steps to realize the United Nations Development Agenda beyond 2015. We further request the Secretary-General to **[make recommendations to –EU, ROK]** integrate the three dimensions of sustainable development in the United Nations Development Agenda beyond 2015 [and establish a coordinated process / **, and to establish and coordinate a process –EU; Switzerland retain**] with a view to establishing a set of coherent global goals in 2015. This process should be [a country-driven process guided by the General Assembly and be –EU, US, Switzerland delete] inclusive, transparent, open to participation of all relevant stakeholders, including the UN System, and draw on relevant expert advice and science-based evidence. [We also propose that any SDGs be agreed by the UN General Assembly. –EU, Japan, Switzerland delete; US reserves] –G77, Turkey delete para]

[SDG 6 alt. We agree to establish an intergovernmental process on SDGs under the United Nations General Assembly that is inclusive, transparent and open to all stakeholders. The process needs to be coordinated and coherent with the processes considering the post-2015 development agenda. –G77, Turkey]

[SDG 7. We underline that progress towards the SDGs should be measured by [an agreed and appropriate set of / **a menu of global –US, Norway**] indicators and [assessed on the basis of specific –US delete] targets [that could be differentiated **[by countries –EU]** depending on [countries' / **their –EU**] levels of development and national specificities –US delete]. **[We call on the Secretary-General of the United Nations to make recommendations also in this regard. –EU, ROK]** –G77 delete para; Turkey, Switzerland retain original text]

[SDG 8. We recognize that there is a need for an integrated and [scientifically-credible / **science and evidence-based –EU**] global sustainable development report, to support the decision-making process at appropriate levels and assist countries in identifying policy options and achieving the agreed SDGs. Such an outlook could draw upon and synthesize the elements of existing outlooks produced by various UN and other international institutions, depending on theme, and should foster closer collaboration among them. [In this regard, we call on the Secretary-General of the United Nations to make proposals for such a report to the UNGA for the subsequent consideration by member States. –US reserves] –G77 delete para; Turkey, Norway retain original text]

[SDG 8 alt. We recognize that there is a need for global, integrated and scientifically-based information on sustainable development. In this regard, we request the relevant bodies of the United Nations System, within their respective mandates, to support regional economic commissions to collect and compile national inputs in order to inform this global effort. We further commit to mobilizing financial resources and capacity building, particularly for the developing countries to achieve this endeavor. –G77]

[SDG 9. We recognize the limitations of GDP as a measure of well-being and sustainable development. As a complement to GDP, we resolve to further develop science-based and rigorous methods of measuring sustainable development, natural wealth and social well-being, including the identification of appropriate indicators for measuring progress. We further [recognize the need to / **resolve to –EU, Norway**] test and refine these methods **[and to introduce them –EU]** [[so as to be able / **and –EU**] to use them effectively in our national decision-making systems –US delete] to better inform policy decisions. [In this regard, we recognize the need for appropriate technical support to developing countries to develop the capacity and information to undertake these efforts. –US delete] We request the [Secretary-General / **United Nations Statistical Commission –US**] to coordinate the further development of such methods with existing efforts and preparation of such indicators in consultation with the UN System and all other relevant organisations, having regard to the UN system of economic and environmental accounts. -EU, US, Australia, Iceland, Norway *move to Section V. A.*; G77 delete para; Turkey retain original text]

Appendix 19:
OWG Proposed Text—
G77 and China Coordinator,
June 14, 2012

[SDG 6. We reiterate our request to the Secretary-General to make recommendations in his annual reports for further steps to realize the United Nations Development Agenda beyond 2015. We further request the Secretary-General to **[make recommendations to –EU, ROK]** integrate the three dimensions of sustainable development in the United Nations Development Agenda beyond 2015 [and establish a coordinated process /, **and to establish and coordinate a process –EU; Switzerland retain]** with a view to establishing a set of coherent global goals in 2015. This process should be [a country-driven process guided by the General Assembly and be –EU, US, Switzerland delete] inclusive, transparent, open to participation of all relevant stakeholders, including the UN System, and draw on relevant expert advice and science-based evidence. [We also propose that any SDGs be agreed by the UN General Assembly. –EU, Japan, Switzerland delete; US reserves] –G77, Turkey delete para]

[SDG 6 alt. We agree to establish an intergovernmental process on SDGs under the United Nations General Assembly that is inclusive, transparent and open to all stakeholders. The process needs to be coordinated and coherent with the processes considering the post-2015 development agenda. –G77, Turkey]

Note: SDG 6 and SDG 6 alt should remain as two distinct options

Facilitators SDG 6 alt. We agree to establish an intergovernmental process on SDGs under the United Nations General Assembly that is inclusive, transparent and open to all stakeholders with a view to proposing global sustainable development goals to be agreed by the UN General Assembly. An Intergovernmental Steering Committee will oversee and guide this process. It shall com-

prise XX members nominated by Member States through the five UN regional groups and serving in their own personal capacity with the aim of achieving fair, balanced and equitable geographic representation. At the outset, this Committee will decide on its method of work including developing modalities for the involvement of relevant stakeholders and expertise including Major Groups in its work. It will produce an interim report to the UNGA in 2013 and a final report with recommendations to the UNGA in 2014.

Facilitators SDG alt. bis. The process needs to be coordinated and coherent with the processes considering the post-2015 development agenda. In order to provide technical support to this process and to the work of the ISC, we request the United Nations Secretary-General to establish an inter-agency technical support team, drawing on all relevant expert advice.

[SDG 7 alt. We underline that progress towards the SDGs should be measured by [an agreed and appropriate set of / a menu of global –US, Norway] indicators and [assessed on the basis of specific –US delete] targets [that could be differentiated [by countries –EU] depending on [countries' / their –EU] levels of development and national specificities –US delete]. [We call on the Secretary-General of the United Nations to make recommendations also in this regard. –EU, ROK] –G77 delete para; Turkey, Switzerland retain original text]

[NOTE: suggest placing before SDG 6]

Facilitators SDG 7 alt. We recognize that progress towards the implementation of the goals needs to be measured and accompanied by indicators while taking into account different national circumstances, capacities and levels of development.

Appendix 20:
Facilitator's Proposed
Negotiation Text,
June 15, 2012

B. Sustainable Development Goals [and Measuring Progress beyond GDP –G77, Australia delete / in a Post-2015 Development Framework –US

SDG 1. We underscore that the MDGs are a useful tool in focusing achievement of specific development gains as part of a broad development vision and framework for the development activities of the United Nations, for national priority setting and for mobilisation of stakeholders and resources towards common goals. We therefore remain firmly committed to their full and timely achievement. [**agreed ad ref**]

SDG 2. We recognize that the development of goals could also be useful for pursuing focused and coherent action on sustainable development. We further recognize the importance and utility of a set of sustainable development, which are based on Agenda 21 and JPOI, fully respect the Rio Principles, in particular common but differentiated responsibilities, build upon commitments already made, respect international law and contribute to the full implementation of the outcomes of all major Summits in economic, social and environmental fields, taking into account that these goals should ensure a holistic coherence with the goals set out in Agenda 21. These goals should address and incorporate in a balanced way all three dimensions of sustainable development and their inter-linkages. These goals should be incorporated and integrated in the United Nations Development Agenda beyond 2015, thus contributing to the achievement of sustainable development and serving as a driver for implementation and mainstreaming of sustainable development in the United Nations system as a whole. The development of these goals should not divert focus or effort from the achievement of the Millennium Development Goals.

SDG 5. We also recognize that the goals should address and be focused on priority areas for the achievement of sustainable development. We also underscore that

SDGs should be action-oriented, concise and easy to communicate, limited in number, aspirational, global in nature and universally applicable to all countries while taking into account different national realities, capacities and development priorities and respecting national policies and priorities. Implementation should be driven by governments with the involvement of all relevant stakeholders, as appropriate.

[SDG 5 bis. We also recognize that the [goals / SDGs –EU] should address and be focused on priority areas for the achievement of sustainable development [including / **which could include –Canada I/ such as –EU, Japan, Australia, Switzerland, Norway**] [, inter alia –EU, Japan delete], energy, water, food security, [**/and –US**] oceans [and sustainable consumption and production –US delete] as well as crosscutting issues like [equity and –US delete] social inclusion, [**decent work, –EU, ROK**] rule of law and good governance, gender equality and women's empowerment. –US reserves; G77 delete para; Norway retain]

Facilitator Proposal SDG 5 and 5bis. We also underscore that SDGs should be action-oriented, concise and easy to communicate, limited in number, aspirational, global in nature and universally applicable to all countries while taking into account different national realities, capacities and development priorities and respecting national policies and priorities. Implementation should be driven by governments with the involvement of all relevant stakeholders, as appropriate.

Facilitator Proposal SDG 5ter. We also recognize that the goals should address and be focused on priority areas for the achievement of sustainable development, including a limited number of the priority areas identified in section V.a. of this document which could include water, food security, oceans and cities.

[SDG 6. We reiterate our request to the Secretary-General to make recommendations in his annual reports for further steps to realize the United Nations Development Agenda beyond 2015. We further request the Secretary-General to [**make recommendations to –EU, ROK**] integrate the three dimensions of sustainable development in the United Nations Development Agenda beyond 2015 [and establish a coordinated process /, **and to establish and coordinate a process –EU; Switzerland retain**] with a view to establishing a set of coherent global goals in 2015. This process should be [a country-driven process guided by the General Assembly and be –EU, US, Switzerland delete] inclusive, transparent, open to participation of all relevant stakeholders, including the UN System, and draw on relevant expert advice and science-based evidence. [We also propose that any SDGs be agreed by the UN General Assembly. –EU, Japan, Switzerland delete; US reserves] –G77, Turkey delete para]

[**SDG 6 alt. We agree to establish an intergovernmental process on SDGs under the United Nations General Assembly that is inclusive, transparent and open to all stakeholders. The process needs to be coordinated and coherent with the processes considering the post-2015 development agenda. –G77, Turkey**]

Note: SDG 6 and SDG 6 alt should remain as two distinct options

Facilitators SDG6 alt. We resolve to establish an inclusive and transparent intergovernmental process on SDGs that is open to all stakeholders with a view to proposing global sustainable development goals to be agreed by the United Nations General Assembly. A Steering Committee shall be constituted no later than the opening of the 67ᵗʰ session of the UNGA and shall comprise XX experts nominated by Member States through the five UN regional groups with the aim of achieving fair and balanced geographic representation. At the outset, this Committee will decide on its method of work including developing modalities to ensure the full involvement of relevant stakeholders and expertise from civil society in its work in order to provide a diversity of perspectives and experience. It will submit a report to the 68ᵗʰ session of the UNGA containing a proposal for sustainable development goals.

Facilitators SDG6 alt bis. The process needs to be coordinated and coherent with the processes considering the post-2015 development agenda. The initial input to the work of the Committee will be provided by the United Nations Secretary-General. In order to provide technical support to this process and to the work of the Steering Committee we request the UN Secretary-General to ensure all necessary input and support team, drawing on all relevant expert advice.

[SDG 7 alt. We underline that progress towards the SDGs should be measured by [an agreed and appropriate set of / **a menu of global –US, Norway**] indicators and [assessed on the basis of specific –US delete] targets [that could be differentiated [by countries –EU] depending on [countries' / **their –EU**] levels of development and national specificities –US delete]. [**We call on the Secretary-General of the United Nations to make recommendations also in this regard. –EU, ROK**] G77 delete para; Turkey, Switzerland retain original text]

[**NOTE: suggest placing before SDG 6**]

Facilitators SDG 7 alt. We recognize that progress towards the achievement of the goals needs to be assessed and accompanied by targets and indicators while taking into account different national circumstances, capacities and levels of development.

[SDG 8. We recognize that there is a need for an integrated and [scientifically-credible / **science and evidence-based –EU**] global sustainable development report, to support the decision-making process at appropriate levels and assist countries in identifying policy options and achieving the agreed SDGs. Such an outlook could draw upon and synthesize the elements of existing outlooks produced by various UN and other international institutions, depending on theme, and should foster closer collaboration among them. [In this regard, we call on the Secretary-General of the United Nations to make proposals for such a report to the UNGA for the subsequent consideration by member States. –US reserves] –G77 delete para; Turkey, Norway retain original text]

[**SDG 8 alt. We recognize that there is a need for global, integrated and scientifically-based information on sustainable development. In this regard, we request the relevant bodies of the United Nations System, within their respec-**

tive mandates, to support regional economic commissions to collect and compile national inputs in order to inform this global effort. We further commit to mobilizing financial resources and capacity building, particularly for the developing countries to achieve this endeavor. –G77]

Facilitator's 8 alt: We recognize that there is a need for global, integrated and science and evidence-based information on sustainable development, including through the possible preparation of a periodic global sustainable development report. To inform this effort, we encourage closer collaboration among the relevant bodies of the United Nations System at international and regional levels, as well as other relevant international institutions within their respective mandates. We further commit to mobilizing financial resources and capacity building, particularly for the developing countries to achieve this endeavor.

PLACEMENT:

[SDG 9. We recognize the limitations of GDP as a measure of well-being and sustainable development. As a complement to GDP, we resolve to further develop science-based and rigorous methods of measuring sustainable development, natural wealth and social wellbeing, including the identification of appropriate indicators for measuring progress. We further [recognize the need to / **resolve to** –EU, Norway] test and refine these methods [**and to introduce them** –EU] [so as to be able /**and** –EU] to use them effectively in our national decision-making systems –US delete] to better inform policy decisions. [In this regard, we recognize the need for appropriate technical support to developing countries to develop the capacity and information to undertake these efforts. –US delete] We request the [Secretary-General / **United Nations Statistical Commission** –US] to coordinate the further development of such methods with existing efforts and preparation of such indicators in consultation with the UN System and all other relevant organisations, having regard to the UN system of economic and environmental accounts' –EU, US, Australia, Iceland, Norway *move to Section V.A.*; G77 delete para; Turkey retain original text]

Appendix 21:
Brazilian Presidency
Proposed Negotiation Text,
June 16, 2012

B. Sustainable Development Goals

248. We underscore that the MDGs are a useful tool in focusing achievement of specific development gains as part of a broad development vision and framework for the development activities of the United Nations, for national priority settings and for mobilization of stakeholders and resources towards common goals. We therefore remain firmly committed to their full and timely achievement. [agreed ad ref]

249. We recognize that the development of goals could also be useful for pursuing focused and coherent action on sustainable development. We further recognize the importance and utility of a set of sustainable development goals, which are based on Agenda 21 and Johannesburg Plan of Implementation, fully respect the Rio Principles, in particular common but differentiated responsibility and international law, build upon commitments already made, and contribute to the full implementation of the outcomes of all major Summits in economic, social and environmental fields including this outcome document. These goals should address and incorporate in a balanced way all three dimensions of sustainable development and their interlinkages. They should be coherent with and integrated in the United Nations Development Agenda beyond 2015, thus contributing to the achievement of sustainable development and serving as a driver for implementation and mainstreaming of sustainable development in the United Nations system as a whole. The development of these goals should not divert focus or effort from the achievement of the Millennium Development Goals.

250. We also underscore that the SDGs should be action-oriented, concise and easy to communicate, limited in number, aspirational, global in nature and universally applicable to all countries while taking into account different national realities, capacities and levels of development and respecting national policies and priorities.

Governments should drive implementation with the active involvement of all relevant stakeholders, as appropriate.

251. We resolve to establish an inclusive and transparent intergovernmental process on SDGs that is open to all stakeholders with a view to developing global sustainable development goals to be agreed by the United Nations General Assembly. A Steering Committee shall be constituted no later than the opening of the 67th session of the UNGA and shall comprise thirty experts nominated by Member States through the five UN regional groups with the aim of achieving fair and balanced geographic representation. At the outset, this Committee will decide on its method of work including developing modalities to ensure full involvement of relevant stakeholders and expertise from civil society in its work in order to provide a diversity of perspectives and experience. It will submit a report to the 68th session of the UNGA containing a proposal for sustainable development goals.

252. The process needs to be coordinated and coherent with the processes considering the post-2015 development agenda. The initial input to the work of the Committee will be provided by the United Nations Secretary General. In order to provide technical support to this process and to the work of the Steering Committee, we request the UN Secretary-General to ensure all necessary input and support to this work from the UN system including through establishing an inter-agency technical support team and expert panels as needed, drawing on all relevant expert advice.

253. We recognize that progress towards the achievement of the goals needs to be assessed and accompanied by targets and indicators while taking into account different national circumstances, capacities and levels of development.

254. We recognize that there is a need for global, integrated and scientifically-based information on sustainable development. In this regard, we request the relevant bodies of the United Nations system, within their respective mandates, to support regional economic commissions to collect and complete national inputs in order to inform this global effort. We further commit to mobilizing financial resources and capacity building, particularly for developing countries, to achieve this endeavor.

Appendix 22:
Fourth Concept Paper on SDGs—
Colombia, Peru, United Arab Emirates,
April 23, 2012

1. The concept of the SDGs has gained increasing support and there have been many recommendations on thematic areas that the SDGs could cover. The SDGs can contribute to framing complex development challenges, generating renewed commitment to address them, and defining practical means for effective implementation. Based on the recommended lists as well as the many informal dialogues on the SDGs that have taken place over the past months, our governments consider that it is possible to identify, at least preliminarily, a list of indicative thematic areas that can help to guide the process to develop the SDGs. These would be centered on issues that are widely regarded as politically mature.*

2. The preliminary definition of an indicative list would enable the process to engage on substantive work from as early as possible (Rio+1). An open-ended process to identify all the SDGs could be protracted and there is a growing sense of urgency and need for action. Work on a preliminary, indicative set of SDGs would start to yield important lessons on the SDG model and linkages between issues. It is submitted that the development of each SDG will require expert guidance and inputs, but that the selection of the thematic areas that could inform the SDGs is a political decision. This preliminary list of SDGs would not limit nor prejudge the work undertaken through the process, which will be driven by Member States.

3. SDGs must be guided by Agenda 21, the Rio Principles—including CBDR—and the JPOI. They should contribute to poverty eradication, catalyze implementation, address existing gaps in implementation of SD, integrate the three dimensions of sustainable development, be few in number and be easily communicated, and

---

*For this reason, it is strongly recommended that the SDGs do not encompass climate change. The UNFCCC negotiations are at a difficult and critical juncture, and need to be resolved within the established framework. Bringing climate change issues into fora outside of the UNFCCC will complicate the negotiations and generate bottlenecks in other processes.

improve ability to track progress. Application of the SDGs will allow for varied country and regional circumstances and priorities. The SDGs build upon the MDGs.

Visualizing Sustainable Development Goals

4. Sustainable Development Goals are integrated sets of voluntary, universally applicable global goal statements organized by thematic areas, with time-bound, quantitative targets and a suite (dashboard) of indicators to be adopted at national level, that aim to catalyze sound pathways to sustainable development, and to balance economic, social and environmental dimensions, and reflect the interconnections between them.

- The goals should be aspirational and universal in scope, and follow up must be tailored to the circumstances and priorities of each country.
- The application of the SDGs will reflect and enhance the principle of equity.
- Their implementation will build capacity in developing countries to address identified issues in a lasting manner
- The development of targets and indicators should incorporate the three dimensions of sustainable development.
- Targets should also serve to characterize linkages between SDGs. An example of this is the linkage between water, energy and food security issues.

The Process to Develop the SDGs

5. The process to follow up a political decision in the Rio Conference needs to be focused and well structured. The components of the SDGs and the SDGs themselves must be defined through targeted consultations and deliberations by Member States, and not negotiated prima facie.

6. The development of the SDGs must be informed by: i) existing information; ii) work already undertaken on indicators and goals, in particular the MDGs; and iii) technical inputs from national experts, regional organizations and specialized agencies.

7. The process would:
- further elaborate the SDGS
- develop targets and indicators
- assess required support for implementation for each SDG in terms of, inter alia,
  - o technology transfer and assistance
  - o capacity building
  - o financial support and investments
  - o institutional architecture (international and regional)

Linkages to the MDGs

The relation between the MDGs and the SDGs is crucial and needs further discussion, in particular with regard to the post 2015 agenda. The definition of new thematic areas for SDGs supposes also a clear commitment in Rio to strengthening the Millennium Development Goals and their core mission of poverty eradication. As part of the Post 2015 process, including the 2013 review of the Millennium Development Goals, updated MDGs and new thematic areas identified for SDGs will be made complementary and mutually supportive, where appropriate. For example, gender is a cross-cutting issue that informs development of the SDGs, yet consideration may also be given to defining new targets to gender MDG. Overall, the planned and ongoing processes on the Post 2015 framework need to be harmonized so as to ensure coherent and consistent outputs.

Indicative Listing of SDGS

8. The Governments that present this proposal do not have their own list of priority SDGs. Based on recommended lists and inputs from informal dialogues there appears to be broad consensus around a core of issues as reflected in the table below. These issues are considered to be politically mature and to address widely acknowledged needs. **The following are proposed as an initial, preliminary and indicative list of SDGs for adoption at the Rio Conference.** Additional thematic areas might be identified, or recommendations emerge on clustering different areas through the process that follows upon Rio.

9. **Poverty eradication is an overarching goal to which all SDGs contribute.**

10. Each SDG would include an assessment of specific requirements for effective implementation (**means of implementation**).

- **Food security: production, access and nutrition**
  ⇨ **Potential issue areas:**
    - o Reduction in food waste and food losses
    - o Achieve zero net land degradation (Increase in productive land)
    - o Increased global food production (Close yield gaps in agriculture and achieve MSY in fisheries)
    - o Improved provision of daily nutritional requirements for all
    - ⇨ MDG Linkage: Halve the proportion of people who suffer from hunger

- **Integrated water management for sustainable growth**
  ⇨ **Potential issue areas:**
    - o Increased access to water supply and sanitation
    - o Improved quality of water resources and ecosystems
    - o Increased water efficiency
    - o Reduced health risks from water-related diseases
    - ⇨ MDG Linkage: Halve, by 2015, the proportion of the population without sustainable access to safe drinking water and basic sanitation

- **Energy for sustainable development**
  ⇨ **Potential issue areas:**
    - o Ensured access to basic energy services for all
    - o Improved energy efficiency
    - o Increase in the share of renewable energy in the global energy mix (differentiated approaches)

- **Sustainable and resilient cities**
  ⇨ **Potential issue areas:**
    - o Improvements in quality of life (water, energy, housing, transport, air quality)
    - o Improved resource productivity in cities and urban systems
    - o Improved integrated planning for cities
    - ⇨ MDG Linkage: By 2020, achieve a significant improvement in the lives of at least 100 million slum-dwellers

- **Healthy and productive oceans**
⇨ **Potential issue areas:**
  - o Global fish stocks sustainably and effectively managed
  - ▪ Reductions in marine pollution from land-based sources
  - o Marine and coastal ecosystems sustainably managed and protected

- **Enhanced capacity of natural systems to support human welfare**
⇨ **Potential issue areas:**
  - o Reduced rate of destruction of critical and provisioning ecosystems
  - o Reduced rate of species/ genus loss (note links to food security)
  - o Local sustainable livelihoods supported

- **Improved efficiency and sustainability in resource use** (Sustainable consumption and production patterns)
⇨ **Potential issue areas:**
  - o Sustainable public procurement
  - o Promotion of life cycle approaches (including sound chemical management)
  - o Promotion of cleaner production approaches

- **Enhanced Employment and Livelihood Security**
⇨ **Potential issue areas:**
  - o Social protection floors tailored to national needs and capacities promoted
  - o Supportive economic, social and environmental policies for employment generation
  - o Promotion of entrepreneurship and sustainable enterprise development
  - o Enabling environment for full participation of women and youth in labor markets
    - ⇨ MDG Linkage: Halve the proportion of people living on less than $1 a day 4 Concept Note on SDGs
    - ⇨ MDG Linkage: Achieve decent employment for women, men, and young people

Table A22.1   Examples of Recommended Thematic Areas for SDGs

	Poverty	SCP	Food	Water	Energy	Cities	Oceans	Growth and Jobs	Natural Resources	Gender	Climate Change	Technology	Education	Disasters	Biodiversity	Land Degradation	Forests
JPOI	X	X							X								
GSP	X	X	X	X	X	X	X		X		X						
Major Groups	X	X	X	X	X	X	X	X	X	X	X	X		X	X	X	X
SG of UNCSD	X	X	X	X	X	X	X	X		X				X			
Zero Draft	X	X	X	X	X	X	X	X	X	X	X	X		X	X	X	X
Rio CSO Dialogues	X	X	X	X	X	X	X	X									X

Notes: JPOI = Johannesburg Plan of Implementation. GSP = Global Sustainability Panel. UN Major Groups = Stakeholders Forum. SG of UNCSD = Secretary General of the UNCSD. Rio Dialogues = Thematic issues proposed by Brazil as host of UNCSD for dialogues with civil society.

Appendix 23:
Colombian Proposal on the Transitional Committee as a Model for the SDGs, Version 1

Agreement on a process to develop the SDGs will be a key outcome of Rio+20. There are concerns that the process is not defined, after Rio we could face protracted negotiations on this issue. Therefore, it is submitted that a simple and useful way forward would be to adopt a recent model that delivered:

The Transitional Committee of the UNFCCC was able, in one year, to define the operational modalities for the Green Climate Fund (GCF), a very complex undertaking. Therefore, this model could be replicated for the SDG process.

If there is agreement on this, there would only be a need to insert a single sentence in the Zero Draft: *The SDG process will follow the model of the Transitional Committee established under the UNFCCC to develop the GCF.*

How Did the Transitional Committee Work?*

At UNFCC COP 16 (Cancun) Member States decided to establish the Green Climate Fund (GCF). The COP decision defined that the GCF was to be designed by a **Transitional Committee** (TC) composed of 40 members: 15 members from developed country Parties and 25 members from developing country Parties. All members were nominated through their UN regional groups.

Structure of the TC
- The TC members were to have the necessary experience and skills (finance and climate change).
- The TC meetings were open to observers.

---

*Information on the TC: http://unfccc.int/cancun_agreements/green_climate_fund/items/6038.php.

- The COP requested that the UNFCCC Secretariat make arrangements with relevant UN agencies to second staff to support the work of the TC. A **Technical Support Unit** (TSU) was established by the UNFCCC Secretariat.
- A document was prepared with the working arrangements for the TC.

Meetings of the TC

- Through 2011, the TC met four times and agreed to a governing instrument for the GCF (later adopted by the COP 17, Durban, 2011).
- For each meeting of the TC a set of background papers and notes and scoping papers were prepared by the TSU.
- The work of the TC was arranged in four work-streams, and participants were divided into the different groups to take forward the specific tasks. Each work-stream had two co-facilitators.
- The TC produced a meeting report for each one of the four meetings detailing the TC's progress.

Functions and Work of the TC

- COP 16 adopted the terms of reference for the TC, as an appendix to its decision creating the GCF.
- The TC was mandated to develop and recommend all the necessary arrangements for its design, including legal and institutional arrangements, for periodic evaluation, financial accountability, among others.
- TC was to encourage input from all Parties and relevant international organizations and observers, as well as take into account the relevant reports.
- The TC successfully produced a report to the COP, and an agreed governing instrument for the GCF, that included all the necessary arrangements for its operationalization.

Appendix 24:
Colombian Proposal on the
Transitional Committee as
a Model for the SDGs
Version 2—Revised June 7, 2012

Agreement on a process to develop the SDGs will be a key outcome of Rio+20. Therefore, it is important that a well-structured process be established to ensure the success of the SDGs as a legacy of Rio+20. In general, parties agree that a process for establishing the SDGs should strike a balance amongst the following important characteristics:

- It should be **intergovernmental**, in the sense that it should involve mechanisms for input and participation from all interested member States
- It should be **focused and well-structured**, to ensure that elaboration of the SDGs avoids protracted negotiations that would delay their implementation and in a way that ensures alignment with the post-2015 process, and
- It should be **informed** by reviews of existing information, including work already undertaken on indicators and goals, in particular the MDGs, as well as technical inputs from national experts, regional organizations and specialized agencies

There are a number of precedents for processes balancing these criteria. One recent example is the Transitional Committee (TC) of the UNFCCC. The TC successfully defined the operational modalities for the Green Climate Fund (GCF), a very complex undertaking, in a year. Its key characteristics were:

- It was intergovernmental and geographically balanced, with all members nominated through their UN regional groups. Specifically, it was composed of 40 members: 15 members from developed country Parties and 25 members from developing country Parties.

- It encouraged input from all Parties and relevant international organizations and observers, as well as taking into account all relevant reports and prior work.
- It was structured in such a way as to facilitate quality inputs and concrete outputs, e.g.:
  - Members were to have the necessary experience and skills;
  - Meetings were open to observers;
  - The COP requested that the UNFCCC Secretariat make arrangements with relevant UN agencies to second staff to support the work of the TC, and establish a **Technical Support Unit** (TSU);
  - For each meeting of the TC a set of background papers and notes and scoping papers were prepared by the TSU to inform its work and compile relevant existing information;
  - The work of the TC was arranged in four work-streams under a set of co-facilitators; providing clear divisions of responsibility and more detailed work on selected issues; and
  - The TC clearly documented its work; such documentation included initial elaboration of its working arrangements, as well as reports for each of its meetings detailing its progress.

We propose that a process sharing similar features should be established for the SDG process.

If there is agreement on this, the following **text** could be inserted into the outcome document:

SDG6alt. We agree that an intergovernmental process should be established to develop SDGs as a key contribution to the post 2015 framework and,
  a) Agree to establish a working group of governmental experts having the necessary experience and skills, on the basis of equitable geographical distribution, to develop recommendations on Sustainable Development Goals; the group shall submit its working arrangements to the General Assembly at its sixty-sixth session, and submitting a report on its work to the General Assembly at its sixty-seventh session;
  b) Request the Secretary-General to make arrangements to provide assistance and services that may be required to support the working group, including secondment of staff from relevant agencies and institutions.

Appendix 25:
Brazilian Presidency Proposed
Negotiation Text,
June 17, 2012

B. Sustainable Development Goals

248. We underscore that the MDGs are a useful tool in focusing achievement of specific development gains as part of a broad development vision and framework for the development activities of the United Nations, for national priority setting and for mobilisation of stakeholders and resources towards common goals. We therefore remain firmly committed to their full and timely achievement.

249. We recognize that the development of goals could also be useful for pursuing focused and coherent action on sustainable development. We further recognize the importance and utility of a set of sustainable development goals, which are based on Agenda 21 and Johannesburg Plan of Implementation, fully respect all Rio Principles, taking into account different national circumstances, capacities and priorities, are consistent with international law, build upon commitments already made, and contribute to the full implementation of the outcomes of all major Summits in the economic, social and environmental fields, including this outcome document. These goals should address and incorporate in a balanced way all three dimensions of sustainable development and their inter-linkages. They should be coherent with and integrated in the United Nations Development Agenda beyond 2015, thus contributing to the achievement of sustainable development and serving as a driver for implementation and mainstreaming of sustainable development in the United Nations system as a whole. The development of these goals should not divert focus or effort from the achievement of the Millennium Development Goals.

250. We also underscore that SDGs should be action-oriented, concise and easy to communicate, limited in number, aspirational, global in nature and universally applicable to all countries while taking into account different national realities, capacities and levels of development and respecting national policies and priorities. We also recognize that the goals should address and be focused on priority areas for

the achievement of sustainable development, being guided by this outcome document. Governments should drive implementation with the active involvement of all relevant stakeholders, as appropriate.

251. We resolve to establish an inclusive and transparent intergovernmental process on SDGs that is open to all stakeholders with a view to developing global sustainable development goals to be agreed by the United Nations General Assembly. An open working group shall be constituted no later than the opening of the 67th session of the UNGA and shall comprise of thirty representatives, nominated by Member States through the five UN regional groups with the aim of achieving fair, equitable and balanced geographic representation. At the outset, this open working group will decide on its method of work, including developing modalities, to ensure the full involvement of relevant stakeholders and expertise from civil society, the scientific community and the UN system in its work in order to provide a diversity of perspectives and experience. It will submit a report to the 68th session of the UNGA containing a proposal for sustainable development goals for consideration and appropriate action.

252. The process needs to be coordinated and coherent with the processes considering the post-2015 development agenda. The initial input to the work of the working group will be provided by the United Nations Secretary General in consultations with national governments. In order to provide technical support to this process and to the work of the working group, we request the UN Secretary-General to ensure all necessary input and support to this work from the UN system including through establishing an inter-agency technical support team and expert panels as needed, drawing on all relevant expert advice. Reports on the progress of work will be made regularly to the General Assembly.

253. We recognize that progress towards the achievement of the goals needs to be assessed and accompanied by targets and indicators while taking into account different national circumstances, capacities and levels of development.

254. We recognize that there is a need for global, integrated and scientifically-based information on sustainable development. In this regard, we request the relevant bodies of the United Nations system, within their respective mandates, to support regional economic commissions to collect and compile national inputs in order to inform this global effort. We further commit to mobilizing financial resources and capacity building, particularly for developing countries, to achieve this endeavor.

Appendix 26:
Secretariat Comparative Table of the Negotiation Text: State of Play, June 15, 2012

[Authors' Note: The left-hand column is a detailed compendium of the state-of-play of the negotiation text across all the tracks. The right-hand column is the Secretariat's proposal for consensus text for the final outcome document at Rio+20 and reflects a deep technical and political understanding across all the negotiations tracks.]

1. Our Common Vision	1. Our Common Vision
B. Sustainable Development Goals [and Measuring Progress beyond GDP –G77, Australia delete / in a Post-2015 Development Framework –US]	B. Sustainable Development Goals
SDG 1. We underscore that the MDGs are a useful tool in focusing achievement of specific development gains as part of a broad development vision and framework for the development activities of the United Nations, for national priority setting and for mobilisation of stakeholders and resources towards common goals. We therefore remain firmly committed to their full and timely achievement. **[agreed ad ref]**	SDG 1. We underscore that the MDGs are a useful tool in focusing achievement of specific development gains as part of a broad development vision and framework for the development activities of the United Nations, for national priority setting and for mobilisation of stakeholders and resources towards common goals. We therefore remain firmly committed to their full and timely achievement. **[agreed ad ref]**
SDG 2. We recognize that the development of goals could also be useful for pursuing focused and coherent action on sustainable development. We further recognize the importance and utility of a set of sustainable development goals, which are based on Agenda 21 and JPOI, fully respect the Rio Principles, in particular common but differentiated responsibilities, build upon	SDG 2. We recognize that the development of goals could also be useful for pursuing focused and coherent action on sustainable development. We further recognize the importance and utility of a set of sustainable development goals, which are based on Agenda 21 and JPOI, fully respect all Rio Principles and international law, build upon commitments already

continues

1. Our Common Vision

commitments already made, respect international law and contribute to the full implementation of the outcomes of all major Summits in economic, social and environmental fields, taking into account that these goals should ensure a holistic coherence with the goals set out in Agenda 21. These goals should address and incorporate in a balanced way all three dimensions of sustainable development and their inter-linkages These goals should be incorporated and integrated in the United Nations Development Agenda beyond 2015, thus contributing to the achievement of sustainable development and serving as a driver for implementation and mainstreaming of sustainable development in the United Nations system as a whole. The development of these goals should not divert focus or effort from the achievement of the Millennium Development Goals.

made, and contribute to the full implementation of the outcomes of all major Summits in economic, social and environmental fields including this outcome document. These goals should address and incorporate in a balanced way all three dimensions of sustainable development and their inter-linkages. They should be coherent with and integrated in the United Nations Development Agenda beyond 2015, thus contributing to the achievement of sustainable development and serving as a driver for implementation and mainstreaming of sustainable development in the United Nations system as a whole. The development of these goals should not divert focus or effort from the achievement of the Millennium Development Goals.

SDG 5. We also recognize that the goals should address and be focused on priority areas for the achievement of sustainable development. We also underscore that SDGs should be action-oriented, concise and easy to communicate, limited in number, aspirational, global in nature and universally applicable to all countries [problematic to one delegation according to facilitator] while taking into account different national realities, capacities and development priorities and respecting national policies and priorities. Implementation should be [involve a – swiss] driven by [governments with the involvement of – swiss delete] all relevant stakeholders, as appropriate. **[voluntary action in line w national realities –us]**

[facilitator; seems to be agreement, maybe para could agree ad ref]

SDG 3. We also underscore that SDGs should be action-oriented, concise and easy to communicate, limited in number, aspirational, global in nature and universally applicable to all countries while taking into account different national realities, capacities and levels of development and respecting national policies and priorities. Governments should drive implementation with the active involvement of all relevant stakeholders, as appropriate.

[SDG 5 bis. We also recognize that the [goals / **SDGs – EU**] should address and be focused on priority areas for the achievement of sustainable development [g77 seems fine w text till here] [including / **which could include – Canada / such as –EU, Japan, Australia, Switzerland, Norway**][, inter alia –EU, Japan delete], energy, water, food security [, / **and – US**] oceans [and sustainable consumption and production – US delete] as well as cross-cutting issues like [equity and –US delete] social inclusion, **[decent work, –EU, ROK]** rule of law and good governance, gender equality and women's empowerment. –US reserves; G77 delete para; Norway retain]

continues

1. Our Common Vision	1. Our Common Vision
[eu: two previous para in one; fine with sdg 5, and retain 5 bis or incl ref to priority areas and cross-cutt issues n sdg 5] [g77: identifying some areas risks not looking at issues which are relevant for sd in future] [premature to indicate areas – us] [should indicate areas – swiss] [how will we implement this agenda w existing resources? – Venezuela] [facilitator: far apart]	
Facilitator Proposal SDG 5 and 5bis. We also underscore that SDGs should be action-oriented, concise and easy to communicate, limited in number, aspirational, global in nature and universally applicable to all countries while taking into account different national realities, capacities and development priorities and respecting national policies and priorities. Implementation should be driven by governments with the involvement of all relevant stakeholders, as appropriate.	
Facilitator Proposal SDG 5 ter. We also recognize that the goals should address and be focused on priority areas for the achievement of sustainable development, including a limited number of the priority areas identified in section V.a. of this document which could include water, food security, oceans and cities.	
[SDG 6. We reiterate our request to the Secretary-General to make recommendations in his annual reports for further steps to realize the United Nations Development Agenda beyond 2015. We further request the Secretary-General to [make recommendations to –EU, ROK] integrate the three dimensions of sustainable development in the United Nations Development Agenda beyond 2015 [and establish a coordinated process /, and to establish and coordinate a process –EU; Switzerland retain] with a view to establishing a set of coherent global goals in 2015. This process should be [a country-driven process guided by the General Assembly and be –EU, US, Switzerland delete] inclusive, transparent, open to participation of all relevant stakeholders, including the UN System, and draw on relevant expert advice and science-based evidence. [We also propose that any SDGs be agreed by the UN General Assembly. –EU, Japan, Switzerland delete; US reserves] – G77, Turkey delete para]	
[SDG 6 alt. We agree to establish an intergovernmental process on SDGs under the United	

continues

Nations General Assembly that is inclusive, transparent and open to all stakeholders. The process needs to be coordinated and coherent with the processes considering the post-2015 development agenda. –G77, Turkey]

Note: SDG 6 and SDG 6 alt should remain as two distinct options

---

Facilitators SDG 6 alt. We resolve to establish an inclusive and transparent intergovernmental process on SDGs that is open to all stakeholders with a view to proposing global sustainable development goals to be agreed by the United Nations General Assembly. A Steering Committee shall be constituted no later than the opening of the 67th session of the UNGA and shall comprise XX experts nominated by Member States through the five UN regional groups with the aim of achieving fair and balanced geographic representation. At the outset, this Committee will decide on its method of work including developing modalities to ensure the full involvement of relevant stakeholders and expertise from civil society in its work in order to provide a diversity of perspectives and experience. It will submit a report to the 68th session of the UNGA containing a proposal for sustainable development goals.

SDG 4. We resolve to establish an inclusive and transparent intergovernmental process on SDGs that is open to all stakeholders with a view to developing global sustainable development goals to be agreed by the United Nations General Assembly. A Steering Committee shall be constituted no later than the opening of the 67th session of the UNGA and shall comprise XX experts nominated by Member States through the five UN regional groups with the aim of achieving fair and balanced geographic representation. At the outset, this Committee will decide on its method of work including developing modalities to ensure the full involvement of relevant stakeholders and expertise from civil society in its work in order to provide a diversity of perspectives and experience. It will submit a report to the 68th session of the UNGA containing a proposal for sustainable development goals.

Facilitators SDG 6 alt bis. The process needs to be coordinated and coherent with the processes considering the post-2015 development agenda. The initial input to the work of the Committee will be provided by the United Nations Secretary General. In order to provide technical support to this process and to the work of the Steering Committee, we request the UN Secretary-General to ensure all necessary input and support to this work from the UN system through establishing an inter-agency technical support team, drawing on all relevant expert advice.

SDG 5. The process needs to be coordinated and coherent with the processes considering the post-2015 development agenda. The initial input to the work of the Committee will be provided by the United Nations Secretary General. In order to provide technical support to this process and to the work of the Steering Committee, we request the UN Secretary-General to ensure all necessary input and support to this work from the UN system including through establishing an inter-agency technical support team and expert panels as needed, drawing on all relevant expert advice.

[SDG 7 alt. We underline that progress towards the SDGs should be measured by [an agreed and appropriate set of / **a menu of global –US, Norway**] indicators and [assessed on the basis of specific –US delete] targets [that could be differentiated **[by countries –EU]** depending on [countries' / **their –EU**] levels of development and national specificities –US delete]. **[We call on the Secretary-General of the United Nations to make recommendations also in this regard. –EU, ROK]** –G77 delete para; Turkey, Switzerland retain original text]

continues

276

1. Our Common Vision

1. Our Common Vision	1. Our Common Vision
[NOTE: suggest placing before SDG 6] Facilitators SDG 7 alt. We recognize that progress towards the achievement of the goals needs to be assessed and accompanied by targets and indicators while taking into account different national circumstances, capacities and levels of development	SDG 6. We recognize that progress towards the achievement of the goals needs to be assessed and accompanied by targets and indicators while taking into account different national circumstances, capacities and levels of development.
[SDG 8. We recognize that there is a need for an integrated and [scientifically-credible / **science and evidence-based –EU**] global sustainable development report, to support the decision-making process at appropriate levels and assist countries in identifying policy options and achieving the agreed SDGs. Such an outlook could draw upon and synthesize the elements of existing outlooks produced by various UN and other international institutions, depending on theme, and should foster closer collaboration among them. [In this regard, we call on the Secretary-General of the United Nations to make proposals for such a report to the UNGA for the subsequent consideration by member States. –US reserves] –G77 delete para; Turkey, Norway retain original text]	
[SDG 8 alt. We recognize that there is a need for global, integrated and scientifically-based information on sustainable development. In this regard, we request the relevant bodies of the United Nations System, within their respective mandates, to support regional economic commissions to collect and compile national inputs in order to inform this global effort. We further commit to mobilizing financial resources and capacity building, particularly for the developing countries to achieve this endeavor. –G77]	SDG 7. We recognize that there is a need for global, integrated and science and evidence-based information on sustainable development, including through the possible preparation of a periodic global sustainable development report. To inform this effort, we encourage closer collaboration among the relevant bodies of the United Nations System at international and regional levels, as well as other relevant international institutions within their respective mandates. We further commit to mobilizing financial resources and capacity building, particularly for the developing countries, to support this endeavor.
Facilitator's 8 alt: We recognize that there is a need for global, integrated and science and evidence-based information on sustainable development, including through the possible preparation of a periodic global sustainable development report. To inform this effort, we encourage closer collaboration among the relevant bodies of the United Nations System at international and regional levels, as well as other relevant international institutions within their respective mandates. We further commit to mobilizing financial resources and capacity building, particularly for the developing countries to achieve this endeavor.	

continues

PLACEMENT:

[SDG 9. We recognize the limitations of GDP as a measure of well-being and sustainable development. As a complement to GDP, we resolve to further develop science-based and rigorous methods of measuring sustainable development, natural wealth and social well-being, including the identification of appropriate indicators for measuring progress. We further [recognize the need to / **resolve to – EU, Norway**] test and refine these methods **[and to introduce them –EU]** [[so as to be able / **and –EU]** to use them effectively in our national decision-making systems –US delete] to better inform policy decisions. [In this regard, we recognize the need for appropriate technical support to developing countries to develop the capacity and information to undertake these efforts. –US delete] We request the [Secretary-General / **United Nations Statistical Commission –US**] to coordinate the further development of such methods with existing efforts and preparation of such indicators in consultation with the UN System and all other relevant organisations, having regard to the UN system of economic and environmental accounts. -EU, US, Australia, Iceland, Norway *move to Section V. A.*; G77 delete para; Turkey retain original text]

[NOTE: to move to another section before Voluntary Commitments]

Chair SDG 9 alt: We recognize the need for broader measures of progress to complement GDP, and in this regard request the UN Statistical Commission in consultation with relevant UN System entities and other relevant organizations to launch a programme of work in this area building on existing initiatives.

Appendix 27:
The Future We Want—
Outcome Document on the United Nations Conference on Sustainable Development, Rio de Janeiro, Brazil, June 20–22, 2012 (SDGs Section)

B. Sustainable development goals

245. We underscore that the Millennium Development Goals are a useful tool in focusing achievement of specific development gains as part of a broad development vision and framework for the development activities of the United Nations, for national priority-setting and for mobilization of stakeholders and resources towards common goals. We therefore remain firmly committed to their full and timely achievement.

246. We recognize that the development of goals could also be useful for pursuing focused and coherent action on sustainable development. We further recognize the importance and utility of a set of sustainable development goals, based on Agenda 21 and the Johannesburg Plan of Implementation, which fully respect all the Rio Principles, taking into account different national circumstances, capacities and priorities, are consistent with international law, build upon commitments already made and contribute to the full implementation of the outcomes of all major summits in the economic, social and environmental fields, including the present outcome document. The goals should address and incorporate in a balanced way all three dimensions of sustainable development and their interlinkages. they should be coherent with and integrated into the United Nations development agenda beyond 2015, thus contributing to the achievement of sustainable development and serving as a driver for implementation and mainstreaming of sustainable development in the United Nations system as a whole. The development of these goals should not divert focus or effort from the achievement of the Millennium Development Goals.

247. We also underscore that sustainable development goals should be action-oriented, concise and easy to communicate, limited in number, aspirational, global in nature and universally applicable to all countries, while taking into account different national realities, capacities and levels of development and respecting

national policies and priorities. We also recognize that the goals should address and be focused on priority areas for the achievement of sustainable development, being guided by the present outcome document. Governments should drive implementation with the active involvement of all relevant stakeholders, as appropriate.

248. We resolve to establish an inclusive and transparent intergovernmental process on sustainable development goals that is open to all stakeholders, with a view to developing global sustainable development goals to be agreed by the General Assembly. An open working group shall be constituted no later than at the opening of the sixty-seventh session of the Assembly and shall comprise thirty representatives, nominated by Member States from the five United Nations regional groups, with the aim of achieving fair, equitable and balanced geographical representation. At the outset, this open working group will decide on its methods of work, including developing modalities to ensure the full involvement of relevant stakeholders and expertise from civil society, the scientific community and the United Nations system in its work, in order to provide a diversity of perspectives and experience. It will submit a report, to the Assembly at its sixty-eighth session, containing a proposal for sustainable development goals for consideration and appropriate action.

249. The process needs to be coordinated and coherent with the processes to consider the post-2015 development agenda. The initial input to the work of the working group will be provided by the Secretary-General, in consultation with national Governments. In order to provide technical support to the process and to the work of the working group, we request the Secretary-General to ensure all necessary input and support to this work from the United Nations system, including by establishing an inter-agency technical support team and expert panels, as needed, drawing on all relevant expert advice. Reports on the progress of work will be made regularly to the General Assembly.

250. We recognize that progress towards the achievement of the goals needs to be assessed and accompanied by targets and indicators, while taking into account different national circumstances, capacities and levels of development.

251. We recognize that there is a need for global, integrated and scientifically based information on sustainable development. In this regard, we request the relevant bodies of the United Nations system, within their respective mandates, to support the regional economic commissions in collecting and compiling national inputs in order to inform this global effort. We further commit to mobilizing financial resources and capacity-building, particularly for developing countries, to achieve this endeavour.

Bibliography

Brondizio, E. S., J. Settele, S. Díaz, and H. T. Ngo, eds. "Global Assessment Report on Biodiversity and Ecosystem Services." IPBES, 2019. https://doi.org/10.5281/zenodo.3831673.

Caballero, Paula. "The SDGs: Changing How Development Is Understood." *Global Policy* 10 (suppl 1) (2019).

Caballero, Paula. "A Short Story of the SDGs." *IMPAKTER*, September 20, 2016. https://impakter.com/sdg-story-insider-account-came.

Chasek, Pamela, and Lynn M. Wagner, eds. *The Roads from Rio: Lessons Learned from Twenty Years of Multilateral Environmental Negotiations.* London: Routledge, 2012.

Climate Action Tracker. Warming Projections Global Update, November 2021. Climate Analytics and New Climate Institute. www.climateactiontracker.org.

Coal 2021. Analysis and Forecast to 2024. International Energy Agency. www.iea.org.

Discussion Paper. High-level Dialogue on Strengthening the Institutional Framework for Sustainable Development. Solo, Indonesia, July 19–21, 2011.

Dodds, F., D. Donoghue, and J. Leiva-Roesch. *Negotiating the Sustainable Development Goals: A Transformational Agenda for an Insecure World.* London: Earthscan Routledge, 2017.

Dodds, F., J. Laguna-Celis, and L. Thompson. *From Rio+20 to a New Development Agenda: Building a Bridge to a Sustainable Future.* London: Routledge, 2014.

Dupont, Christophe. "Negotiation as Coalition Building." *International Negotiation* 1, no. 1 (1996): 47–64. https://doi.org/10.1163/157180696X00287.

Farrell, Mary. "Group Politics in Global Development Policy: From the Millennium Development Goals to the Post-2015 Development Agenda." *Hague Journal of Diplomacy* 12, nos. 2 and 3 (2017): 221–248.

"Financing for Sustainable Development in the Global Partnership Beyond 2015." Thematic Think Piece. OHCHR, OHRLLS, IFAD, IOM, UNCTAD, UNDESA, UNDP, UNEP, UNESCO, UNFCCC, UNFPA. UN System Task Team on the Post-2015 Developing Agenda, 2013.

Fukuda-Parr, Sakiko. "From the Millennium Development Goals to the Sustainable Development Goals: Shifts in Purpose, Concept, and Politics of Global Goal Setting for Development." *Gender & Development Journal* 24, no. 1 (2016): 43–52.

"Fulfilling the Rio+20 Promises: Reviewing Progress Since the UN Conference on Sustainable Development Report." Stakeholder Forum for a Sustainable Future and Natural Resources Defense Council, New York, September 2013. http://stakeholderforum.org.

GEO5. "Global Environment Outlook, Summary for Policy Makers." United Nations Environment Programme, 2012. http://unep.org.

"The Green Economy: Trade and Sustainable Development Implications." Report of the Ad Hoc Expert Meeting, Palais des Nations, Geneva, October 7–8, 2010. United Nations Department of Economic and Social Affairs, UNCTAD Secretariat, Background Paper Second Preparatory Committee Meeting /2011/BP1 of the UN Conference on Sustainable Development Preparatory Process. Second Preparatory Meeting, New York, March 7–8, 2011.

Hawden, John G., and Johan Kaufman. *How United Nations Decisions Are Made*. Leiden: Sijthoff, 1962.

Hazlewood, Peter. "Discussion Note 1—Linking the SDGs, MDGs and the Post-2015 Development Agenda." Retreat on the SDGs, Rio+20 and the Post-2015 Development Agenda, Tarrytown, New York, January 22–24, 2012. World Resources Institute, 2012.

IPBES. "Summary for Policymakers of the Global Assessment Report on Biodiversity and Ecosystem Services." In *Intergovernmental Science-Policy Platform on Biodiversity and Ecosystem Services*, edited by S. Díaz et al. Bonn, Germany: IPBES Secretariat. https://doi.org/10.5281/zenodo.3553579.

IPCC. "Summary for Policymakers." In *Climate Change 2021: The Physical Science Basis. Contribution of Working Group I to the Sixth Assessment Report of the Intergovernmental Panel on Climate Change*, edited by V. Masson-Delmotte et al. Cambridge: Cambridge University Press, 2021. https://www.ipcc.ch/report/ar6/wg1/downloads /report/IPCC_AR6_WGI_SPM.pdf.

Ivanova, Maria. *The Untold Story of the World's Leading Environmental Institution: UNEP at Fifty*. Cambridge, MA: MIT Press, 2021.

Jaramillo Correa, Luis Fernando, and Patti Londoño Jaramillo. *La Política Multilateral de Colombia y el Mundo en Desarrollo—NOAL*. Bogotá: Universidad Externado de Colombia, 1995.

Jaramillo Correa, Luis Fernando, and Patti Londoño Jaramillo. *Naciones Unidas a través de la mirada de sus Secretarios Generales*. Bogotá: Universidad Externado de Colombia, 2006.

Kamau, M., P. Chasek, and D. O'Connor. *Transforming Multilateral Diplomacy: The Inside Story of the Sustainable Development Goals*. London: Routledge, 2018.

Kelly, Liz, ed. *Biodiversity and Ecosystem Services: A Business Case for Re/insurance.* Zurich: Swiss Re Institute, 2020. https://www.swissre.com/dam/jcr:a7fe3dca-c4d6 -403b-961c-9fab1b2f0455/swiss-re-institute-expertise-publication-biodiversity-and -ecosystem-services.pdf.

Kennedy, Paul. *The Parliament of Man: The Past, Present, and Future of the United Nations*. New York: Random House, 2006.

Khan, Farrukh. "The SDG Story: An Insider Account of How It All Came About." *IMPAKTER*, December 13, 2016. https://impakter.com/sdg-story-insider-account-came/.

Lawson, Max, Man-Kwun Chan, Francesca Rhodes, Anam Parvez Butt, Anna Marriott, Ellen Ehmke, Didier Jacobs, Julie Seghers, Jaime Atienza, and Rebecca Gowland. "Public Good or Private Wealth?" Policy Paper, OXFAM International, January 21, 2019. http://www.oxfam.org/en/research/public-good-or-private-wealth.

Meilstrup, P. "The Runaway Summit: The Background Story of the Danish Presidency of COP15, the UN Climate Change Conference." In *Danish Foreign Policy Yearbook*, edited by N. Hvidt and H. Mouritzen. Copenhagen: Danish Institute for International Studies, 2010, 113–135.

"Monterrey Consensus (2002) on Financing for Development." UN International Conference on Financing for Development, Monterrey, Mexico, March 18–22, 2002.

O'Callaghan, Brian J., and Em Murdock. "Are We Building Back Better? Evidence from 2020 and Pathways to Inclusive Green Recovery Spending. Summary for Policy Makers." Global Recovery Observatory, Oxford University, and United Nations Environment Programme, 2020. https://wedocs.unep.org/bitstream/handle/20.500 .11822/35282/AWBBB_ES.pdf.

OECD. *Global Outlook on Financing for Sustainable Development 2021: A New Way to Invest for People and Planet.* Paris: OECD, 2021. https://www.oecd-ilibrary.org/sites /6ea613f4-en/index.html?itemId=/content/component/6ea613f4-en#endnotea0z2.

OECD and UNDP. "Framework for SDG Aligned Finance." OECD and UNDP, 2020. http://www.oecd.org/development/financing-sustainable-development/Framework -for-SDG-Aligned-Finance-OECD-UNDP.pdf.

Partnerships for Sustainable Development—The Stockholm Call for Action. Stockholm+40 Partnership Forum for Sustainable Development. April 25, 2012.

Pirlea, A. F., U. Serajuddin, D. Wadhwa, M. Welch, and A. Whitby, eds. "Atlas of the Sustainable Development Goals 2020." In *World Development Indicators.* Washington, DC: World Bank, 2020. https://datatopics.worldbank.org/sdgatlas/.

"Preparations for the UN Conference on Sustainable Development: 19–27 March 2012." *Earth Negotiations Bulletin* 27, no. 17 (March 19, 2012). http://www.iisd.ca/uncsd/ism3/.

"Preparing the Summit, Paper 1: Focusing the Summit Agenda." Stakeholder Forum for a Sustainable Future, Rio+20 Workshop, New York, October 22–24, 2009. http:// www.stakeholderforum.org.

"Preparing the Summit, Paper 2: Organizational Options for the 2012 Sustainable Development Summit." Stakeholder Forum for a Sustainable Future, Rio+20 Workshop, New York, October 22–24, 2009. http://www.stakeholderforum.org.

"Preparing the Summit, Paper 3: Intergovernmental Roadmap to 2012." Stakeholder Forum for a Sustainable Future, Rio+20 Workshop, New York, October 22–24, 2009. www.stakeholderforum.org.

"Review of Implementation of Agenda 21 and the Rio Principles Synthesis." Stakeholder Forum for a Sustainable Future, United Nations Department of Economic and Social Affairs, Division for Sustainable Development, Sustainable Development in the 21st Century (SD21), New York, January 2012.

"Report 2009, the Workshop on Options for a Rio+20 High Level Event New York, 22–23 October 2009." Workshop on a possible 2012 Earth Summit, Stakeholder Forum for a Sustainable Future, London, November 1, 2009. www.stakeholderforum.org.

"Report 2011, the High-Level Dialogue on Institutional Framework for Sustainable Development." Submission by the government of the Republic of Indonesia to the Zero Draft of UNCSD 2012 Outcome Document. Solo, Indonesia, July 19–21, 2011.

"Report 2011, the Regional Preparatory Meeting for the United Nations Conference on Sustainable Development." s' Summary and Closure of the Meeting, Addendum E/ECE/RPM/2011/2/Add.1, Economic Commission for Europe, Regional Preparatory Meeting for the United Nations Conference on Sustainable Development, Geneva, December 1 and 2, 2011, December 7, 2011.

"Report 2012, Realizing the Future We Want for All: Equality, Sustainability and Human Rights." United Nations System Task Team to the Secretary-General on the Post-2015 Development Agenda, New York, June 2012. http://www.un.org/en/development /desa/policy/untaskteam_undf.

"Report 2014, The Open Working Group of the General Assembly on Sustainable Development Goals." Letter of transmittal dated August 1, 2014, from the Permanent Representatives of Hungary and Kenya to the United Nations addressed to the President of the General Assembly, A/68/970, New York, August 12, 2014.

"Report 2014, The Open Working Group Proposal for Sustainable Development Goals." Full Report of the Open Working Group of the General Assembly on Sustainable Development Goals, A/68/970. Letter of transmittal dated August 1, 2014, from the Permanent Representatives of Hungary and Kenya to the United Nations addressed to the President of the General Assembly, New York, August 12, 2014. http://undocs.org/A/68/970.

"Retreat on Sustainable Development Goals, Rio+20 and the Post-2015 Development Agenda." Chair's Summary. Tarrytown, New York, January 23–24, 2012.

"Rio+20: Sustainable Development Goals." Proposal by the governments of Colombia and Guatemala for consideration by the participating countries. LC/L.3366/Rev.1, August 30, 2011. Latin American and Caribbean Regional Meeting, Preparatory to the United Nations Conference on Sustainable Development Meeting of the member countries of the Rio de Janeiro Platform for Action on the Road to Johannesburg 2002: Latin America and the Caribbean in preparation for Rio de Janeiro 2012, Santiago de Chile, September 7–9, 2011.

Rockström, J., W. Steffen, K. Noone, Å. Persson, F. S. Chapin III, E. Lambin, . . . and J. Foley. "Planetary Boundaries: Exploring the Safe Operating Space for Humanity." *Ecology and Society* 14, no. 2 (2009). https://www.stockholmresilience.org/research/planetary-boundaries.html.

Sachs, Jeffrey D. *The UN Millennium Project Investing in Development: A Practical Plan to Achieve the Millennium Development Goals.* New York: Earthscan, 2005.

Stalley, Phillip. "Norms from the Periphery: Tracing the Rise of the Common but Differentiated Principle in International Environmental Politics." *Cambridge Review of International Affairs* 31, no. 2 (2018): 141–161.

"State of the Planet Declaration." Co-chairs of the Planet Under Pressure Conference, Lidia Brito and Mark Stafford Smith, supported by the Conference Scientific Organizing Committee, Planet Under Pressure: New Knowledge Towards Solutions, London, March 26–29, 2012.

Statement by President Juan Manuel Santos at the UNCSD Rio+20 Conference, Rio de Janeiro, Brazil, June 21, 2012.

Statement by President Juan Manuel Santos at the United Nations General Assembly on the adoption of the Sustainable Development Goals, New York, September 25, 2015.

Statement by Mr. Sha Zukang, Under-Secretary-General for Economic and Social Affairs, Secretary-General of the 2012 UN Conference on Sustainable Development. 2nd Intersessional Meeting of UNCSD, New York, December 15, 2011.

Statement on behalf of the European Union and its Member States. Istvan Teplan, Senior Adviser to the State Secretary for the Environment Republic of Hungary, Second Preparatory Committee of the 2012 United Nations Conference on Sustainable Development, United Nations, New York, March 7, 2011.

Statement on behalf of the Group of 77 and China. H. E. Ambassador Jorge Argüello, Permanent Representative of Argentina to the United Nations, Chairman of the Group of 77, at the Second Preparatory Committee meeting of the UN Conference on Sustainable Development, New York, March 7, 2011.

Summary by H. E. Mr. In-kook Park and H. E. Mr. John Ashe, Co-chairs of the Bureau for the Preparatory Process of the UNCSD. First Informal Intersessional Meeting for the United Nations Conference on Sustainable Development, New York, January 10–11, 2011.

Summary of the First Intersessional Meeting of the UNCSD (January 10–11, 2011) and Summary of the Second Session of the Preparatory Committee (PrepCom) for UNCSD (March 7–8, 2011).

Summary of the insights from the Informal Consultations on the SDG Proposal. Respecting Chatham House Rule. Bogotá, Colombia, November 4–5, 2011.

Summary of the Second Intersessional Meeting by the Co-chairs. UN Conference on Sustainable Development, New York, December 15–16, 2011.

Summary of the Second Preparatory Committee Meeting, by Co-chair H. E. Dr. John Ashe of Antigua and Barbuda. United Nations Conference on Sustainable Development, New York, March 7–8, 2011.

"Summary of the Third Round of UNCSD Informal Informal Consultations: 29 May–2 June 2012." *Earth Negotiations Bulletin* 27, no. 40 (2012): 16. http://www.iisd.ca /uncsd/iinzod3/.

"Summary of the UNCSD Informal Informal Consultations and Third Intersessional Meeting, 19–27 March 2012." *Earth Negotiations Bulletin* 27, no. 24 (2012). http:// www.iisd.ca/uncsd/ism3.

"Summary of the UNCSD Informal Informal Consultations 23 April–4 May 2012." *Earth Negotiations Bulletin* 27, no. 35 (2012). http://www.iisd.ca/uncsd/iinzod2/.

"Summary of UNCSD Prepcom III: Friday, 15 June 2012." *Earth Negotiations Bulletin* 27, no. 44 (2012). http//www.iisd.ca/uncsd/rio20/ENB.

"Summary of the United Nations Conference on Sustainable Development, 13–22 June 2012." *Earth Negotiations Bulletin* 27, no. 51 (2012).

Talberth, John, and Erin Gray. "Discussion Note 2—Sustainable Development Challenges as Thematic Areas of Common Concern." Retreat on SDGs, Rio+20, and the Post-2015 Development Agenda, Tarrytown, New York, January 22–24, 2012. World Resources Institute, 2012.

Talberth, John, and Erin Gray. "Discussion Note 3—A Conceptual Architecture for Sustainable Development Goals." Retreat on SDGs, Rio+20, and the Post-2015 Development Agenda, Tarrytown, New York, January 22–24, 2012. World Resources Institute, 2012.

TFCD. "Climate Change Presents Financial Risks for the Global Economy." Task Force on Climate-Related Financial Disclosures, 2021. https://www.fsb-tcfd.org.

United Nations Conference on Sustainable Development (UNCSD). Minutes of the Bureau Meetings Preparatory Process, New York, April 18, 2011, 10 am–1:15 pm; June 14, 2011, 10 am–12:30 pm; September 12, 2011, 9 am–2:00 pm; November 8, 2011, 9:00 am–2:30 pm; December 14, 2011, 9 am–1:15 pm; December 22, 2011, 10 am–12:30 pm and 3:00 pm–4:30 pm; January 9, 2012, 9:30 am–12:30 pm; January 26, 2012, 1:15 am–3:00 pm.

UNDESA. "The Millennium Development Goals Report 2011: We Can End Poverty." UNDESA et al., 2011. https://www.un.org/millenniumgoals/pdf/(2011_E)%20MDG %20Report%202011_Book%20LR.pdf.

UNDESA. "Back to Our Common Future, Sustainable Development in the 21st Century (SD21) Project Summary for Policymakers." UNDESA, May 2012a. https:// sustainabledevelopment.un.org/content/documents/UN-DESA_Back_Common _Future_En.pdf.

UNDESA. "The Millennium Development Goals Report 2012." UNDESA, July 2012b. https://www.un.org/millenniumgoals/pdf/MDG%20Report%202012.pdf.

UNDESA. "World Social Report 2020: Inequality in a Rapidly Changing World." UNDESA, 2020. http://www.un.org/development/desa/dspd/wp-content/uploads /sites/22/2020/01/World-Social-Report-2020-FullReport.pdf.

UN Draft resolution submitted by the President of the General Assembly. Report of the Open Working Group on Sustainable Development Goals established pursuant to General Assembly resolution 66/288, A/68/L.61, Agenda item 14: Integrated and coordinated implementation of and follow-up to the outcomes of the major United Nations conferences and summits in the economic, social and related fields. New York, September 8, 2014.

UNEP. "Towards a Green Economy: Pathways to Sustainable Development and Poverty Eradication—A Synthesis for Policy Makers." UNEP, 2011. http://www.unep.org /greeneconomy.

UNEP. "Global Environment Outlook—GEO-6: Healthy Planet, Healthy People." UNEP, 2019. https://www.unep.org/resources/global-environment-outlook-6.

UNEP. "Emissions Gap Report 2020." UNEP, 2020. http://www.unep.org/interactive /emissions-gap-report/2020/.

UNICEF. 2017. "Building the Future: Children and the Sustainable Development Goals in Rich Countries." Innocenti Report Card no. 14, UNICEF Office of Research Innocenti, Florence, 2017.

UN Resolution A/RES/25/2626, adopted by the General Assembly on October 24, 1970. Declaration on Principles of International Law Concerning Friendly Relations and Co-operation Among States in Accordance with the Charter of the United Nations.

UN Resolution 2009/28 adopted by the Economic and Social Council on July 31, 2009. The role of the United Nations system in implementing the ministerial declaration on the internationally agreed goals and commitments in regard to sustainable development adopted at the high-level segment of the substantive session of the Economic and Social Council in 2008.

UN Resolution A/RES/60/1 adopted by the General Assembly on September 16, 2005. 2005 World Summit Outcome.

UN Resolution A/RES/64/236 adopted by the General Assembly on December 24, 2009 (published in official document on March 31, 2010). Implementation of Agenda 21, the Programme for the Further Implementation of Agenda 21 and the outcomes of the World Summit on Sustainable Development.

UN Resolution A/RES/66/288—Rio Declaration adopted by the General Assembly on July 27, 2012. *The Future We Want*.

UN Resolution A/RES/70/1 adopted by the General Assembly on September 25, 2015. Transforming Our World: The 2030 Agenda for Sustainable Development.

United Nations Department of Economic and Social Affairs, Financing for Development Office, 2003. http://www.un.org/en/events/pastevents/pdfs/MonterreyConsensus.pdf.

United Nations/Rio+20 United Nations Conference on Sustainable Development. Zero Draft, January 10, 2012.

United Nations. *The Future We Want*. Negotiated Draft as of March 28, 2012, with Co-chairs' Suggested Text, April 17, 2012.

UNSG. "Report—Resilient People, Resilient Planet: A Future Worth Choosing, Overview." United Nations Secretary-General's High-Level Panel on Global Sustainability, 2012.

UNSG. "Report—A New Global Partnership: Eradicate Poverty and Transform Economies Through Sustainable Development." United Nations Secretary-General's High-Level Panel of Eminent Persons on the Post-2015 Development Agenda, 2013.

UN System Task Team. "Review of the Contributions of the MDG Agenda to Foster Development: Lessons for the Post-2015 UN Development Agenda." Concept Note, UN System Task Team on the Post-2015 Development Agenda, March 2012.

"The Water, Energy and Food Security Nexus." Solutions for a Green Economy, Policy Recommendations, Bonn2011 Conference, February 13, 2012.

World Bank. "Poverty and Shared Prosperity 2018: Piecing Together the Poverty Puzzle." World Bank, 2018. https://www.worldbank.org/en/publication/poverty-and-shared-prosperity-2018.

World Economic Forum, in collaboration with McKinsey & Company. "Nature and Net Zero 2021." World Economic Forum, May 2021. https://www.weforum.org/reports/consultation-nature-and-net-zero.

Index

287

About the Book

This extraordinary first-person story of what can be achieved through informal diplomacy traces the improbably successful struggle to achieve acceptance of the Sustainable Development Goals (SDGs)—and thus transform the global development agenda—against all odds.

Moving from the framing of the SDGs concept through the entire negotiation process (including a trove of key documents), Paula Caballero and Patti Londoño's vibrant narrative provides rare insight into informal diplomacy and multilateralism in action. Their insiders' account provides a unique perspective on how global movements and agendas can be built and impelled forward. Not least, it also serves to prove that just a few committed individuals can generate radical change.

During the period covered in this book, **Paula Caballero** was director for economic, social, and environmental affairs, and **Patti Londoño** was vice minister for multilateral affairs in the Colombian Ministry of Foreign Affairs.